ESSENTIALS FOR SPIRIT-EMPOWERED MINISTRY

Early Release Edition

The final editorial phase of this book has not yet been completed.

ESSENTIALS FOR SPIRIT-EMPOWERED MINISTRY

J. Randolph Turpin, Jr.

Declaration Press

Essentials for Spirit-Empowered Ministry

Early Release Edition

Contents

Very truly I tell you,
whoever believes in me will do the works I have been doing,
and they will do even greater things than these,
because I am going to the Father.
(Jesus Christ, John 14:12)

PREFACE

Long ago in the Clinch River Valley of East Tennessee, God in His providence began a work of grace that would eventually lead to the ministry which this book represents. As far as the Turpin family is concerned, the Pentecostal experience began with a woman named Laura Turpin in 1906—the same year that the Azusa Street Revival began. Aunt Laurie, as she was called, passed the legacy on to King Turpin who was her nephew and my grandfather. It was King who used to sit for hours exhorting me to earnestly desire spiritual gifts. That emphasis was only reinforced by my parents, Jim and Betty Turpin, who over the years so sacrificially supported many of my educational and ministerial endeavors. For these family members, I am so grateful.

At the height of my ministerial and academic pursuits, pastoral mentors like Calvin Rogers of the Assemblies of God and Reginald Spooner of the Church of God encouraged me to expect the supernatural in ministry. Both of these men are now in heaven, and someday I will thank them face-to-face. Colleagues in ministry, such as Kevin Porter and Kevin Matthews, contributed much to my understanding and appreciation of the *charismata* as they shared many biblical and practical insights.

For over thirty years I have labored among men and women who have had to come to grips with what they will do with this Holy Spirit who wants to take over their lives and ministries. Some choose to exclude Him. Others choose to embrace Him wholeheartedly. At several points in my ministry I have found myself caught in the tension between both kinds of people, and in those situations leadership had to emerge that would do the right thing. As a leader, I have come to realize that the right thing is to *tenderly* teach and guide people, whatever their opinion might be, deeper into the things of the Spirit.

Having committed to this cause, the journey has been both rewarding and costly. Some have followed; others have resisted. It was in the pain of trial that the beginning phase of this writing project started about fifteen years ago. It is my hope that the work at hand is more the product of a healing than it is of personal woundedness, for most assuredly, God has been gracious and merciful.

For a number of years, it has been a particular concern of mine that believers not distance themselves from the power of the Spirit. Few seem to have much of a problem with His person, His purity or His presence, but the moment someone starts talking about the *power* of the Spirit released through charismatic gifts, in some contexts the caution flag starts waving.

A way must be found to encourage God's people to allow themselves a full engagement with the gifts of grace—the *charismata*. For a people requiring a reasonable basis for faith and practice, it is hoped that this book might prove palatable as a training and discipleship tool—one that *tenderly* leads them to that heavenly River of the Spirit. May those who hunger for a ministry that is holy and supernatural be helped by lessons learned in this attempt at honoring the person, purity, presence and power of the Holy Spirit.

The research supporting this material was conducted from 2001 to 2005 during my Doctor of Ministry program at the Pentecostal Theological Seminary in Cleveland, Tennessee.[1] I have traveled many life and ministry miles since that time; consequently, I am finding that my understanding of the things of the Spirit is being continually challenged and expanded. In other words, I am still a student—a lifetime learner, and I am sure that whatever conclusions I have formed in the pages that follow are not my concluding conclusions. I *am* trying to be true to my current convictions; however, as I write these words, the revival movements rising out of Bethel Church

---

[1] The research supporting this material was conducted from 2001 to 2005 during my Doctor of Ministry program at the Pentecostal Theological Seminary in Cleveland, Tennessee. To review the complete documentation of the noted doctoral work, the reader may refer to the resulting dissertation, entitled, *A Training Model for Transitioning Classical Pentecostal Churches Toward the Intentional Integration of the Charismata in the Exercise of Prayer Ministry*.

(Redding, California), the Appalachian Awakening (Southern West Virginia) and the ministry of Pastor Rod Parsley (Columbus, Ohio) are powerfully impacting my life. Hopefully the benefit I am gaining from these Presence-saturated environments will show through in what I have composed. It is my hope that many will find this material helpful for the equipping of God's people in the exercise of Spirit-empowered prayer ministry.

Prior to publication, the training models that this book promotes were field tested in numerous ministry contexts. Those churches include Royal Ridge Church of God (Scarborough, Maine), Princeton Church of God (Princeton, North Carolina), Oleander Avenue Church of God (Fort Pierce, Florida) and City Church (Chattanooga, Tennessee). The members of those churches who participated in training sessions provided much feedback that contributed to the shaping and reshaping of the model. I do thank God for these wonderful brothers and sisters in the Lord.

I commend the congregation that I served at the time I prepared the first draft of large portions of this manuscript—Solid Rock Church of God in Grand Rapids, Minnesota. Their receptivity to this teaching was very rewarding. May the Lord greatly increase His anointing upon the prayer servants of the Minnesota Northland.

My wife and five children deserve a standing ovation for patiently enduring what at times seemed a wilderness journey leading up to the completion of my doctoral program and the production of multiple drafts of this publication. My wife, Kerry King Turpin, has by far contributed more to the support of this endeavor than anyone else. Not only has she been a great wife and mother through the duration of the project, but she has also been my proofreader and most immediate dialogue partner. Her insights into the Scriptures, her prophetic voice and her personal devotion to the things of the Spirit have been profoundly refreshing.

The students of Valor Christian College are the most recent influencers upon this project. At this moment, I am only days away from standing before them to teach a new course, Essentials for Spirit-Empowered Ministry. I am placing into their hands a pre-release edition of this text, inviting them to give feedback as we progress through the semester. Their input will be seriously considered as I prepare the final draft of the public release edition. I feel so blessed to serve and lead this rising generation of world changers.

Above all, to God be the glory. I am living proof that He does graciously choose and use the foolish and weak things of this world (1 Corinthians 1:27). May the fruit of this endeavor rightly demonstrate that He is the powerful God and loving Father that He truly is.

J. Randolph Turpin, Jr., D.Min.
Canal Winchester, Ohio
August 15, 2016

Introduction

The Master's words provoke unsettling thought: "I tell you the truth, anyone who has faith in me will do what I have been doing."[2] What had Jesus been doing? The context makes it clear: He was talking about signs, wonders and miracles. He was saying that anyone who has faith in him would function in the realm of the supernatural and the miraculous. He is saying to people of faith, "You will do what I have been doing!"

As though Jesus' declaration were not enough to challenge preconceived notions, He continued, saying, "He will do even greater things than these...."[3]

---

[2] John 14:12.

[3] Ibid. Biblical commentators have struggled with the idea that believers might do "greater" works than Jesus. R. Jamieson, A. R. Fausset and D. Brown suggest that the "greater" works are not greater in degree; rather, they are greater in kind: i.e., evangelism. R. Jamieson, A. R. Fausset, & D. Brown, "John 14:8-13," *A Commentary, Critical and Explanatory on the Old and New Testaments* [CD-ROM] (Oak Harbor, Washington: Logos Research Systems, Inc., 1997). C. F. Pfeiffer holds that the text could not mean greater in quality; rather, it must mean greater in extent. Theological worries over this matter are lifted when one notes that the "greater" works are nothing other than the continued and extended works of Christ; the disciples will not work independent of Him. Pfeiffer has this understanding when he notes, "The restrictions imposed on Jesus by incarnation would be removed. His position with the Father would be related to the greater works in two ways: answering the prayers of his own, and sending the Paraclete as the unfailing source of wisdom and strength. The works, then, would not be done in independence of Christ. *He* would answer prayer; *he* would send the Spirit." C. F. Pfeiffer, "John 14:11-12," *The Wycliffe Bible Commentary* [CD-ROM] (Chicago: Moody Press, 1962). The *Theological Dictionary of the New Testament* notes the basis of these "greater" works: "This going to the Father gives Him the possibility of greater efficacy exercised through the disciples."

Now, that statement boggles the mind. It seems too grand to be true, but it is Jesus talking here, and what He says is always true.

The call to supernatural ministry is also seen in Matthew 10:7-8 where Jesus commissioned the Twelve Apostles, saying,

> "As you go, proclaim this message: 'The kingdom of heaven has come near.' Heal the sick, raise the dead, cleanse those who have leprosy, drive out demons. Freely you have received; freely give."

Concerning these words, some are careful to argue that this commission was specific to the Twelve Apostles and should not be considered normative for all believers. In response to that objection, note that later in the same Gospel, in Matthew 28:18-20, Jesus said,

> "All authority in heaven and on earth has been given to me. Therefore go and make disciples of all nations, baptizing them in the name of the Father and of the Son and of the Holy Spirit, and *teaching them to obey everything I have commanded you*. And surely I am with you always, to the very end of the age."

Jesus said to His original disciples, "Teach new disciples to obey everything I have commanded you." Whatever it was that Jesus had commanded His original disciples, those same commands were supposed to be transmitted on to future disciples. What had Jesus commanded His original disciples? He had given His original disciples a lot of instructions, and one of those instructions was the command to heal the sick, raise the dead, cleanse lepers and drive out demons.

Jesus promised, "You will do what I have been doing. You will even do greater things."[4] Later in the biblical narrative, the Holy Spirit came, enabled the fulfillment of Jesus' pledge[5] and manifested powerful spiritual gifts through those who were eager to receive.[6] Empowered by the Holy Spirit, the

---

Theological Dictionary of the New Testament, ed. G. Kittel, G. W. Bromiley, et al., [CD-ROM] (Grand Rapids, Michigan: Eerdmans, 1964-1976), 4:536.

[4] John 14:12.

[5] John 14:16-17, 26; 15:26; 16:7-15; Luke 24:49, and Acts 1:8.

[6] Luke 11:9-13; 1 Corinthians 12:31; 14:1, 12, and 39.

church was then propelled into supernatural ministry. Today, by the agency of the same Spirit, Jesus still works signs and wonders in, among and through those who believe.

The New Testament, especially the Acts of the Apostles, portrays the Spirit of God shaping and directing ministry in dramatic and supernatural ways that until recently have seemed foreign to much of the western church. It is encouraging to see that once again the church is witnessing the same demonstrations of God's love and power that those first century pioneers experienced. This generation is seeing signs, wonders and miracles that are bringing great glory to the Lord Jesus. For a long time, such was not the case, but now the Lord has been so pleased to manifest much more than what the modern church had previously known.

In 2001 when I began my doctoral research on the subject of supernatural ministry, I felt that abuses and misunderstandings of the Gifts of the Spirit (the *charismata*[7]) and the infrequency of signs and wonders signaled for the reexamination of the biblical call to Spirit-empowered ministry. I could not escape this question: What would happen if the church of the twenty-first century were to *fully* embrace the dynamic of the Holy Spirit in the practice of ministry?

For years I had believed that biblically-informed *Spirit-empowered* ministry models would produce more authentic and more effective outcomes than programs and plans devised without regard for the Spirit. I believed that the intentional training of believers in the function of the charismatic gifts combined with planned opportunities for the exercise of those gifts would increase the number of people capable of ministering confidently in the power

---

[7] "*Charismata,*" meaning "grace gifts," is found in Romans 12:61 and Corinthians 12:4, 9. C. Peter Wagner and others have identified as many as twenty-seven spiritual gifts in which believers may function. C. Peter Wagner, *Your Spiritual Gifts Can Help Your Church Grow* (Ventura, California: Regal Books, 1997). While these twenty-seven gifts are worthy of attention, this project is focused on just a few: i.e., the manifestation gifts of 1 Corinthians 12-14 and their related signs and wonders.

of the Spirit. In other words, teach it, trust God for it, make room for it, and it will happen.

What is meant by "Spirit-empowered" ministry? The Spirit-empowered approach is one that relies heavily on the dynamic of the Holy Spirit, integrating specific gifts and resources that the Spirit provides. This approach delivers authentic and effective results. An "authentic" ministry is defined as that which closely resembles Jesus' own example of what ministry should be. It is also a ministry without pretense and self-serving motivations. It is a ministry initiated by the Spirit, the Word and the heart of the Father. An "effective" ministry is defined as one that truly fulfills or accomplishes the divine mandates of the Gospel: to minister salvation, healing and deliverance to the world.

The dogma of many churches affirms belief in the charismatic gifts, yet in some of those religious bodies, knowledge and experience in the practice of the full spectrum of these gifts has been limited to a few. The perception has been that the preacher is the one who has such an anointing. A broader understanding is needed. The manifestation gifts should be embraced and intentionally integrated into the *overall* life and mission of the church. Workings of the Spirit should be showing up in church administration, pastoral care, evangelism, youth ministry, the nursery, teaching ministries, missions, worship and in every other area of the church.

Let us take this a step further and consider how the life of the church interfaces with the world. Taking that perspective, the work of the Spirit should also be showing up outside the walls of the church—in business, industry, education, the arts, the media, the entertainment industry, science, technology, politics, government and so forth. We are talking about every sphere of influence being impacted by the presence and power of the Holy Spirit!

This book is designed to encourage the embracing of the Father's heart in the work of the ministry. To make His heart known to the world, the Father has placed gifts of revelation and power in the church. To rightly represent His heart and to manifest His power to the world, it is necessary for the church to intentionally integrate the *charismata* into our works of ministry.

CHAPTER 1

KINGDOM VALUES AND MINDSETS

Spirit-empowered ministry requires values and mindsets that are not of this world. The values and mindsets necessary for signs, wonders and miracles are derived from the kingdom of heaven. Unless a person was born into a culture of supernatural Jesus-centered life and ministry, in all likelihood, an intentional effort will be needed to adopt the new values and mindsets of heaven.

Values and mindsets affect how we carry and steward what God as given us. Many people experience powerful spiritual impartations, but how many are able to sustain what they have gained? How many find themselves a month later back in the same patterns of weakness and mediocrity that they thought they had abandoned? Why is it that for some individuals and even some congregations, spiritual advances seem so hard to hold on to?

I think that the answer is found in the possibility that complete repentance has not yet taken place. Repentance is not just saying "I am sorry" about a thing. It is an entire change of mindset regarding the matter. It is a change of thinking. It is even a change of beliefs. The word "repentance" carries the idea of thinking differently after an encounter with truth. Repentant people start thinking differently about the direction of their life, and as a result of the changed mindset, they start living differently. Their lives turn *from* one thing and *unto* another. They repent *from* sin, and they repent *unto* God's ways. They turn *from* lies, and they turn *unto* truth.

Repentance is not just for unsaved people who need to come to faith in Christ. Anytime any of us encounter a God-given truth that challenges already established ways of thinking, we need to repent. When we change our mind, our actions will change. There are many Christians who have the life of heaven—eternal life—inside of them, yet they are still living as though they are bonded to earth. They seem unaware of who they truly are and what they possess. They seem unaware that they have access to life of heaven in the here and now. They seem unaware that they are authorized and empowered to release the life of heaven into the world around them. Christians whose minds are still so earth-bound need to repent of powerless thinking and turn their focus toward the one who has empowered them to bring heaven to earth.

The biblical imagery of wineskins represents such needed change.[7] Our mindset or belief system is a wineskin, and that wineskin carries the new wine of what God is doing. Too often we try to carry new wine in old wineskins. That will not do. Old wineskins cannot contain the new wine. New wine will leak through old wineskins because the old wineskins are old and brittle. In a sense, the new wine of the Spirit needs to be allowed to create its own wineskins. New mindsets and core values are needed to sustain the new wine of God's work.

Here we are not talking about shifting with the moral and cultural trends of our world, but we are most definitely talking about shifting with the movements of heaven. Too many try to hold on to what heaven *was* doing at the expense of missing what God *is* doing in the present. It is time to move *with* Him.

Neither are we talking about moving away from the truths of God's Word, but we are most definitely talking about revisiting how we interpret and apply what God has revealed. Too many hold their *understanding* of God's Word as a higher authority than God's Word itself. It is in the realm of understanding that change needs to take place.

As we approach the subject of Spirit-empowered life and ministry, what old mindsets and values need to be abandoned or at least modified? What are the mindsets and core values that will rightly carry the spirit of revival? What are the mindsets and core values that will rightly cultivate and deliver Spirit-empowered ministry?

---

[7] See Matthew 9:17 for the biblical context.

Often the adopting of new mindsets requires the discarding of old ones. Steve Backlund of Bethel Church in Redding, California often quotes Francis Frangipane, saying, "Every area of your life not glistening with hope is under the influence of a lie."[8] The only way to crush hopelessness is to identify the lies that sustain our hopeless thoughts and to counter those lies with truth.

Be careful to *not* believe the internal lies that sometimes bombard the minds of people—lies such as these:

"It is too late for my situation."

"It is too late for our nation."

"It is not always God's will to heal."

"Signs, wonders and miracles were for the first century church, but they are not for today."

"The ability to minister supernaturally is only given to an elite group of people—God's select few."

"Some people have what it takes for God to work through them, and others don't. I don't."

"I'm not anointed."

These statements are so far from the truth that they are laughable.[9] Thoughts such as these do not come from the heart and mind of God. If God is not thinking these kinds of thoughts concerning you, you should not be thinking these kinds of thoughts concerning you either.

---

[8] Steve Backlund notes that he learned this concept from Francis Frangipane. Steve Backlund, "Renewing the Mind," Igniting Hope Ministries, last modified 2015, accessed August 8, 2015, available from http:// ignitinghope.com/ renewing-the-mind/. See also Romans 15:13 and Hebrews 10:23.

[9] In my Success in College class at Valor Christian College, I read these "lies" aloud to the class, and after reading each lie, I say, "Let's laugh at that!" Then the class laughs at the lie, as a faith action to break its power off of their minds.

The Power of Your Words

If you want to know the direction a person's life is taking, just listen to the way they talk. The Bible speaks of the tongue as being like a small rudder that steers the direction of a ship.[10] Words that we speak determine the direction of our life. When people declare a thing, they increase the likelihood that it will happen. That principle can have a positive or negative impact on a person's life, depending on whether a person's words are positive or negative. When you make a declaration of a desired outcome based on God's truth, you increase the likelihood that the truth you have spoken will be manifested in your life.

Spiritual dynamics are at play when we speak. Things that we say can actually affect the activities of spiritual forces and entities. However, even if nothing spiritual were at work, words still affect outcomes. When a person speaks a thing, the brain immediately goes to work to make arrangements for that thing to be fulfilled. Once again, this principle can work both positively and negatively.

Our words and our thoughts are important because they affect our whole being. The good news is that negative mindsets can be transformed into positive mindsets whenever people decide to intentionally renew their minds. The Bible says that we are to "be transformed by the renewing of our minds."[11]

To intentionally renew the mind, one must take negative thoughts captive. The Bible says, "We take captive every thought to make it obedient to Christ."[12] Catch that thought the moment that it shows up in your brain, and say, "You don't belong here! Get out!" Then replace that lie with truth by declaring the truth.

---

[10] James 3:4-5a.

[11] Romans 12:2.

[12] 2 Corinthians 10:5.

Personalized Declarations

One of the most powerful Bible reading exercises is to personalize verses of Scripture, converting them into prayers or declarations. In the college where I teach, my book entitled, *Gateway to the Christian College Experience,*[13] is required reading for all entering students who have not had previous college experience. Much of that text's content is stated verbatim in this section. It is my belief that God's people greatly increase the likelihood that they will succeed when they declare biblical truth into their own lives. In the *Gateway* text, I demonstrate how to compose personalized declarations of truth. A few examples of converted Bible passages into declarations of truth are provided below. Read each of the noted verses, and then speak the corresponding declaration. Afterwards, open your Bible and locate some of God's promises that you have already underscored or highlighted. Practice converting those promises into declarations, and speak them aloud.

1 John 5:4
"Everyone born of God overcomes the world. This is the victory that has overcome the world, even our faith."

Declaration: "I am born of God, and I am overcoming the world. My life originates from Him. The world cannot defeat me."

Romans 8:37
"No, in all these things we are more than conquerors through him who loved us."

Declaration: "I am more than a conqueror through Jesus, and He loves me."

---

13 J. Randolph Turpin, Jr., *Gateway to the Christian College Experience* (Canal Winchester, Ohio: Declaration Press, 2015).

Isaiah 41:10
"So do not fear, for I am with you;
do not be dismayed, for I am your God.
I will strengthen you and help you;
I will uphold you with my righteous right hand."

Declaration: "I am not afraid. God is with me. I refuse to be discouraged. He is my God. He strengthens me. He helps me. He upholds me with His righteous right hand."

Philippians 2:13
"For it is God who works in you to will and to act in order to fulfill his good purpose."

Declaration: "God has created in me the desire to do His will. My decisions are wise. My actions are powerful. My desires are pleasing to God and fulfill His good purpose."

Romans 6:14
"For sin shall no longer be your master, because you are not under the law, but under grace."

Declaration: "Sin is not my master. I am ruled by grace."

Philippians 4:19
"And my God will meet all your needs according to the riches of his glory in Christ Jesus."

Declaration: "My God meets all my needs according to the riches of His glory in Christ Jesus."

Romans 12:2
"Do not conform to the pattern of this world, but be transformed by the renewing of your mind. Then you will be able to test and approve what God's will is—his good, pleasing and perfect will."

Declaration: "The world does not shape my life. My mind is being renewed, and my renewed mind is transforming my life. With a renewed mind, I test and approve what God's will is. With a renewed mind, I know what He desires of me. His will is good. His will is pleasing. His will is perfect."

1 Corinthians 6:19
"Do you not know that your bodies are temples of the Holy Spirit, who is in you, whom you have received from God? You are not your own."

Declaration: "My body is a temple—a holy dwelling for the Holy Spirit. He lives in me. I am not my own. I belong to Him."

1 Peter 5:7
"Cast all your anxiety on him because he cares for you."

Declaration: "I cast all of my worries and fears on Jesus. He cares for me."

Matthew 28:20
"[Teach] them to obey everything I have commanded you. And surely I am with you always, to the very end of the age."

Declaration (directed to Jesus): "I will do everything you command me."

Declaration: "Jesus is always with me."

Galatians 6:9
"Let us not become weary in doing good, for at the proper time we will reap a harvest if we do not give up."

Declaration: "I will not become weary of doing good works. I *will* reap a harvest. I will not give up."

John 10:10
"The thief comes only to steal and kill and destroy; I have come that they may have life, and have it to the full."

Declaration: "The devil may try to steal from me, kill me and destroy me, but he will not prevail. Jesus came to give me life. I have that life, and it is a *full* life."

John 5:19
"Jesus gave them this answer: 'Very truly I tell you, the Son can do nothing by himself; he can do only what he sees his Father doing, because whatever the Father does the Son also does.'"

Declaration: "I can do nothing of eternal worth by myself. I watch for what my Father is doing. Then I align my actions with His. Whatever the Father does, that is what I want to do."

Declaration (directed to the Father): "Father, where you go, I go. What you say, I say. What you do, I do."

Be aware that with your attitude, actions and words, you have the power to change your environment and shift the atmosphere around you. Collective mindsets of others affect us more than we realize. You can walk into a room of negative thinking people and feel it. Likewise, you can walk into a room of positively thinking people and feel it. With one word spoken in faith, you can shift the atmosphere. You can make a difference in the mental and emotional orientation of the people around you. [14]

Releasing the Kingdom with Our Words

Steve Backlund teaches that nothing in the kingdom happens without someone first making a declaration. Jesus made declarations to storms. He spoke to the paralytic, saying, "Pick up your mat and walk."[15] He stood outside of Lazarus' tomb and commanded, "Lazarus, come out!"[16]

Generally, if something has happened, it is because something has been spoken. If something is going to happen, then something needs to be spoken to make it happen. Just because you say something that does not necessarily mean that it will happen, yet many things will never happen unless something is said.

Core Values

Core values are the guiding principles of our life. They represent the things that are most important to us. For some people, things like "fun" or "friendship" may be core values. For others, "success" and "security" may be core values. Still others may say that "honesty" and "sincerity" are the key principles that guide their lives.

Followers of Jesus typically discover that they are guided by a set of core values that are very different from those of non-believers. Take a few moments to consider the values listed below. Do any of them reflect the way

---

[14] Much of this section's content has been taken verbatim from the author's previous work in *Gateway to the Christian College Experience* (Canal Winchester, Ohio: Declaration Press, 2015).

[15] John 5:8.

[16] John 11:43.

you would like to conduct your life and ministry? Place a check mark beside any that seem relevant to you.[17]

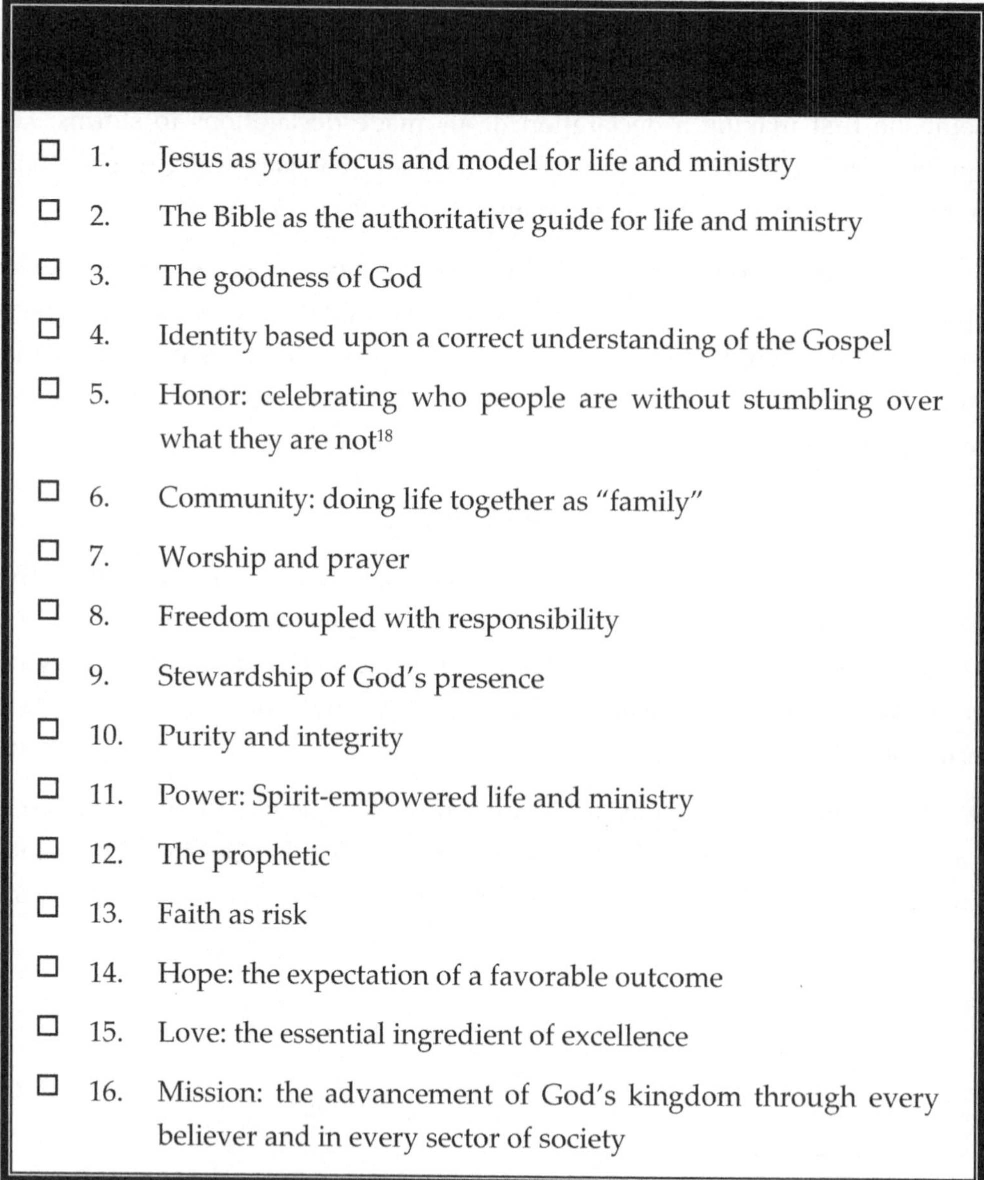

- ☐ 1. Jesus as your focus and model for life and ministry
- ☐ 2. The Bible as the authoritative guide for life and ministry
- ☐ 3. The goodness of God
- ☐ 4. Identity based upon a correct understanding of the Gospel
- ☐ 5. Honor: celebrating who people are without stumbling over what they are not[18]
- ☐ 6. Community: doing life together as "family"
- ☐ 7. Worship and prayer
- ☐ 8. Freedom coupled with responsibility
- ☐ 9. Stewardship of God's presence
- ☐ 10. Purity and integrity
- ☐ 11. Power: Spirit-empowered life and ministry
- ☐ 12. The prophetic
- ☐ 13. Faith as risk
- ☐ 14. Hope: the expectation of a favorable outcome
- ☐ 15. Love: the essential ingredient of excellence
- ☐ 16. Mission: the advancement of God's kingdom through every believer and in every sector of society

---

[17] Much of this section's content has been taken verbatim from the author's previous work in *Gateway to the Christian College Experience* (Canal Winchester, Ohio: Declaration Press, 2015).

Let us now consider more in-depth a few of these core values that are especially important for the conduct of Spirit-empowered ministry. Much of my thinking regarding these values has been heavily influenced by Bill Johnson and the leaders of the great church that he leads—Bethel Church in Redding, California.

1. Jesus is our model. Jesus is our model for everything. If we want an accurate picture of any area of truth, we look first to Jesus. If we want a clearer understanding of the Old Testament, we look first to Jesus: what did He say about it? If we want a guide for how we are to live our lives, we look to Jesus. If want to know how to conduct ourselves in the work of ministry, we look to Jesus.

When Jesus summoned His first disciples, He said things like, "Follow me" and "Come, and see." To heed the call, "Follow me," means *to be with* Him, but it also means *to adhere to His teachings* and *to follow His example.* To heed the call, "Come, and see," means something similar. It means to be with Him, to follow Him and to observe Him with the intent of learning from Him—even to the point of learning to be like Him.

In John 14:12, Jesus taught us that the work He did, we would also do. He even implied that we would take what He delivered to us and go even further with it. This great promise strongly implies that we need to pay attention to how Jesus healed the sick, raised the dead, cast out demons and performed every other aspect of the Gospel. We are to honor and observe Him as our model for Spirit-empowered ministry. As we take all of this to heart, we need to realize that we are in fact learning to minister like Jesus.

2. The Holy Spirit is our guide. We are dependent on revelation from Him. We do not want to go where He is not going, do not want to do what He is not doing and do not want to say what He is not saying. Sensitivity to the leading of the Holy Spirit is a core value for the person desiring to live a Spirit-Empowered life.

---

[18] This understanding of honor has been popularized by leaders at Bethel Church in Redding, California.

3. The Bible is our objective authoritative reference. The Bible is the written word of God. We may receive many subjective prophetic words, but every subjective word is subject to the authority of the already-written objective word of God as contained in the Holy Bible. Not every model and method for ministry has to be explicitly stated in Scripture, but the principles guiding those models and methods are to be derived from those pages. If a particular approach to ministry should come into question, go back to the Book.

4. God is good. The fundamental nature of this core value calls for a more extensive treatment of its meaning, in comparison with our discourse on the other core values. What is meant by the statement, "God is good"? Yes, He is good in his essence, in the sense that he is qualitatively good and not bad,[19] but He is also good in all that He does[20] and consistently good or favorable in His disposition toward mankind and toward each of us individually. In fact, nearly all biblical references to the goodness of God relate to His favorable disposition toward mankind.[21]

Everything about God is good. The goodness of God is a character trait which applies to every other attribute. God's wrath is good. God's holiness is good. God's righteousness is good. God is good in His entirety. There is nothing about God that is not good. There is nothing God purposes for His children that is not good. God gives to His children only that which is good, and He withholds nothing good from us. God is good, and He is at work in our lives for good.

In Psalm 73, the psalmist affirms the fact that God is good—especially to Israel—especially to such as are of a clean heart. However, while the writer of this Psalm, Asaph, believed biblically and theologically that God was good, he struggled with the issue of God's goodness on a personal level. Look carefully at where he goes with this psalm:

---

[19] Psalm 119:68; 1 John 1:5.

[20] Genesis 1:31; Psalm 33:5; 84:11; James 1:17.

[21] See Psalm 31:19; 73; 107:1.

> 1 Surely God is good to Israel,
> to those who are pure in heart.
> 2 But as for me, my feet had almost slipped;
> I had nearly lost my foothold.

Asaph is saying, "Yes, God is good, but look at me! I'm far from good. I nearly lost it!" How did Asaph almost blow it? He had begun to doubt the goodness of God. He had been looking at the difficulties of life. He had been comparing the troubles of his life with the trouble-free lives of others. Asaph's thought was, "Yes, God is good, *but* look at how the wicked prosper!" Read further in the text:

> 3 For I envied the arrogant
> when I saw the prosperity of the wicked.
> 4 They have no struggles;
> their bodies are healthy and strong.
> 5 They are free from common human burdens;
> they are not plagued by human ills.
> 12 This is what the wicked are like—
> always free of care, they go on amassing wealth.

Look at how the wicked live—they dishonor God, yet it looks like all of the good things happen to them.

> 13 Surely in vain I have kept my heart pure
> and have washed my hands in innocence.

Asaph's thought was, "Yes, God is good, *but* look at my life! Where are the evidences that God is good? What good has it done for me to live a godly life? What do I have to show for it all?"

The doubts of Asaph sound just like the doubts people have today. Not everyone agrees with the idea that God is entirely good. Many live their lives thinking, "God does not have my good in mind." That thought should sound familiar to us, because it echoes the thoughts of Adam and Even at the point of their decision to rebel against God. Satan's first attack in the Garden was against the God's goodness—against His good intentions toward Adam and Eve:

> God has forbidden you to eat from the tree of the knowledge of good and evil because He knows that in the day you eat from it your eyes will be

opened, and you will be like Him, knowing good and evil. God is withholding something good from you, and if He is withholding something good from you, how could *He* be good?[22]

By the time Satan had finished, Eve had come to view God as One who is less than good, and the forbidden fruit as that which is good. Once Eve doubted the goodness of God, it was a great deal easier for her to disobey Him. If God was not good and was not acting for her good, then why should she obey Him? Indeed, why should she not act independently of God in seeking her own good—the forbidden fruit?

Such is the mindset of many. They think that the God of the Christians is less than good. They think that the things He forbids are the things that are good; in other words, they think that He is an oppressive God. They think, "Since He is not good and does not act for our good, why should we obey Him? Every person needs to seek his own good, being independent of this God."

How strange it seems to the Christian's ears to hear such things. We know Him as the God who frees men from oppression—the things that bring death. How strange it is to our ears to hear people say that our God is not good, for we know and believe God to be entirely good.

Some may still object, saying, "But how could a good God allow evil and suffering?" The question reflects an ignorance of the fact that all of the trouble of the world is a result of man's doings—not God's. God is not responsible for the evil and suffering which plague our planet. God manifested all of His goodness to man. God gave to man dominion over all the earth. Man sinned against the goodness of God. Man surrendered his dominion to Satan—the destroyer. The destroyer and fallen humanity have been at work ever since.

What about wars? They are the result of the fallen state of man. How about hurricanes; are they not "acts of God"? The Bible speaks of the devil as being the prince of the power of the air.[23] What about death? Satan has been a

---

[22] An expanded paraphrase of Genesis 3:1-5.

[23] Ephesians 2:2.

murderer from the beginning, and God names death as an enemy,[24] not an ally. Besides, it is the devil who steals, kills and destroys; if is Jesus who came to give life—even life more abundantly.[25]

If it were not for the goodness and mercies of God, the human race would have totally self-destructed by now, and whatever man could not mess up, Satan himself would have destroyed it. The Creator gave us freedom of choice, but he is not accountable for our abuse. As Wayne Jackson states, "Blaming God for our current woes is about like charging Henry Ford with the responsibility for the death of a person mortally wounded in a drunk-driving accident."[26]

What has God done about all of this evil in the world? Titus 2:11 states, "The grace of God that brings salvation has appeared to all men." Romans 2:4 says, "The goodness of God leads you to repentance." Psalm 86:5 declares, "You, Lord, are forgiving and good, abounding in love to all who call to you." In His goodness, He is ready to forgive. I love the King James Version wording of 107:8 that reads, "O, that men would praise the Lord for His goodness, and for His wonderful works to the children of men."

Returning to our consideration of Psalm 73, Asaph he had came close to confessing that it does not matter how godly a person tries to live—his life is still destined to be miserable. As it might be said in our day, "How can we say that God is good? Look at our lives? Look at our world? Where is His goodness?" The thing that held the psalmist back was his sense that such a confession would have been an act of betrayal against God's children. In essence, He said in his psalm, "If I had voiced that I doubted the goodness of God, I would have betrayed your children."[27] God's people trusted him to be

---

[24] 1 Corinthians 15:26.

[25] John 10:10.

[26] Wayne Jackson, "Reflections on the Goodness of God," ChristianCourier.com, accessed July 30, 2016, https://www.christiancourier.com/articles/444-reflections-on-the-goodness-of-god.

[27] Psalm 73:15.

one who would lead them in the worship of God—he was not to be one who propagated doubt in the goodness of God.

Asaph finally climbed out of this hole of doubt and concluded with some profound insights that I believe bring great encouragement and strength to us today:

> 16 When I tried to understand all this,
> it troubled me deeply
> 17 till I entered the sanctuary of God;
> then I understood their final destiny.

Until Asaph entered the sanctuary of God, until he entered the place of God's presence, until he had divine encounter, he doubted the goodness of God. Once he entered the sanctuary of God, once he entered the place of God's presence, once he had divine encounter, his doubts disappeared! Then he had insight and understanding. Then he had clarity and a correct perspective. Then he had an eternal perspective.

We need a renewed view of our *present* situation in Christ—seated with Him in heavenly places. We need a renewed view of our *future* situation in Christ—literally with Him throughout the eternal ages. An *eternal* view of this *temporal* life must always be kept in view. That is the only way that much in this life can be rightly understood. When Asaph took the eternal perspective, he rightly perceived the end of the wicked, and he realized how wrong he had been regarding the goodness of God. No matter how bad things get, here is what Asaph came to realize:

> 23 Yet I am always with you;
> you hold me by my right hand.
> 24 You guide me with your counsel,
> and afterward you will take me into glory.
> 25 Whom have I in heaven but you?
> And earth has nothing I desire besides you.
> 26 My flesh and my heart may fail,
> but God is the strength of my heart
> and my portion forever.

Finally, listen closely as the psalmist defines in Psalm 73:28 the ultimate goodness that a man or woman can experience: "As for me, it is good to be near God." The intended message behind those words is more clearly heard in this rendering: "As for me, the nearness of God is my good."

Here is a key concept: the nearness of God is our good. It is very important that we come to the point in life where the nearness of God is all that we need. With that, we are content. Whatever interferes with our nearness to God is evil—not good. Whatever draws us into deeper fellowship with God is good.

Because God is good, we are accepted in His beloved son.[28] His eyes are upon us, and His ears are attentive to our cry.[29] He withholds nothing good from those who walk uprightly.[30] He is our stronghold in the day of trouble,[31] and He works all things together for our good.[32] Because God is good, He is rich in grace,[33] rich in mercy,[34] rich in supplying needs,[35] rich in giving things to enjoy[36] and rich in the strength He provides.[37]

The belief that God is good is essential to Spirit-empowered ministry. If we do not believe that He is good, we will doubt whether or not He desires to heal, deliver or work miracles. If we do not believe that He is good, we run the risk of prophetic ministry delivering something other than His goodness. If we do not believe that God is good, we have no basis for moving forward with confidence and hope in any area of our mission.

---

[28] Ephesians 1:6.

[29] Psalm 34:15.

[30] Psalm 84:11.

[31] Nahum 1:7.

[32] Romans 8:28.

[33] Ephesians 1:7.

[34] Ephesians 2:4.

[35] Philippians 4:19.

[36] 1 Timothy 6:17.

[37] Ephesians 3:16, 21.

5. Abounding hope is normative. Prior to the Christian usage of the word "hope," it simply meant "expectation." It could have been an expectation of good or an expectation of something bad. However, once Christians started using the word, it took on the more positive definition. Now the word "hope" in commonly understood as an expectation of good or an expectation of a favorable outcome.

Almost anything I will ever say about hope has been conceived under the influence of Steve Backlund.[38] Every time I have heard Steve speak to a new audience on this subject, he quickly goes to Romans 15:13: "May the God of hope fill you with all joy and peace as you trust in him, so that you may overflow with hope [abound in hope] by the power of the Holy Spirit." The original language does not say, "as you trust in him"; rather, it says "in believing." There is something about *the way* in which we believe or *what* we believe that is critical. It is not just about the general placing of our trust in Jesus, as important as that may be.

Let us consider what the writer is emphasizing in this text. God is a God of hope or expectation. He is forward-looking and is fixated on where everything is heading. A right belief system will hold that God does in fact have our future in mind—a favorable future. When we truly believe that he cares for us in that way, it brings us joy and peace. Wrong beliefs about God and His way with us will rob us of joy and peace. Joy and peace only come by right beliefs. There is something here that is important about believing *rightly*. Right beliefs or mindsets will lead to greater *joy* and *peace*, and right mindsets accompanied by joy and peace lead cause us to experience the life of abounding hope that the passage emphasizes.

---

[38] I will attempt to site the specific works of Steve Backlund, but if I make a statement that I believe to be my own original thought and you, the reader, think that it actually originated with Steve Backlund, please email me, and I will attempt to provide to correct citation in the next edition of this text. However, please understanding, many of Steve's teachings have so powerfully impacted my life that those concepts have actually become integrated into my own thinking and speaking. Sometimes it is difficult to distinguish between his words and my own.

Why are joy and peace so important? Emotions are an indicator of beliefs. If we have no joy, and if we have no peace, it could be an indication that something is amiss in our beliefs. Read the book of Philippians sometime. It is a book that is almost entirely about how our mindset, beliefs and thoughts have a direct bearing on joy.

Hope is a barometer. If what I believe creates hope, it is from God. If what I believe creates hopelessness, it is not from God. No matter how negative the situation, when we believe what God has to say about Himself, about us, about others and about our circumstances, our prevailing attitude concerning the matter at hand will be one of hope.

6. Honor is the currency of heaven. The Bible teaches that we are to honor one another above ourselves.[39] We typically have no problem honoring people who have made great accomplishments or have risen to positions of authority, but the biblical concept of honor is more inclusive. Yes, the Bible teaches that we are to honor people in authority,[40] and we are to honor those to whom honor is due,[41] but we are also instructed to honor everyone.[42]

I have heard Bill Johnson, Danny Silk and others say that "honor is the currency of heaven," but what does that expression mean? When I honor another person, it opens the way for an exchange of life to take place between me and that other person. When I honor people, it increases the likelihood that I will receive from them the grace that they carry, and they will be more likely to receive from me as well.

What is honor? Again it is Bill Johnson and Danny Silk from whom I draw wisdom to construct my answer. Honor is acknowledging the value of another person. Honor is celebrating what or who a person is without stumbling over what or who that person is not. Too often the value of other people is missed because of our preoccupation with what or who they are not.

---

[39] Romans 12:10.

[40] 1 Peter 2:17.

[41] Romans 13:7.

[42] 1 Peter 2:17.

Think about it: the list of what any person *is not* is an infinite list. Take myself for instance. I am not athletic. I am not a genius. I am not an engineer. I am not an acrobat. I am not a marine biologist. I am not good at calculus. I am not a lion tamer. I am not an astronaut. I am not a sculptor. I am not an accountant. I am not a physicist. I am not a comedian. I am not a geologist. I am not an architect. Do I need to continue? I could continue on for millions of pages listing the things I am not, but the list of things that *I am* would be a much shorter list. That list would easily fit on half a page, yet it would speak volumes concerning my value. The same would be true of you.

What are we to honor about other people? One of the reasons the church has been given the gift of the discerning of spirits[43] is that we might discern the things that should be affirmed in others—the spiritual graces and gifts that they carry. Yes, the gift of the discerning of spirits does help us in discerning demonic activity, angelic activity and Holy Spirit activity, but it also serves the purpose of helping us to honor that which is worthy of honor among us. The Apostle Paul once indicated that he had determined to know no person merely on the basis of natural knowledge—after the flesh.[44] The implication is that he had determined to know people on the basis of what he perceived them to be in spirit as a new creation. The Holy Spirit will reveal what we should honor in one another.

When we spiritually discern and honor the body of Christ, we contribute to the unity and health of the church.[45] Consider a time when someone in the church may need a miracle. The particular anointing for that miracle may be resting on the person sitting next to you or it may be resting on someone across the room. Through the discerning and honoring of that gift, you are able to introduce the person with the need to the person with the gift. Without the ability to recognize the gift that God has placed within them, you cannot draw from what they bring to benefit the situation. We need the ability to see the Spirit of God upon other people for the sake of the church.

---

[43] 1 Corinthians 12:10.

[44] 2 Corinthians 5:16.

[45] 1 Corinthians 11:29-30.

Honor is also the factor that causes the five-fold equipping gifts to strengthen and improve the health of the church.[46] The five-fold equipping gifts—apostles, prophets, evangelists, pastors and teachers—are gifts that Jesus has given to His people.[47] Jesus taught us that when we receive a prophet in the name of a prophet, we receive a prophet's reward.[48] In other words, when we receive or honor a prophet on the basis of the anointing that is on his or her life, we increase the likelihood that we will receive from the grace that is on that prophet's life. The same principle applies to the other four equipping gifts as well. If I do not receive a person on the basis of the grace or anointing that is on his or her life, then I shut down the exchange of blessing.

The Spirit of God is attracted to environments where mutual honor is taking place. When every person is valued and esteemed on the basis of what they bring to the rest of us, it is then that we become open to what God wants to do in our midst. A culture of honor is the culture in which Spirit-empowered ministry thrives.

7. Faith is risk. Romans 10:17 teaches that faith comes by hearing, and hearing comes through the word of God. In other words, when God speaks, the sound of His voice creates within a person the ability for those very words to be received and heard. God creates the ability for His message to be heard at the moment that He speaks to a person. That is why the Gospel can still impact the hearts of people who even say that they do not believe the Gospel. The Gospel is spoken, and it creates its own potential for being heard and received. When the ability to hear has been created, then faith comes.

When faith comes, then it calls for a response. Faith without some outworking of that faith is dead.[49] My heart may be stirred by a scripture or a prophetic word. I may sense that through what I am hearing, God is calling me to action. I must act. It may require a risk, but I must act, if it is truly God speaking. At times I may not be absolutely sure that it is God speaking, but

---

[46] Ephesians 4:7-16.

[47] Ephesians 4:8.

[48] Matthew 10:41.

[49] James 2:17.

somehow I must put it to the test. For instance, I may think that I have just received a word of knowledge, word of wisdom or prophecy that is to be spoken to a particular person. Acting on that word will require risk. I have got to press beyond internal barriers to speak that word. What if it is not a true word from God? What if it is not received? What if I look foolish?

The same principle of risk is required in all functions and aspects of Spirit-empowered ministry. We take a risk when we make a healing declaration over a person. We take a risk when we speak out in tongues over a congregation, hoping that someone will interpret. We take a risk when we give our last dollar in an offering simply because we felt that God said to give it. We take a risk when we take an action based on something we saw in a dream or vision. We take a risk when we try to witness to the stranger on the street.

In my experience, I have found that one of the reasons supernatural things do not happen more frequently in and through the church is that people are not given the opportunity to take risks. It can get messy when we allow people to do supernatural things, but we need to be willing to deal with the mess. People need a safe place to take risks in the exercise of spiritual gifts. They need a safe place to make mistakes, such as in small group training sessions. If they make a mistake while trying to exercise what they think to be faith, they should not be judged or condemned. They actually need to be applauded for taking the risk. Yes, corrective guidance may be needed, but at least they are trying to grow in the exercise of spiritual gifts. Faith is risk.

CHAPTER 2

PERSONAL PREPARATIONS FOR SPIRIT-EMPOWERED MINISTRY

The Spirit-empowered approach to ministry is not just about learning new methods. Although methodology is involved, preparation for this ministry is first a matter of preparing the heart, attitudes and the mind. The ministry trainee should be asking questions like, "What is the heart of God toward the people I will be serving? What new concepts and attitudes do I need to embrace? What will be the necessary spiritual disciplines for this pursuit?" To bring the heart and mind to a state of readiness, this chapter suggests several conceptual and experiential preparations.[50]

Conceptual Preparations

In order to be authentic and effective in Spirit-empowered ministry, there are several essential concepts to embrace. Depending upon the reader's background, some of these concepts may require more attention than this book alone can address. Here the presentation of these concepts should cause one to ask, "Have I already embraced this attitude or belief? Do I need to explore this matter further?"

1. A Worldview that Includes the Supernatural. A word of warning may be in order: Preconceived notions are about to be challenged. Erroneous

---

[50] Portions of this chapter have been adapted from J. Randolph Turpin, Jr., "A Synthesis and Critique of 'The Prophetic Journey': The 2005 Prophetic Ministry Conference Conducted at Westmore Church of God" (an unpublished paper, Church of God Theological Seminary, 2005).

thinking has been a major hindrance to the work of the Spirit in churches of technological societies. A change of thinking is needed.

Obviously, if one is to rely upon the Holy Spirit for ministry empowerment, and if a supernatural outcome is to be expected, then it is required to have a worldview that includes belief in the supernatural. Most Christians would probably respond, "No problem! I believe in the supernatural." However, we who have been so influenced by the Age of Reason or the Enlightenment do not even realize how severely we have been biased to exclude the supernatural from our lives.

Are we really ready to believe in things that we cannot prove, are not able to analyze, do not understand or cannot see? Are we ready to renounce the little adage, "Seeing is believing"? If you are a typical American or European, you are likely to feel a little internal tension even pondering these questions. That small bit of intellectual resistance is the same mindset that often hinders the working of the supernatural among us. Due to the fact that the western worldview is largely scientific and naturalistic in its orientation, the mindset of western Christianity needs to be reoriented toward embracing the reality of supernatural signs and wonders.

We need to overcome naturalistic thinking. In the industrialized world there is a need for a change in the patterns and models that govern thought regarding the way the natural and supernatural realms impact one another. Westerners tend to think of the spiritual and the natural as distinctly separate and unrelated realms. The Eastern mindset (the mindset of the Scriptures) sees the two realms as intricately interrelated.

I will illustrate what I am talking about. Today if a region of the world were to experience a drought, we would most likely explain the cause and effect of that crisis in scientific terms. However, in ancient times, when droughts occurred, pagans assumed that the gods had withheld the rain, while Jews or Christians would have assumed that somehow the God of Abraham, Isaac and Jacob was involved. To resolve dilemmas in nature, both pagans and Christians would take spiritual action. Even in our own not-too-distant past, natural disasters were referred to as "acts of God." In one sense, it is not a good idea to blame God for the bad things that happen in nature; I am more inclined to think that the prince of the power of the air is somehow involved. On the other hand, when the term "act of God" was used, at least it acknowledged that spiritual causes were sometimes at work behind phenomena in nature.

2 Chronicles 7:13-14 demonstrates the validity of this point. This passage offering prayer instruction for the healing of the "land" is often used as a basis for crying out for revival and the healing of a nation. In principle, such application may be permissible; however, "land" is not a reference to the nation; here "land" literally means the physical ground—the soil in which plants grow. The passage is all about what God's people are to do in times of drought. The result of prayer, humility and repentance would be that the Lord would heal the drought-stricken land. The implication is that He would heal the land by sending rain. What is to be noted is the connection between issues in the visible realm and the influence of the invisible realm.

Now that the scientific age is here, the church can do such a good job at explaining everything away that they seldom seek out what the underlying spiritual causes might be. I am not suggesting that we all get preoccupied with demon hunting, but the point is that we need an increased awareness of the spiritual realm and how it interfaces with our day to day reality. People have drawn a line between the spiritual and natural realms that is a much thicker line than what really exists. In reality, the line between the spiritual and the natural is very thin. Far too many oppressed and afflicted people have remained oppressed and afflicted because the church has failed to properly discern the integral relationship between the spiritual and physical realms. May Spirit-filled believers stop making statements like these:

"Ah, she's just prone to get sick."

"It's just the flu."

"You know, that heart condition just runs in the family."

"I guess he just caught a virus."

Rather, may God's people humble themselves, pray and repent with worshipful faith-filled hearts. May Spirit-filled believers recognize the power and the authority that has been given to them in Jesus' name to nullify the oppressive works of darkness. The Lord of heaven is to be magnified above all earthly circumstances.

Another negative ramification of naturalistic thinking is that people think of science and the medical professions as the final authorities on health.[51] While God does expect man to use the intellect that He gave him, at the same time, that intellect must include the integration of supernatural thinking. Of course, such thinking is not possible apart from the work of the Spirit. Spirit-filled believers do have the ability to be spiritually minded on such matters,[52] holding the Word of the Lord as a higher authority than scientific reasoning.

While our natural thinking processes are a gift from God, they are also limited. Spiritual realities need to be engaged intellectually, but they can only be comprehended spiritually. The Bible says 1 Corinthians 2:14-16,

> The man without the Spirit does not accept the things that come from the Spirit of God, for they are foolishness to him, and he cannot understand them, because they are spiritually discerned. The spiritual man makes judgments about all things, but he himself is not subject to any man's judgment: "For who has known the mind of the Lord that he may instruct him?" But we have the mind of Christ.[53]

How does spiritual understanding come to us? A few verses earlier, Paul says,

> However, as it is written: "No eye has seen, no ear has heard, no mind has conceived what God has prepared for those who love him"—but God has revealed it to us by his Spirit. The Spirit searches all things, even the deep things of God.

The understanding that we need comes supernaturally. It comes by revelation through the Holy Spirit. Back up a little further in chapter two, and

---

[51] People who serve in the healing and medical professions should be highly esteemed. Often it has been the divine-human partnership between God and physician that has resulted in the needed healing breakthrough. Even Jesus affirmed the need for physicians (Mark 2:17).

[52] 1 Corinthians 2:1-5, 9-10, 14-16.

[53] 1 Corinthians 2:14-16.

Paul tells us why God has chosen to manifest such understanding solely through the Spirit:

> When I came to you, brothers, I did not come with eloquence or superior wisdom as I proclaimed to you the testimony about God. For I resolved to know nothing while I was with you except Jesus Christ and him crucified. I came to you in weakness and fear, and with much trembling. My message and my preaching were not with wise and persuasive words, but with a demonstration of the Spirit's power, so that your faith might not rest on men's wisdom, but on God's power.[54]

Here it is clearly stated. God does not want our faith to be based in human reason. Our faith is to rest on God's power.

2. The Father Heart of God. If we are going to minister to people with any degree of confidence that God is going to meet their needs, then we need to have a pretty good grasp of the heart of God the Father. Do we as a needy people have a benevolent God in heaven? Yes, we do! His goodness and grace are far beyond our comprehension.

Jesus came to reveal to the world the heart of the Father. When we receive the revelation of the Father's great heart for His children, then we are able to love Him in return. Furthermore, that revelation of His heart causes us to believe that He is both loving enough and strong enough to grant us salvation, sanctification, the fullness of His Spirit, healing, deliverance, encouragement and whatever else divine providence might bring.

Several years ago I was approached by some individuals who felt uncomfortable with my message regarding the loving heart of the Father. They were afraid that too much of a focus on God's love and mercy would make people think that they could get away with living a sinful life. There was no need for concern, for as 2 Corinthians 6:17-18 demonstrates, the call to holiness and the extension of the Father's love to humanity are inseparable. In 2 Corinthians 6, verse 18 speaks to us regarding the father-heart of God; however, verse 17 says, "Come out from them and be separate, says the Lord. Touch no unclean thing, and I will receive you." These words are an essential prelude to that which follows in verse 18. The Father seeks us out, and He

---

[54] 1 Corinthians 2:1-5.

calls, "Come out from where you are! Separate yourself from lesser things, and be exclusively mine!" We heed His call, answering, "Yes!" No more is needed. He has been waiting all of our lives for that moment. His heart is pounding, eager to embrace us. When we make that decision to forsake sin and follow Him, He draws us into His arms, calls us His children, and assures us by saying, "I will be a Father to you, and you will be my sons and daughters" (2 Corinthians 6:18). The final word is that Father loves and accepts all who will turn to Him.

Years ago when I was a student at Lee College (now Lee University) in Cleveland, Tennessee, Floyd McClung, Jr. came through and conducted a special series of services on campus. At that time he worked with Youth With A Mission in Amsterdam, Holland. In those meetings, every message he delivered was about the father-heart of God. It changed my life. Here I am over thirty years later, and I still remember the personal revival that I and many others experienced that week. Since that time, I have also acquired the book that Floyd McClung wrote on the subject, entitled, *The Father Heart of God.*[55]

Floyd McClung brought attention to the fact that Jesus reveals to us the father-heart of God. Jesus said, "Anyone who has seen me has seen the Father."[56] We find many examples of how Jesus revealed the Father to us in the Bible. For instance, on one occasion some mothers wanted Jesus to bless their little children, but the disciples stood in the way, saying, "Jesus can't be bothered right now." They didn't understand. Jesus reprimanded His disciples for holding the children back, took those children in His arms, and talked to them. He had time for them. He had time to listen to their stories. He had time to play their games. He didn't mind being "bothered." In fact, He wasn't bothered. He wanted to be with them. It was for this very reason that

---

[55] Floyd McClung, Jr., *The Father Heart of God* (Harvest House Publishers, 1985).

[56] John 14:9.

He came into the world: to embrace us all as children. It is through seeing that Jesus had time for the children that we learn that *God has time for us!*

Another day came in the ministry of Jesus when He met a Samaritan woman at a well. Jesus knew that she was an immoral person, yet He was not ashamed to be seen with her. Jesus actually *wanted* to talk with her. He saw past her sin and hardness of heart, and He kept loving her and reaching to her. The result was that she in turn received His love, because He helped her to see God in a way that she had never seen Him before.

As we see Jesus, there is much that we learn about God our Father: (1) He seeks us with all of His heart. (2) We are the center of the Father's affection. (3) He is with us all the time. (4) We always have His undivided attention.

I am a father with five children, and I remember the first time that I held our first child, Tiffany, in my arms. The emotion that filled my heart was indescribable. Suddenly it occurred to me that if this is the way that I feel about this child, how much more the heavenly Father feels this way about me!

There is more to this than meets the eye. I believe that God made the family the way He made it with all of its emotional ties so that we could learn something about *His* love for us! If you are a parent, you can relate to what I am saying. Think about the way that you care for your children, and then apply that sense of care to the picture of Father God's care for you as His child.

When my children were smaller, there were times when they were out playing that they came in covered with sand and mud. What was I going to do about it? Now, I rejected the mud, but I didn't reject the child. I despised the mud, but I love that child. Make the application to God's heart for us. Yes, we were sinners. Yes, we still sometimes fail God and get dirty, but it does not change His great love for us! What He wants to do is be the loving Father who doesn't get too concerned about that spiritual mud that is dripping all over the place. Oh yes, He despises that muddy sin stuff, but Jesus, His Son, bled and died to take care of it. He wants to wash us clean. He wants to give us a new start. We can start all over because we have a loving Father who makes it so.

I remember the first time that I preached on this subject. In preparation for that sermon, I searched through the Bible for every passage that I could find that conveyed the heart of the Father toward His children. Compiling those passages was such an enriching experience. Out of a wealth of biblical passages, we can hear the call of our Father's voice to all who have set their love on Him. In this composite rendering of the Father's message to His children, we hear Him saying,

> My child, I have loved you with an everlasting love. With lovingkindness I have drawn you.[57] I washed you from your sins in the blood of my own Son, and now, you are my child.[58] I rejoice over you with joy. I joy over you with singing.[59] Always know that I will never forsake you.[60] I preserve all who set their love on me.[61] I will deliver you. I will set you on high.[62] I will fill your treasures.[63] I will crown you with life.[64] You have never seen, you have never heard, it has never even entered your heart what I have prepared for you.[65] I will love you unto the end.[66] Yes, that is true, for neither death nor life, neither angels nor demons, neither the present nor the future, nor any powers, neither height nor depth, nor anything else in all creation, will ever keep me from loving you.[67]

---

[57] Jeremiah 31:3.

[58] Revelation 1:5; 1 John 3:1.

[59] Zephaniah 3:17.

[60] Psalm 37:28.

[61] Psalm 145:20.

[62] Psalm 91:14.

[63] Proverbs 8:21.

[64] James 1:12.

[65] 1 Corinthians 2:9.

[66] John 13:1.

[67] Romans 8:38-39.

Yes, it is true, "We love Him, because He first loved us."[68] As someone once said, "It is in the light of such mercy that our stony hearts are made tender and that our wounded hearts are healed." It is in light of such mercy that we can believe that God the Father would delight in manifesting supernatural answers to our prayers through the power of the Holy Spirit.

As we perceive God as our loving heavenly Father, it is fitting for us to respond to that revelation by becoming more like little children. A revival of signs and wonders would more likely occur in an environment filled with child-like believers. Matthew 18:1-4 says,

At that time the disciples came to Jesus and asked, "Who is the greatest in the kingdom of heaven?" He called a little child and had him stand among them. And he said: "I tell you the truth, unless you *change* and *become like little children*, you will never enter the kingdom of heaven. Therefore, whoever *humbles* himself like this child is the greatest in the kingdom of heaven.

In light of this passage, to enter the realities of God's kingdom,[69] believers must be willing to yield to change, humble themselves and become like little children. Children are typically readable, open and real. They are not reluctant to express their wants and emotions. They are known for their simple ability to trust. Do you see any qualities here that we as believers should emulate? We will more easily access the life of the kingdom when we stop making the Christian life so complicated. Let's just be the Father's children.

3. The Goodness of God. This divine quality has been addressed previously, but it is repeated here for emphasis in the context of the discussion at hand. The goodness of God is a concept closely related to the revelation of the Father heart of God. Simply stated, we need to be thoroughly convinced that God is entirely good, and the devil is entirely bad. Too often, God gets blamed for the afflictions and misfortunes that overtake people. God

---

[68] 1 John 4:19.

[69] Luke 11:20 indicates that signs and wonders such as the delivering of the oppressed are evidences that the kingdom of God has come.

does not work evil. God is good, and His works are good.[70] The following passages accent the distinction between the works of the Lord and the work of the evil one:

> **John 10:10**
> The thief comes only to steal and kill and destroy; I have come that they may have life, and have it to the full.
>
> **James 1:17**
> Every good and perfect gift is from above, coming down from the Father of the heavenly lights, who does not change like shifting shadows.
>
> **1 John 5:19**
> We know that we are children of God, and that the whole world is under the control of the evil one.
>
> **1 John 3:8b**
> The reason the Son of God appeared (was manifested) was to destroy the devil's work.

We need to know that God's works are good because He is essentially good. Yes, He is good in His essence, but He is also good in the sense that His disposition toward us is one of goodness or favor.

4. The Will of God to Heal. Those who would desire to enter a ministry of signs, wonders and miracles need to be convinced that it is God's will to heal. Those who say that it is not always God's will to heal will be hard pressed to prove their point on the basis of Scripture. In the Bible, all afflictions were associated with the work of the devil, and God's will was to overthrow the devil's oppressive work. The burden of proof rests upon those who would take exception to that belief.

---

[70] In those cases where God is the dispenser of affliction, it is with a view toward judgment or chastisement. God's ultimate will in such times is not that the afflicted continue to suffer; rather, He would desire them to repent, call upon His name and be restored.

Rather than remain in the erroneous experientially-formed beliefs that downplay the work of the Lord our Healer, the church would do well to become reacquainted with passages such as these:

> **Exodus 15:26**
> He said, "If you listen carefully to the voice of the Lord your God and do what is right in his eyes, if you pay attention to his commands and keep all his decrees, I will not bring on you any of the diseases I brought on the Egyptians, for *I am the Lord, who heals you*" [emphasis mine].
>
> **Hebrews 11:6**
> And without faith it is impossible to please God, because anyone who comes to him must believe that he exists and that *he rewards those who earnestly seek him*" [emphasis mine].

But some still object, saying, "What about Paul's thorn in the flesh mentioned in 2 Corinthians 12:7?" Paul's thorn in the flesh was not a physical affliction. Paul's thorn in the flesh was either a person or a group of people that had become a constant annoyance to him. That was the meaning of the expression, "thorn in the flesh" or "thorn in the side," in Paul's day.

5. The Present-Day Work of the Spirit. In some cases, a rethinking of theology and doctrine is needed. For instance, many have been taught against the belief that signs and wonders continued beyond the days of the first apostles. That erroneous doctrine is referred to as cessationism. Cessationists teach that the charismatic gifts ended with the deaths of the first Apostles, yet both the Scriptures and church history testify otherwise.[71]

Attitudinal Preparations

1. Mutual Love and Respect. The Apostle Paul called the Corinthian church to the integrated exercise of nine manifestation gifts in a context of mutual love and respect. These gifts of the Spirit were given to individuals for the benefit of the body. Paul teaches the believer to earnestly desire spiritual gifts; they are necessary for the edification of the church.

---

71 Michael L. Brown, *Israel's Divine Healer* (Grand Rapids, Michigan: Zondervan Publishing Company, 1995), 63, 64 and 291.

After noting that there is a diversity of grace gifts (*charismata*), ministries and divine powers, operating by the "same Spirit," Paul states, "Now to each one the manifestation of the Spirit is given for the common good."[72] Have the gifts been given to *individuals* or to the *corporate church*? Paul's words imply that both are true. The gifts have been given "to each one" or to individuals, but they have been given to those individuals for the good of the faith community or the "common good."

Stated another way, God gives gifts to individuals so that those individuals in turn might have something to give to the faith community. Allow me to illustrate. When my children were very young, they did not have the ability on their own to purchase Christmas gifts for their siblings. My wife and I would often give each of the children gifts that they could wrap and place under the Christmas tree. If we had not placed those gifts in their hands, they would have had nothing to give to one another. Likewise, when God gives us spiritual gifts, He has given them to us so that we might have some manifestation of His goodness and grace to impart to others. Otherwise, we would have nothing to give.

Paul proceeds to list nine manifestations of the Spirit that are given to individuals *for the common good*: word of wisdom, word of knowledge, faith, gifts of healing, operations of miraculous powers, prophecy, distinguishing between spirits, various kinds of tongues, and interpretation of tongues. These gifts are not based in natural abilities. They are supernatural, for they are in fact manifestations of the Spirit, and they have been given for the good of the body of Christ. What prevailing attitudes are needed to ensure that these gifts are manifested in a way that benefits the body? We can list them:

1. Concern for the common good
2. Appreciation and understanding of how the parts of the body work together in mutual care for one another
3. An earnest desire for spiritual gifts
4. The most excellent virtue—love

---

[72] 1 Corinthians 12:7.

In 1 Corinthians 13 Paul proceeds to teach about "the most excellent way"[73] or the most excellent manner in which the gifts should operate. He is *not* speaking of a *gift* that is more excellent than those noted in chapter twelve. He is speaking of a *manner* or *way* of functioning in those gifts that is more excellent than a manner characterized by dishonor and division.

A lot of people think that charismatic gifts caused a problem in the Corinthian church. Such is not the case. Gifts were not the problem. The problem is to be found in the manner in which the people treated one another. The gifts will not function properly in an atmosphere that is not dominated by love.

First Corinthians 13 is a monument to the virtue of love. In that chapter, Paul teaches that love is patient and kind. Love does not envy, boast or act rudely. Love is not proud or self-seeking. Love is not easily angered, and it keeps no record of wrongs. Love does not enjoy seeing people mess up. It looks for opportunities to protect, and it is more inclined to bear part of the blame than it is to join the mob of accusers. Love always moves in the direction of trust. It always hopes, and it always perseveres. Love never fails; it never gives up.

Such love is to be the prevailing attitude in the atmosphere of the local church. Without it, the gifts of the Spirit will not function properly. Without love, ministry will be severely handicapped. With love, our service unto Christ becomes powerful.

2. Compassion. Be a person of love and compassion—the two dispositions of the heart are inseparable. Faith works by love,[74] and the only way that any of the grace gifts can function properly is when they are motivated by love.[75]

Jesus is our example in all things. His compassion is one of the most consistent reoccurring features of His ministry. In Luke 7:11-17, Jesus saw a

---

[73] 1 Corinthians 12:31.

[74] Galatians 5:6.

[75] 1 Corinthians 12:31; 13:1-13.

mother at Nain whose only son had died. He had compassion on her and comforted her saying, "Don't cry."[76] Jesus then touched the bier and said, "Young man, I say to you, get up!" The young man sat up alive. The working of this miracle follows this pattern:

1. Jesus saw the need,
2. He was moved with compassion,
3. He ministered comfort,
4. He touched, and
5. He spoke the word which affected the miracle.

Whether the manifestation of grace results in a son being raised from the dead or in someone being encouraged and strengthened by a prophetic word, compassion is always the driving force behind Spirit-empowered ministry.

3. Earnest Desire. I have heard some well-intentioned individuals say, "We are not supposed to seek gifts. We are to seek the Giver of the gifts."

The heart of what they are trying to say is probably correct, in that they are attempting to bring a needed focus to the very personal and intimate fellowship that we share with the Holy Spirit. However, I am more inclined to say, "Seek the Giver *and* the gifts." Rather than downplay a pursuit of the charismatic gifts, the Bible actually encourages it. The Apostle Paul instructed even the dysfunctional Corinthian church to "eagerly desire spiritual gifts, especially the gift of prophecy."[77]

4. Patience with the Process of Preparation. Be patient with the process of preparation. Cindy Jacobs notes, "The greater the calling and responsibilities God plans to give a prophet, the more exacting, and at times lengthy, the preparation for the call."[78]

---

[76] Luke 7:13.

[77] 1 Corinthians 14:1.

[78] Cindy Jacobs, *The Voice of God: How God Speaks Personally and Corporately to His Children Today* (Ventura, California: Regal Books, 1995), 43.

Michael Sullivant observes,

> God has normally prepared His prophetic vessels in the solitude of some kind of wilderness environment. Today, many people get their first taste of a season of prophetic anointing and immediately want to minister on platforms with microphone in hand! This kind of overexposure can be dangerous to all. God may choose to hide the glory inside of you for lengths of time and in various ways that may be confusing if you don't understand this principle. If He is presently choosing to hide you, find contentment in knowing Him, and let your roots go down deep into the rich soil of His transcendent kingdom. Then you will be ready to 'manifest' in His perfect time.[79]

5. Humility. Stay humble.[80] God gives grace to the humble, and the charismatic gifts are manifestations of grace. In fact, the word *charismata* actually means the "things of grace" or the "grace gifts." Spiritual giftedness is not an indication of a person's greatness; it is an evidence of God's mercy and grace. God speaking to and working through a believer is not dependent on who he or she is or how mature the person might be. It has more to do with God's commitment to get through to His people. If believers will walk humbly with God, He will get His message and ministry through to them. [81]

Humility will cause us to honor and respect the ministry of others. We will not get caught up in comparing one gifted person against another. Humility will also cause us to function in a mutually submissive manner in relationship with all of the equipping gifts—apostle, prophet, teacher, pastor and evangelist. Have a servant's heart. A humble person will approach Spirit-

---

[79] Michael Sullivant, *Prophetic Etiquette: Your Complete Handbook on Giving and Receiving Prophecy* (Lake Mary, Florida: Charisma House, 2000), 109.

[80] Jack Deere, *Surprised by the Voice of God: How God Speaks Today through Prophecies, Dreams, and Visions* (Grand Rapids, Michigan: Zondervan Publishing House, 1996), 317.

[81] Floyd McClung, Jr., "The Prophetic Journey," a prophetic ministry conference, Westmore Church of God, Cleveland, Tennessee, 2005.

empowered ministry with a teachable spirit and with a willingness to be corrected.[82] Be submissive in your relationships within the local church.[83]

6. An Ear to Hear. Have an ear to hear what the Spirit is saying. Live your life every day expecting to hear His voice. Listen for Him. Learn to recognize Him. With a particular view toward the prophetic, Michael Sullivant has stated, "We mustn't forget that listening, not speaking, is the basis of the prophetic."[84] The prophet Isaiah said,

> The Sovereign Lord has given me an instructed tongue,
> to know the word that sustains the weary.
> He wakens me morning by morning,
> wakens my ear to listen like one being taught.[85]

In the New Testament, James elevated the virtue of hearing or listening above the fleshly habit of undisciplined speech, stating, "Everyone should be quick to listen, slow to speak..."[86]

How can we be certain that it is God's voice that we are hearing? Over time, we can learn to recognize the voice of the Shepherd; Jesus said that His sheep hear His voice.[87] We will hear something in our spirit, and we will automatically think, "That sounds like the Shepherd's voice!"

When God speaks, what He has to say will agree with Scripture. However, His message may contradict the opinions or beliefs of others.[88] There is also a consistent character to words that come from God,[89] and His words will always

---

[82] 1 Corinthians 14:32.

[83] Jacobs, 133.

[84] Sullivant, 168.

[85] Isaiah 50:4.

[86] James 1:19.

[87] John 10:27.

[88] Deere, 323.

[89] Ibid., 324.

bear good fruit.[90] Remember that New Testament prophetic ministry is redemptive in nature; therefore, when God speaks, He always has some redemptive purpose in mind. Paul told the Corinthians that true prophecy results in people being strengthened, encouraged and comforted;[91] therefore, the implication is that when God speaks, I will feel stronger, I will have more courage, and I will gain a great sense that the Holy Spirit—the great Comforter—is with me. Prophetic hearing is essential to the faithful exercise of all aspects of Spirit-empowered ministry.

Experiential Preparations

Spiritual formation and ministry development are most certainly dependent upon the impact of the Scriptures upon our lives. The Bible provides us with indispensable concepts essential to the functions of Spirit-empowered ministry. However, our development as ministers also calls for *experiential encounters* with God.

Years ago I used to hear the criticism, "You Pentecostals are all about *experiences*." I answer without apology, "That is correct." We are all about experiences—having ongoing unceasing experiences of encounter with God. Biblically speaking, that is what the knowledge of God is all about. Knowing Him is not just a cognitive adventure. While it does include the engaging of the human brain, the knowledge of God is primarily a matter of allowing God to encounter us in the real stuff of life. This God is real. He is not just an idea. He wants to be known relationally—even face-to-face. Experiential encounters with His Presence transform the whole person—mind, body and spirit. Here we will describe several spiritual experiences that are essential to the development of Spirit-empowered prayer teams.

1. The Baptism of the Holy Spirit. Spirit-empowered ministry calls for us to be immersed or baptized in the Holy Spirit. I like to encourage recruits for ministry to receive the baptism of the Spirit before they start their training. However, an opportunity for receiving the Gift of the Spirit might also be

---

[90] Ibid., 325.

[91] 1 Corinthians 14:3.

provided within their ministry training. Regular opportunities to receive this blessing should actually be a part of normal congregational life.[92]

2. Continual Infilling of the Spirit. The Bible teaches us that being full of the Spirit results in the power of God being manifested through us.[93] It also instructs us to be filled and to be *continually filled* with the Spirit.[94] When Ephesians 5:18 tells us to be continually filled, it is actually saying that we are to *remain in a continual state of being filled* with the Spirit.

What does it look like to remain in a continual state of being filled with the Spirit? How does a person practically enter in to such a state?

The old-timers in the Pentecostal movement used to refer frequently to the practice of "tarrying" in the presence of the Lord. Tarrying involved remaining continually in prayer until a breakthrough was realized. People have been known to tarry before the Lord in fasting and prayer for days. It is a matter of pressing in for a breakthrough and giving God time and space to manifest an answer.

In the midst of the Toronto Revival that began in 1994, the practice of "soaking" in the presence of the Lord became a popular spiritual practice. Soaking is similar to tarrying, but it typically does not involve the same intensity of focus toward a specific breakthrough. Here the seeker says very little to God. It is more about relaxing, listening and allowing the Lord to speak and minister to the seeker. The idea is to absorb or soak in the Holy Spirit. Both tarrying and soaking are practices that prove helpful for posturing oneself for a continual infilling of the Spirit.

Association and regular fellowship with other people who are hungry for the things of the Spirit also positions a person to receive more. Michael Sullivant suggests,

---

[92] The receiving of the Gift of the Spirit should not be perceived as something apart from the normative life of the faith community. Frequent opportunities should be provided for the receiving of the baptism of the Holy Spirit in the context of the regular corporate worship experience.

[93] Acts 1:8; 2:17-18.

[94] Acts 19:6; Ephesians 5:18.

> Place yourself in spiritual environments in which believers are worshiping and waiting upon the moving of the Holy Spirit through the spiritual gifts. Experiences will inevitably come if you do so.[95]

3. Intimacy with and Passion for Jesus. One of the names for the Son of God is the name "Emmanuel"—meaning, "God is with us." Ever since the expulsion of Adam and Eve from the Garden of Eden, the Lord has greatly desired to once again dwell with man. He longs for friendship with us. It boggles the mind when one realizes that this great God actually *wants* to be close to us.

Like Abraham, the desire of many believers is to be called the "friend of God." The good news is that God Himself desires friendship with us. Yes, He wants our obedience too, but He so greatly longs to see that obedience rising out of a heart of passion for Him and His Son.

While many of us desire to be busy about our Master's business, let us not forget the lesson portrayed by the story of Mary and Martha in Luke 10:38-42 where Mary sat at the feet of Jesus clinging to His every word while Martha was busy about her work. Yes, there is work to be done, but what the Savior desires from us more than anything else is the kind of passion that Mary had for His presence.[96] It is out of our intimacy with the Lord that Spirit-empowered ministry will flow.[97]

Pursue intimacy with Christ. So much of Spirit-empowered ministry is guided by the prophetic, and prophetic ministry is more about a deeper relational intimacy with God than it is about receiving specific revelatory details and knowledge. Jack Deere states, "Friendship is the key to recognizing God's voice."[98]

---

[95] Sullivant, 189.

[96] Luke 10:38-42.

[97] Those who want to explore the subject of intimacy with God and passion for Jesus further should study Solomon's Song of Songs from the allegorical perspective.

[98] Deere, 331.

Michael Sullivant testifies,

> Simply being with Him and adoring Him and then seeking to obey Him in the full range of my earthly life and responsibilities has positioned me to hear His voice at the appointed times. When I have tried to get Him to "say something" to me, I have usually been frustrated.[99]

Jesus called His disciples to intimate friendship with Himself. Imagine His earliest days with these young followers. Jesus would eventually send forth these men to proclaim the Gospel and demonstrate its power. To prepare them for this mission, Mark 3:13-15 shows that they needed to be *with* Him.[100] They would live every moment in His company, absorbing His words and coming to know His heart. There was a mystical dimension to this relationship; although they would one day be physically separated, in reality, Jesus would never leave His disciples. Whatever spiritual work they might do, it would actually be the Lord working in and through them by the agency of the Spirit.

4. The Disciplines of the Spiritual Life. Be devoted to the spiritual disciplines.[101] Prayer, meditation, worship and study should be primary disciplines of those who would desire to function in Spirit-empowered ministry. Prayer is the means through which the believer presses into breakthrough and calls upon heaven to be manifested in the earth.[102] Spirit-empowered ministry should be saturated with prayer and intercession. Meditation fine tunes the ear to hear what the Spirit would desire to say. Worship elevates the person into the realm of God's presence and heightens one's sensitivities to the Spirit. Study of the Word fills a person with the sound of God's voice, giving the Spirit more to work with—more to call forth

---

[99] Sullivant, 109.

[100] Intimate communion with Jesus should be regarded as a prerequisite to effectiveness and integrity in charismatic anointing.

[101] Richard J. Foster, *Celebration of Discipline: The Path to Spiritual Growth* (New York: HarperCollins Publishers Inc., 1998).

[102] Matthew 6:10.

prophetically when it is needed. A private devotional life characterized by prayer, meditation, worship and study is key. [103]

Inevitably when I announce that I am going to teach on the spiritual disciplines, someone will express concern that the subject might drift toward legalism. Such a concern is understandable, because the very word "discipline" sounds like nothing but a lot of hard work. Some may even think that we are trying to outlaw smiles and laughter. On the contrary, the disciplines are grace-based and life-giving. Richard Foster, author of *Celebration of Discipline*, points out, "Joy is the keynote of all the Disciplines."[104] In fact, I am inclined to think that we should add laughter to our list of spiritual disciplines.

The disciplines have to do with *liberation* from self-interest and striving so that we may *enjoy* the joy of the Lord. God has given us the disciplines of the spiritual life as a means of positioning ourselves to gain the greatest benefit from the grace that he lavishes upon us. The disciplines allow us to place ourselves before God so that he can transform us.

Galatians 6:8 says, "The one who sows to please his sinful nature, from that nature will reap destruction; the one who sows to please the Spirit, from the Spirit will reap eternal life." The spiritual disciplines are a way of sowing to the Spirit. Foster speaks of the disciplines as a path of disciplined grace. The path does not produce the change; it simply places us where the change can take place.

How do the disciplines relate to Spirit-empowered ministry? *Meditation* trains our spirit to hear the voice of God so that we might rightly know what to do in a ministry encounter. The life of private personal *prayer* is essential before one can effectively engage in a ministry of prayer, for one can only minister out of the overflow of what God is already doing in the heart. *Fasting* assists with the destruction of unbelief, and the humility that it employs

---

[103] Floyd McClung, Jr., "The Prophetic Journey," a prophetic ministry conference, Westmore Church of God, Cleveland, Tennessee, 2005.

[104] Foster, 2.

becomes the invitation for the manifest presence and power of God to show up. God gives enabling grace to the humble. *Study* gives us a biblical and reasonable basis for our ministry. *Simplicity* unclutters our lives from things of lesser worth. *Solitude* removes the distractions. *Submission* makes certain that it is indeed the Lord who is in control. *Service* is the fruit and outworking of the submissive heart. *Confession* keeps the heart pure and healed. *Worship* keeps us intimately connected with the One seated on the throne—the source of all authority and power. *Guidance* protects us from presumptuous action in ministry. Finally, *celebration* both honors the One who deserves all the glory and provides the environment in which the Father will bless those who have sought to faithfully serve Him.[105]

5. A Renewed Prayerfulness. In Mark 11:17 Jesus said, "My house will be called a house of prayer for all nations." On the day that He spoke those words, a lot of other activity was going on in the outer court, but these activities were distracting the people from the priority of prayer. To be even more specific, the busyness was crowding out the *nations*, robbing them of the opportunity to pray and seek the Lord. Jesus confronted this perversion of the temple's purpose and brought a cleansing. Similarly, Jesus wants to drive out of our lives and out of our churches all of the busyness that is crowding out prayerfulness.

In Matthew's version of this episode, he shows that following this cleansing of the temple, the blind and the lame came to Jesus and were healed.[106] Back in the 1980s, Larry Lea observed regarding this passage that here with the healing of the blind and the lame, the "house of prayer" becomes the "house of power." When applying this truth to the way that we do ministry, I believe that we can state it in these words: If we will become a house of prayer, the Lord will make of us a house of miracles.

In light of Jesus' declaration that His Father's house would be known as a "House of Prayer for all nations," we should make prayer a central focus of

---

[105] Foster.

[106] Matthew 21:14.

ministry. For Spirit-empowered ministers, prayer is not a peripheral concern. Prayerfulness fulfills a great desire in the Father's heart.

6. Multiple and Varied Corporate Prayer Experiences. In our ministry we have found it important to offer multiple and varied opportunities for corporate prayer experiences. One approach to prayer may appeal to some but not to others.

While pastoring in the state of Maine, the Lord placed it in my heart that I was to start a Saturday night prayer meeting to prepare the ground for the Sunday morning service. At first there was a good deal of excitement about this call to prayer, but over a few weeks the number of participants began to fall off. One Saturday night I showed up, and I was the only one there. While I paced the floor praying all alone, I cried out, "Lord, am I the only one? Doesn't anyone else care about the mission that You have given this church?"

Immediately I heard the Spirit say, "You just do what I have given you to do, and I will take care of the rest!"

A few days later I was meeting with my good friend, Phil Strout, who at that time was pastoring the Vineyard Christian Fellowship of Greater Portland. I asked him, "Why won't people come together to pray?"

He responded by asking, "How many opportunities do you give them to pray?"

My immediate thought was that if I could not get them to show up for one prayer meeting, how could I possibly get them to show up for other opportunities. Phil proceeded to explain that the success of prayer ministry in his church was partly due to the fact that multiple and varied kinds of prayer experiences were offered to the people. Those who might not be attracted to one form or focus of prayer might be attracted to another. Church members whose schedules might have prohibited them from coming to a Saturday night prayer meeting may be able to attend one conducted on a Monday morning, for instance. In the weeks that followed my meeting with Phil, we began to offer multiple and varied opportunities for prayer ministry, and at that point the cultivation of a culture of prayer began in our congregation.

7. An Extended Corporate Fast. A church will not fully comprehend what it means conceptually to be a "House of Prayer" until they are led into the practices that are characteristic of being such an entity. Corporate fasting is one practice that demonstrates congregational devotion to prayerfulness. After 1995, every year that I was serving in pastoral ministry I made it a point to lead my congregation through some form of meaningful corporate fasting experience. Most often we promoted a twenty-one day experience of prayer and fasting, providing a lot of instruction, support and encouragement along the way.

What is fasting? Before directly addressing that question, let us first consider what fasting is not. Fasting is not a hunger strike. It is not an attempt to manipulate God, and it is not an attempt to get God to love you more. What then is fasting? Fasting is to voluntarily deprive oneself of physical nourishment in order to accomplish a spiritual purpose. In the Old Testament, when people desired to humble themselves before the Lord, they often did so by entering into a fast. The psalmist in Psalm 35:13 said, "I humbled myself with fasting."

Why fast? Fasting serves several purposes. We fast as an expression of turning to God with the whole heart.[107] We fast to humble ourselves before God.[108] We fast to identify with the life and mission of Jesus, and to prepare ourselves for greater works. If Jesus did it, we want to do it! It is part of following Him, even if it means following Him into the wilderness! Jesus fasted forty days in preparation for a great work.

Why fast? We fast to put priorities in proper order. In Matthew 4:4 Jesus said, "Man does not live on bread alone, but on every word that comes from the mouth of God." You will not live the life that Jesus has for you to live as long as you are preoccupied with the temporal—"bread alone." We are to live on "every word that comes from the mouth of God." You can feast while you are fasting! Crave for every word that you can possibly receive from the

---

[107] Joel 2:12.

[108] Psalm 35:13; James 4:6, 10.

mouth of God. Have an appetite that says, "I don't want to miss a thing that He has to say!"

Why fast? We fast to remove unbelief and to become more aligned with and aware of our spiritual authority.[109] We fast as a preparation for hearing God's voice.[110] We fast to seek the Lord's manifest Presence—to become more aware of Him.[111] Bodily appetites can distract us from the awareness of God's Presence. Fasting fine tunes that awareness. We fast to bring the body into subjection to the Spirit and the Word. Fasting assists us in our pursuit of self-control and discipline.[112] We fast as an act of faith to consider ourselves dead to carnal desires.[113] We fast to stimulate a hunger for the things of God—a yearning for intimacy with Him.[114] We fast to make ourselves weak so that we might know His strength. Fasting helps us to come to a point of total reliance on God. Through fasting, our attitude is one that says to the Lord, "It's You or nothing!" Fasting brings to us the realization that we have nothing to offer; our resources are insufficient.

What are the things that can nullify fasting? According to Jesus, desiring to be seen of men can be a hindrance.[115] From the book of Jeremiah we learn that a love for wandering and a lack of restraint can nullify fasting.[116] Isaiah cautions that doing as you please on the day of your fasting can cancel out its impact. Exploiting your employees can nullify fasting. Participation in quarreling and strife can negate the potential benefit.[117] Participation in

---

[109] Matthew 17:19-21; Mark 9:14-29, KJV.

[110] Acts 13:2.

[111] Matthew 9:15.

[112] 1 Corinthians 9:27.

[113] Romans 13:14.

[114] Matthew 5:6.

[115] Matthew 6:16-18.

[116] Jeremiah 14:10.

[117] Isaiah 58:3-4.

accusation and malicious talk can nullify fasting. Finally, neglecting the needy can hinder.[118]

How should we fast? Before getting into how this discipline should be carried out, let us address a very practical concern. From a medical point of view, it would be wise to consult with your physician before pursuing an extended fast, especially if you are already dealing with serious health issues. Having noted this precaution, we can now consider the following guidelines:

First, talk with God about your fast. Ask the Lord how many days or how many meals He wants you to fast. Also, ask the Lord to what degree you should fast. For instance, at times one may want to fast solid food but continue to take in fruit and vegetable juices.

Second, submit to the leading of the Holy Spirit. Let the Holy Spirit drive you into the "wilderness" to fast. The "wilderness" is where God is. There are many biblical examples to establish this truth.

Third, prepare for the fast. In the days leading up to the fast, fine tune your prayer life and Bible reading habits. Adjust your eating habits as well. If you drink coffee, it is a good idea to taper off of the coffee before the fast begins. If you have never fasted before, start with a meal or a day, and let God bless your faithfulness. Then you can move on into a more extended fast as the Lord gives you grace to do so.

Fourth, those who have fasted before might want to ask the Lord for His wisdom regarding an extended fast. Once He gives that wisdom, step out with confidence knowing that you will be sustained by the Holy Spirit.

Fifth, for extended fasts, take heed to a few practical guidelines. Taper in, and taper out. By all means, do not stuff yourself with food the day before the fast begins! The same applies for when the fast has been completed. Gradually taper out of extended fasts with an intake of liquids. Furthermore, for extended fasts, drink fluids. Water should be your primary fluid. Some fruit juice or vegetable juice might be advisable on extended fasts; it is all up to you

---

[118] Isaiah 58:9-10.

and the Lord to make those decisions. As far as drinking milk is concerned, understand that milk is about the most perfect source of nourishment that God created; therefore, satisfying hunger by drinking milk on a fast physically nullifies the effect of the fast.

Sixth, you do not want to draw too much attention to yourself while you are engaged in the fast. Be worshipful, and maintain a joyful countenance and appearance throughout the fast. Furthermore, don't talk about it much.[119]

Seventh, make time during the fast to draw aside and away from others for prayer, Bible reading and reflection. Consider such time as "feasting while you're fasting."

Do not be surprised if the fast becomes both physically and spiritually difficult. Fasting is in many ways a self-imposed wilderness experience. It is in fact an act of offensive spiritual warfare. Do be aware that often it is in such times that our faults begin to surface. If that happens, do not partner with self-condemnation. On the other hand, if the Holy Spirit convicts you, repent, and speak the liberating truth over yourself. Also remember that the sense of breakthrough does not usually come until the fast is over. Jesus' forty days in the wilderness is a good example. Temptations bombarded Jesus during His fast, but when the fast had concluded, the blessing came: angels came and ministered to Him.

8. A "God Encounter" Retreat.[120] Cleansing and healing of the heart may be needed for one considering entry into front-line ministry. In my ministry, I have found that two-day God Encounter retreats facilitate such inner spiritual

---

119 Matthew 6:17-18. While the Bible does advise us to not broadcast the fact that we are fasting, it may be important to tell your immediate family members so that they will understand why you are not coming to the dinner table.

120 Jim Egli and others have created retreat models based on the experience of believers in Bogota, Columbia. A "God Encounter" retreat includes times of solitary reflection, repentance and confession of sin to one another. Participants pray for and affirm one another's cleansing and healing. Opportunity is also given for participants to receive the baptism of the Holy Spirit. This "God Encounter" experience may need to be a prerequisite to participation in the training course. Jim Egli, *Encounter God* (Houston, Texas: Touch Outreach Ministries, 2000).

workings in an excellent way. Sozo[121] sessions or participation in Ancient Paths[122] sessions can produce similar results.

Churches that conduct God Encounter retreats typically center in on the truth conveyed in two key New Testament passages. The first of these is 1 John 1:9, which says, "If we confess our sins, he is faithful and just and will forgive us our sins and purify us from all unrighteousness." From these words we know that any person may come to God, confess their sins to Him, and receive forgiveness and purification.

However, there is another passage that takes this matter of confession a step further. James 5:16 says, "Confess your sins to each other and pray for each other so that you may be healed." What is different here? While confession of sins to God brings healing and purification, confession of sins to other brothers and sisters in the Lord combined with a mutual exchange of prayer brings healing. This principle is the basis of the God Encounter retreat model.

9. Stewardship. Be a good steward of the grace gift that has been entrusted to you.[123] Fan the gift into flame, and do not neglect it.[124] Michael Sullivant writes, "Take whatever steps you must take: Study, pray, seek God's face, put it into practice, but by all means stoke the fire until that gift returns to its original intensity."[125]

10. Association with Other Spirit-Empowered People. Start spending quality time with other believers who share your passion for Jesus and the things of the Spirit. People who desire to advance in the ministry of healing tend to grow in that area as they associate with others who are pursuing the

---

[121] Sozo is an inner healing ministry that is often associated with the work of the Transformation Center at Bethel Church in Redding, California.

[122] Ancient Paths seminars are conducted by Family Foundations International, an organization based in Littleton, Colorado and led by Craig Hill.

[123] 1 Peter 4:10.

[124] 2 Timothy 1:6.

[125] Sullivant, 20.

same thing. Likewise, people desiring to grow in the prophetic tend to become more prophetic as they associate with other prophetic people.

Tending to Personal Character and Spiritual Health

1. Integrity. Related to preparations of the heart is the need to tend to issues of personal character. Be a person of integrity. The call here is for both ministerial and personal integrity. Ministerial integrity as it relates to the prophetic in particular involves being careful not to exaggerate or to go beyond what God is actually saying. Integrity calls for an honoring of the person for whom the prophecy is intended, but it also requires that a prophetic message not be revised just to make it more palatable or understandable to the hearer.

Personal integrity largely relates to the issue of purity. Keep yourself pure. Guard your heart, guard your mind, and be selective in your thought-life. The Apostle Paul describes the selective thought-life in these words:

> Whatever is true, whatever is noble, whatever is right, whatever is pure, whatever is lovely, whatever is admirable—if anything is excellent or praiseworthy—think about such things.[126]

Consider the importance of a selective thought-life, especially for the faithful and effective exercise of prophetic gifts. The imagination must be reserved for that which is holy. Keep the canvas of your mind clear and clean so that the Lord may paint *His* pictures there.

Another aspect of personal integrity relates to what we do with the revelations the Lord gives us. We most certainly are not to indiscriminately broadcast revelations that have the potential to bring harm to others. We are not to use our prophetic gifting to satisfy our own ego—to try to appear spiritual before others. Finally, we need to be totally and promptly obedient to the Lord. When we are obedient with a little, he will most likely entrust us with much more at the appropriate time.

---

[126] Philippians 4:8.

2. Significance and Wholeness. Personal significance and wholeness are important issues for the person desiring to be used of God in Spirit-empowered ministry and leadership. Seek significance only in terms of relationship with Christ. All believers are called to live out of their identity in Him. In order for the integrity of ministry to be preserved, it is important for those who minister to be secure in that identity.[127] Otherwise, you may be inclined to think that how you perform prophetically or supernaturally has something to do with you.

Be whole. People who have not experienced wholeness can be prone to do some foolish things. On this point, Floyd McClung gives the example of one who might try to use prophecy to deal with personal relational conflicts. The prophetic should not be used to deal with relational conflict. Relationship issues should be handled like healthy people would deal with relationship issues. When a person is angry or caught up in a major disagreement, it is not the time to prophesy.[128]

Suggested Assignments

Essential to this study is the promotion of a lifestyle of fellowship or relationship with the Holy Spirit. Such friendship with God moves from an initial baptism in the Holy Spirit to learning to listen for the Holy Spirit's voice. Learning to listen and wait for the Holy Spirit's guidance is the key to success in this time of ministry training. Take time this week to devote yourself to prayer, fasting and meditation. Listen for the Spirit's voice. If He whispers something to you, write it down. Ask the Holy Spirit to manifest His power to you and to the others around you, such as your own ministry team, in the weeks to come.

If you are a ministerial student, seek out an experienced Spirit-empowered minister and offer to accompany him or her in times of ministry. Let that person be your mentor. Simply accompany the minister in supportive prayer and serve in any way that you can. Observe how he or she ministers at

---

[127] Floyd McClung, Jr., "The Prophetic Journey," a prophetic ministry conference, Westmore Church of God, Cleveland, Tennessee, 2005.

[128] Ibid.

the altar or in other contexts. As you watch and learn, expect that the Holy Spirit may begin to impress upon you what is going to happen next in the ministry encounter. If the Spirit impresses something upon you, it does not necessarily mean that you have to act upon it. This is training time. Let the Spirit's impressions serve to confirm what God is doing through your mentor as you observe. In time, your mentor will invite you to act upon things that the Holy Spirit shows you. The Holy Spirit delights in guiding hearts that want to be guided.

CHAPTER 3

THE BAPTISM IN THE HOLY SPIRIT

At the end of Jesus' days on earth with His disciples, He promised, "I am going to send you what my Father has promised; but stay in the city until you have been clothed with power from on high."[129] Then He said, "Do not leave Jerusalem, but wait for *the gift my Father promised,* which you have heard me speak about. For John baptized with water, but in a few days you will be baptized with [in] the Holy Spirit."[130]

What is this *promise of the Father* to which Jesus refers? The writer of the Acts 1 passage, Luke, seems to expect that the reader will know what this promise is. It seems that there must be some previous reference in the Gospel of Luke that could be called the promise of the Father, but what is it? Consider the words found in Luke 11:11-13 as a possibility:

> Which of you fathers, if your son asks for a fish, will give him a snake instead? Or if he asks for an egg, will give him a scorpion? If you then, though you are evil, know how to give good gifts to your children, how much more will your Father in heaven give the Holy Spirit to those who ask him!

Although a number of other passages from both the Old Testament and the Gospels could be cited, it is this one reference that Jesus makes to His Father's desire to give the Holy Spirit that stands out in Luke's writing.

Your heavenly Father *wants* to give you the Holy Spirit. He wants you to *ask* Him for the Holy Spirit. When you ask Him for the Spirit, He will not give

---

129 Luke 24:49.

130 Acts 1:4-5.

you something else instead; He will give you precisely what you have requested: the Spirit Himself.

I often hear it taught and preached that the purpose for the Baptism in the Holy Spirit is to give us power for service. That is true, but I do not think that explanation goes deep enough into the heart of the purpose. The Holy Spirit is much more than a spiritual battery charger. He is not just powering us up so that we can do more work. This blessing goes deeper.

In Acts 1:8, Jesus said, "You will receive power when the Holy Spirit comes on you; and you will be my witnesses in Jerusalem, and in all Judea and Samaria, to the ends of the earth." On the basis of these words, some may still say, "See, there it is! The Holy Spirit is going to power us up that we can go out and do some witnessing all over the planet!"

Look carefully at the passage. It says, "You will receive power when the Holy Spirit comes on you; and you will *be* my witnesses." The Holy Spirit causes us to *be* or *become* something that we could never have become apart from Him. When the power of the Holy Spirit comes upon us, we are brought into immediate contact with God Himself, and that connection transforms us. We are talking about an intimacy with the Almighty that causes us to become eyewitnesses to His person and work. Through the immediacy of His presence, we know Him, and because we know Him, we can rightly represent Him in the world as His witnesses. Our witness or testimony then flows out of a real heart to heart and face to face relationship with God.

My Story

This experience known as the Baptism in the Holy Spirit can happen suddenly and without human effort, or it can occur after an extended time of seeking God's face. For my grandfather, King Turpin, it happened suddenly. While attending a prayer meeting in Lynch, Kentucky, he knelt down at a chair to surrender his life to Christ. When he stood to his feet, he was a new man. It was the thing that happened next that caught him by surprise. He heard a voice that spoke these words: "He is coming. He is coming. He is coming." After hearing those words the third time, the power of God struck his head and swept down through his body to his feet. Then he began speaking in tongues. It was a sovereign move of the Spirit and required no effort on my grandfather's part.

My introduction to the Holy Spirit was more gradual. At the age of ten, I came to faith in Christ. One year later at the age of eleven, I had my first personal encounter with the power of the Holy Spirit. I was sitting in church, and the pastor shared with the congregation a prayer request for a child who had injured her eye. The pastor then said, "I feel that there is someone here tonight who God has healed of an eye injury, and He wants you to join me in this prayer."

I immediately knew that the pastor was talking about me. When I was two years old, the cornea of one of my eyes was cut open by a sharp piece of metal. My parents prayed for me, and I was completely healed within a few hours. "He's talking about me," I said to my parents. Then I stepped forward and joined the pastor in the prayer.

When I returned to my seat and sat down beside my parents, the power of the Holy Spirit came upon me. My body started vibrating, and the pew was shaking with me. My father turned to me and said, "Randy, that is the Holy Spirit on you. Do you want to receive the Baptism in the Holy Spirit?"

I shook my head and said, "No." Although I knew what I was feeling was God, I was afraid. I had never felt anything like that before. The Spirit lifted from me, and the shaking stopped.

I might have resisted receiving the Baptism on that night, but a hunger and thirst for the Holy Spirit remained with me. Within a few months, I felt compelled to pursue the same Spirit who was pursuing me.

At the age of twelve, I knelt in prayer and asked God the Father to fill me with the Holy Spirit. For three consecutive days, I came before Him and prayed the same prayer. On that third day, out of a heart of expectation, I raised my hands and just started praising and thanking Him for the Gift of the Spirit.

As I praised the Lord, I felt something wonderful rise within me, and my words of praise were overtaken by a quivering of my tongue and lips. Altar workers nearby encouraged me to forget English and to speak out the syllables that were coming to me with no concern for how they sounded.

I simply spoke out the sounds that were upon my tongue. It did not sound pretty, and it certainly made no sense. Nevertheless, what I heard coming out of my mouth was awesomely powerful. I was speaking in tongues. I had received the Baptism of the Holy Spirit.

In the days and weeks that followed, a new power dominated my life. I read the Bible with a new depth of insight and understanding. My prayer life became more fervent. My worship became more passionate. My witness became more courageous. In fact, I wanted to share the Gospel with everyone. With this new connection with the Holy Spirit, my deep desire was for every aspect of my life to center upon Jesus.

Personal Instruction for Receiving the Gift of the Spirit

One of the greatest joys of my ministry has been to pray with others to receive this blessing. It is my hope that the following list of questions and answers will prove helpful as you too seek to be clothed in the Spirit's power.

1. Who is the Holy Spirit? The Holy Spirit is God. He is just as much God as the Father is God. He is just as much God as Jesus is God. He is the Third Person of the Trinity.

Throughout the Bible we see that whenever God chooses to do anything in the earth, the Holy Spirit is always involved in one way or another. The Holy Spirit is God's agent on earth.

Before God created life on earth, it was the Holy Spirit who hovered over the waters. Whenever God conveyed a message to mankind, it was the Holy Spirit who came upon prophets, and they in turn spoke and wrote the holy Word. When it was time for God's Son to come to earth, it was the Holy Spirit who came upon the Virgin Mary and caused Jesus to be conceived in her womb. At the initiation of Jesus' ministry, it was the Holy Spirit who settled upon Him in the likeness of a dove, anointing Him for supernatural works. On the day of Pentecost it was the Holy Spirit that was poured out upon the church, empowering God's people for the proclamation and demonstration of the Gospel with signs and wonders following those who believed.

Likewise, in our day, it is by the power of the Spirit that God's eternal purposes are accomplished among men. The Holy Spirit is God's agent in the earth.

2. **What is the Baptism in the Holy Spirit?** Before Jesus returned to heaven, He promised that the Father would send the Holy Spirit to continue and advance the ministry of Jesus in and through believers. Upon the Holy Spirit's arrival, they would be "baptized" into Him. In other words, they would be immersed into the Holy Spirit. Being saturated with the Spirit, they would live a life full of His presence, purity and power.

On the day of Pentecost,[131] Jesus' promise was fulfilled, and 120 believers received this Baptism of the Holy Spirit. Within hours of that initial outpouring, thousands of others came to faith in Christ and were transformed by God's manifest presence and His marvelous grace. From that day forward, the church proclaimed the Gospel of Jesus boldly with miracles accompanying their message.

The Baptism in the Holy Spirit does empower us for serving God, but this encounter with the Third Person of the Trinity also plunges us into the depths of an intimate relationship with Jesus. As a matter of fact, this latter aspect of Holy Spirit baptism is probably the primary reason why every believer should desire to be filled and to be continually filled with the Spirit.

3. **How can a person receive the Baptism in the Holy Spirit?**

a. **First, accept by faith Jesus Christ as Lord and Savior, and turn from sin.** On the day of Pentecost, a crowd of seekers asked Peter what they had to do to receive the great blessing of the Spirit that they were witnessing.

Peter replied, "Repent and be baptized, every one of you, in the name of Jesus Christ for the forgiveness of your sins. And you will receive the gift of the Holy Spirit."[132]

---

[131] Acts 2.

[132] Acts 2:38.

So, your first step is to repent and receive God's forgiveness made available to you through Jesus, His Son. Perhaps you have already taken this step.

b. Second, *believe* that God the Father *wants* you to receive the Baptism in the Holy Spirit. We must believe that our Father truly desires to bless us. Regarding this blessing, Jesus once said, "If you then, though you are evil, know how to give good gifts to your children, how much more will your Father in heaven give the Holy Spirit to those who ask him!"[133]

c. Third, *desire* to be filled. Christians should have a deep hunger and thirst for the Baptism in the Holy Spirit. Jesus promised that those who deeply desire the Spirit will indeed receive the Spirit. In John 7:37-38 He said, "If anyone is thirsty, let him come to me and drink. Whoever believes in me, as the Scripture has said, streams of living water will flow from within him."

In verse 39 John goes on to comment, "By this he meant the Spirit, whom those who believed in him were later to receive."

d. Fourth, ask the Father for the Gift of the Spirit. The Father *wants* you to *ask* Him for the Gift of the Spirit; asking demonstrates that we deem this blessing to be of great worth. Furthermore, the act of asking is evidence of our trust in the love and faithfulness of our Father. Remember, Jesus promised that those who ask for the Spirit will in fact receive the Spirit.[134]

Asking for the Gift of the Spirit does not need to be complicated, and you can probably pray that prayer without anyone coaching you. However, if you feel that you do need help, perhaps the following will prove beneficial:

> Heavenly Father, I belong to you, and Jesus is my Lord. Your word says that if I will ask, I will receive the gift of the Holy Spirit. So, in the name of Jesus, I am asking you to fill me to overflowing with the Holy Spirit. Baptize me with the Holy Spirit. By faith, I receive the Gift of the Spirit, and I thank you for answering my prayer.

---

[133] Luke 11:13.

[134] Ibid.

e. Expect that God will baptize you in the Holy Spirit. Jesus said, "I tell you, whatever you ask for in prayer, believe that you have received it, and it will be yours."[135]

Let your expectation drive you into an "I don't care how long it takes" frame of mind. Although it is entirely possible for believers to fully receive the Holy Spirit baptism the first time they ask, for some it takes time to get to a point where they can be totally open and ready to receive.

Those first recipients of the Holy Spirit in the book of Acts were willing to wait several days for the Gift; they were able to do so because Jesus had *promised* that the Gift would be given.[136] We too are encouraged to persevere in expectant prayer, because the Gift has been promised to us as well.[137]

f. Ask the Father to give to you the ability to pray/speak in tongues. Is the Baptism in the Holy Spirit only about speaking in tongues? No. However, speaking in tongues is normally the first outward evidence that one has received the Gift of the Spirit.[138]

Why should you desire to speak in tongues? The Bible teaches that this gift enables our own spirit to communicate directly to God in a way that surpasses our natural understanding. Have you ever been so full of love and adoration for the Lord that you just could not express it in words? Have you ever had a prayer that you could not quite pull together with your own words? When we pray in tongues, our spirit is bypassing our understanding, and through the power of the Holy Spirit, our spirit prays the perfect will of God.[139]

This function of tongues is also known as "praying in the Spirit." Praying in the Spirit is not the only purpose for tongues, but it is the most immediate

---

[135] Mark 11:24.

[136] Acts 1:4-5.

[137] Acts 2:39.

[138] Acts 2:4.

[139] Romans 8:26-27.

reason why the gift should be desired. When we pray in the Spirit we ourselves are built up and strengthened in our inner being.

To receive tongues, you may want to pray something like the following, and then start giving vocal expression to whatever you are sensing in your spirit.

> Father, I believe the Holy Spirit is within me. Now, Holy Spirit, rise within me as I praise God. I fully expect to speak in tongues as you give me the ability to do so.

g. Speak in tongues. Once you have asked for tongues, expect the Spirit to rise up from within you like a flowing stream (John 7:38). If tongues do not immediately spring forth, you may want to just spend some time offering continuous praise to the Lord in anticipation of the gift that is to come.

Understand that the Holy Spirit is not going to force you to speak in tongues. He enables *you* to do the speaking. He is going to use your lips and mouth to form the words. You supply the sound; the Holy Spirit will supply the words. If strange syllables come to your mind, just speak them out. At first you may think that it is just you making it up, but once you step out in faith with it, the Spirit of God will increase His anointing upon what you are doing.

Perhaps for you tongues may begin to manifest in yet another way. As you are praising the Lord, you may suddenly realize that your native language is getting harder and harder to speak. Your mouth may be trying to do something different. Just go with it, even if it sounds very strange. It does not matter what it sounds like. In a way similar to a child learning to speak, your language in tongues will grow. Remember, you are beginning to pray from your spirit when you speak in tongues; it will not make sense to your mind, but it will make perfect sense to God. Just speak it out.

h. If you do not immediately speak in tongues, continue to receive from the Holy Spirit, and continue to expect your prayer language to begin. Something is happening, even if tongues have not yet manifested. However, do not settle for anything less than the full manifestation of tongues. Just keep on receiving, keep on expecting, and keep on making efforts at speaking out those sounds as they come to you.

4. Once I have received the Baptism in the Holy Spirit, what should then happen?

a. Be continually filled with the Spirit.[140] Before Jesus' identity was revealed to the masses, John the Baptist stood waist-deep in the Jordan River baptizing and preparing a people for the approaching kingdom of heaven. He was ready to identify the Anointed One—the Christ—as revealed by the Holy Spirit. He spoke these words:

> "I baptize [dip / soak] you with [in] water for repentance. But after me will come one who is more powerful than I, whose sandals I am not fit to carry. He [Jesus] will **baptize** you [He will be baptizing you] with [in] the Holy Spirit and [even] with [in] fire."[141]

In effect, he said, "Jesus will be baptizing you in the Holy Spirit, even in *fire*." Imagine how dipping any substance in fire would alter the substance. Applying the metaphor to the person and work of the Holy Spirit, this fire purifies. It refines and strengthens, as in the refining of metals. It provides warmth and light. Fire speaks of fervency, intensity and even passion. Fire is power. The Baptist said that Jesus would immerse people in this fire, and the word choice suggests that he would do so *repeatedly and continuously*!

The Apostle Paul also conveyed this idea of repeated encounters with the Holy Spirit when he said, "Do not get drunk on wine, which leads to debauchery. Instead, be [be being] filled with the Spirit."[142] In the original language, the words translated, "be filled with the Spirit," actually say, "*be being filled* with the Spirit," or "be in a continuous state of being filled with the Spirit." The application is that we should always keep ourselves positioned to be continuously filled with the Holy Spirit. There is always more. Continuous infilling with wine will radically change a person's behavior, removing inhibitions, bringing a temporary sense of happiness and often making them fearless. Continuous infilling with the Holy Spirit will do something similar, except the happiness part is replaced with a joy that will not fade away. Both

---

[140] Ephesians 5:18.

[141] Matthew 3:11.

[142] Ephesians 5:18.

fire and wine provide powerful images of how continuous contact with the Holy Spirit can radically and comprehensively change and redirect a person's life.

The Greek word for "baptize" was used outside of Scripture in reference to the dipping (or baptizing) of fabric in the dying process. The longer that the fabric remained immersed in the dye solution, the more the qualities of the dye that the fabric absorbed. Apply the metaphor to the believer's experience in the Holy Spirit. The longer and more frequent that a person becomes immersed in the presence and power of the Holy Spirit, the more the qualities of the Holy Spirit that the person will absorb. We are talking about soaking in the Holy Spirit, taking on His qualities.

b. Pray in tongues frequently in your personal prayer times. Praying in tongues is one of the ways that we can pray in the Spirit. [143] When you pray in the Spirit, you are praying the will of God.[144] When you pray in the Spirit, you are strengthening your own spirit.[145]

c. Make yourself available to the Holy Spirit for intercession. Intercession is prayer on behalf of others. Tell the Holy Spirit that you are available anytime day or night for Him to awaken you, to stir you and to call you into prayer. You may not even know for whom you are praying, but as you cry out in response to the Spirit's prompting, you are making a difference in somebody's situation.

d. As you receive, give it away. The best way to keep or increase anything that you receive in the kingdom is to give it away. Increase in the things of the Spirit comes with releasing to others. Pray for others. Impart to others. Start serving in your new-found spiritual ability.

e. Ask the Father for other spiritual gifts. The Bible teaches us to eagerly desire the gifts of the Spirit.[146]

---

[143] 1 Corinthians 14:4, 14-15, 18.

[144] Romans 8:26-27.

[145] Jude 1:20.

[146] 1 Corinthians 14:1.

f. Expect the fruit of the Spirit to become more plentiful. The more contact that we have with the Holy Spirit, the more that we can expect His fruit to be produced in and through us. We are talking about more love, joy, peace, forbearance, kindness, goodness, faithfulness, gentleness and self-control.[147]

g. Respect the Spirit. We need to realize that the Holy Spirit is not just a mystical force. He is God. We need to respect environments in which He moves, people whom He may anoint and things that He may touch. We need to respect all things that pertain to Him. As a child of God, even your body belongs to the Holy Spirit. The Bible says, "Do you not know that your bodies are temples of the Holy Spirit, who is in you, whom you have received from God? You are not your own; you were bought at a price. Therefore honor God with your bodies."[148]

Much more could be said about this wonderful blessing of the Spirit, but hopefully these biblical suggestions will provide you with a place to begin in your quest for a deeper walk with God.

---

[147] Galatians 5:22-23.

[148] 1 Corinthians 6:19-20.

CHAPTER 4

THE MEANING OF THE PENTECOSTAL OUTPOURING

The great outpouring of the Holy Spirit on the Day of Pentecost in the second chapter of Acts changed everything. A fearful band of disciples became a fearless force. Supposed barriers to the propagation of the Gospel became insignificant. A God whom many had thought to be unknowable became immediate and tangible in His presence. This in-breaking of heaven into the affairs of earth left onlookers without choice; ignoring the happenings of that day was not an option. It was altar call time. They had to respond, and they did. Many of them responded with the question, "What does this mean?"

There were three initial signs that accompanied the Baptism in the Holy Spirit on the Day of Pentecost: (1) a sound like the blowing of a violent wind, (2) a visible manifestation that resembled flames of fire and (3) the manifestation of supernatural tongues. The sound was a sign. The visible manifestation was a sign. The tongues were a sign. What is a sign? A sign points to or indicates something other than itself. A sign does not point to or refer to itself.

Allow me to illustrate. I currently live in Columbus, Ohio. If my wife and I were to have an appointment in Wheeling, West Virginia, we would start driving east on Interstate 70. After about two hours of driving, we would see a sign that says, "Wheeling." Now, I would not pull over at the sign, stop there and say, "Kerry, we're here! Get out of the car now! We're at Wheeling!"

Would I get out of the car and stand there staring at the sign? No, not even I would do that. That is ridiculous. I did not drive two hours just to see a sign.

The sign is very important, but it is not the most important thing going on. A sign points to something other than itself. It is not about the wood, paint and metal that make up that sign. It is about the city of Wheeling itself.

In similar fashion, the sound of wind, the appearance of fire, and the other tongues were not about wind, fire and tongues. They were signs pointing to or indicating the arrival of Holy Spirit! They were signs indicating that a Baptism in the Holy Spirit was going on there in Acts 2.

When manifestations of the Spirit are occurring, they are indicators or signs that something is going on in the hearts of people and that something is going on in the realm of the Spirit. Now, I want to re-emphasize here that there is great value and purpose to spiritual manifestations such as tongues, but the manifestations are not what I am most interested in. I want to know what is going on in the hearts of people.

For instance, one man approached me after a church service a few years ago and testified about what God did in his life on the previous Sunday when he was baptized in the Holy Spirit. With humility and great joy, all he wanted to talk about was what God had done in His heart. He had received forgiveness and liberation from a longstanding area of struggle. He had been set free. Then he concluded, "Oh, and yes, I almost forgot to mention this. I spoke in tongues too! It was wonderful!"

You see, on the Day of Pentecost, the wind was not about the wind. The fire was not about the fire. The tongues were not about the tongues. It was all about the Holy Spirit, and the Holy Spirit is always all about pointing to Jesus!

Yes, I am excited when I see someone speaking in tongues, because it indicates to me something wonderful is going on there. However, my foremost thought is this: "I wonder what is going on in the heart of that person while the Holy Spirit is burning in her like fire! What is going on in the realm of the Spirit, while she is praying and praising in tongues?" That is what it really is all about.

As we read further in Acts 2, take note of the various responses and reactions of the people in the crowd. In Acts 2:37, after Peter preached his great sermon that day, we read that the people asked, "Brothers, what shall we do?" But before he preached, what were they thinking?

1. Some were disturbed. The onlookers in the crowd were from "every nation under heaven," the text says. When they heard the sound of people speaking in tongues, they came together in bewilderment. Note that the first response of people outside of the church was one of bewilderment; their minds were disturbed. Why? Their minds were disturbed because "each one heard their own language being spoken."[149]

2. Some were amazed. The next verse, Acts 2:7, says that they were "utterly amazed." In other words, they were marveling and wondering. There is even a hint of admiration in their response. They asked, "Aren't all these who are speaking Galileans? Then how is it that each of us hears them in our native language?" Then they exclaimed, "We hear them declaring the wonders of God in our own tongues!" [150]

3. Some doubted. Then Acts 2:12 says that they were "amazed and perplexed." In other words, they were entirely at a loss. They were probably saying, "We don't have a clue as to what is going on here." The King James Version says that they "doubted." The implication is that they were trying to weigh things. They wanted to understand. Their hearts were searching. They had questions. If we do not have searching hearts, we will likely draw immediate and premature conclusions, and in so doing we might miss God's visitation. The doubters were the ones who asked the question, "What does this mean?"

4. Some mocked. Acts 2:13 says that others made fun of them and said, "They have had too much wine." The mockers represent those who jump to immediate premature conclusions.

---

[149] Acts 2:6.

[150] Acts 2:7-8, 11.

5. Many believed, after they received the preached Word. Peter stood and brought the light of Scripture into what was going on. He answered the question, "What does this mean?"

Peter essentially answered, saying,

"This is God's Spirit. This is for all flesh. This means you can expect more. This means that biblical prophesies are being fulfilled. This means that the last days have begun. This means that the great and glorious Day of the Lord is approaching. This means that you had better get saved while there is time!

"Miracles, wonders and signs from God verified the fact that Jesus of Nazareth was a man accredited by God, but of course, you already know that, or at least you should have known that by the signs and wonders that accompanied His life and ministry. But here is something that you would have had no way of knowing until now. On this day in which the Holy Spirit is being poured out as you are seeing and hearing, on this day in which you are asking, 'What Does This Mean?', this is what these signs and wonders are pointing to: Jesus is very much alive!

"You people in the crowd, the message that Jesus is risen may be news to most of you, but we have already been convinced of that for several weeks now. We—His disciples—were all there and saw Him alive.

"But now, here is something that even those of who are His disciples are excited about today. It has not been until this day that we have seen and experienced the evidence—the proof that Jesus is now exalted and seated at the right hand of the Father.

"What does all of this mean—this outpouring of the Holy Spirit? It means Jesus is being unveiled! It means that Jesus is risen. It means that Jesus is exalted and seated at the right hand of the Father. It means that our enemies are beneath His feet! It means that this Jesus, whom you crucified, is both Lord and Messiah! It means the Lord is restoring joy, gladness and hope! It means there is more to life than living and dying! It means He want us to know Him here and now, face to face! It means His face is shining upon us! It means God wants to fill you with Himself! It means less of the works of the flesh, more of the Spirit!"[151]

---

[151] These words are a creative and expanded paraphrase of Acts 2:14-36.

Then the people responded, "Brothers, what shall we do?"[152] The way of salvation was explained, and three thousand souls were saved on that day.

[152] Acts 2:37.

CHAPTER 5

STEWARDING GOD'S PRESENCE

Several years ago my daughter, Miranda, sent me a message from Redding, California. We were living in Scarborough, Maine at the time, and Miranda had moved to Redding to enroll in Bethel School of Supernatural Ministry. Eventually her move to Redding would prove to be providential for the rest of our family, resulting in all of us moving out there. In her note, she had written these words: "I am learning to become more aware of the Dove who sits on my shoulder."

Miranda was echoing the words of Bethel's lead pastor, Bill Johnson. He frequently wrote and spoke about the hosting and stewarding of God's presence, and one of the metaphors he used was the image of a dove sitting on a person's shoulder. If a dove were sitting on my shoulder, I would be very careful and intentional about my movements. Knowing that the dove represents the Holy Spirit, I would also want to make sure that my movements take me only to where the Holy Spirit wants to go. I would want to move in a way that is in keeping with His nature.

The Dove does not rest upon us for our benefit alone. He desires to find a resting place on others as well. Bill Johnson illustrates by going back to the account of Noah releasing the dove from the ark. When he first released the dove, it could not find a resting place, so it returned to the ark. On a third attempt, he sent out the dove, and it did not return. It had found a place to rest.

We are like Noah. We who are aware of the Holy Spirit resting upon us have been authorized to release the Spirit to others and into spiritual atmospheres around us. If we were not aware of His presence, then we could have this kind of influence, but we *are* a people who cultivate this awareness.

Jesus suggested something similar. He spoke of us letting our peace rest upon a house when we enter it, if it is deserving of that blessing. He also said that if that house proves unworthy of the blessing, then we are to let that peace return to us.[153] He speaks as though this peace were something tangible—somewhat like the dove that Noah released. Peace and the presence of the Holy Spirit are nearly synonymous.

The pictures presented in these biblical illustrations motivate us to become increasingly aware of what we carry—the very presence of God. These images also prod us to make ourselves aware of our environments and the people around us. Every day we step into places that need the presence of the Lord. Every day we are within reach of people who need his presence. As Bill Johnson teaches, when we are aware of what we carry, we are then able to release that very thing into atmospheres and onto other people's lives.

Let us learn to live a presence-centered life and to be releasers of God's presence. How can one release His presence? Sometimes His presence can be released by just showing up. One good example is Peter showing up and people getting healed with his shadow falling upon them.[154] Sometimes His presence is released with the utterance of a timely word. Sometimes it is a deed of kindness. Sometimes it may be nothing more than a smile or a touch. Make yourself aware of the Dove resting on your shoulder, and as you become more familiar with His ways, He will show you how, when and where He is to be released.

Suggested Assignments

In my stack of notes from Bethel, I have a lot of things written down that Bill Johnson has said on this subject. Among those notes, I found a number of his suggestions for cultivating an awareness of God's presence. Part of the following list of exercises is based on that material:

1. Become reacquainted with the secret place—that place where it is just you and Jesus, with no one looking to admire you and no one around

---

[153] Matthew 10:13.

[154] Acts 5:15.

to give you an applause. In that place, give thanks, worship, meditate on His word and listen for His heartbeat.

2. To draw the Holy Spirit into your sleeping hours, turn your affections toward Jesus before you fall asleep.[155]

3. Before going into a restaurant, pause and make yourself aware of God's presence. Turn your affections toward Him. Then walk into that restaurant aware of His presence. [156]

4. Before stepping into that next business meeting, make yourself aware of God's presence by turning your affections toward Him. You can expect His peace and wisdom to accompany you.

5. Before going to the mall, make yourself aware of God's presence. Expect divine appointments—opportunities to release His love and peace to someone in need of a blessing. Often prophetic things happen in public places when this awareness has been cultivated.

6. Before stepping into that hospital room, make yourself aware of God's presence. Comfort, peace and healing will accompany you.

7. Preachers and teachers, before stepping in front of that congregation or class, make yourself aware of God's presence. Turn your affections toward Jesus. He will meet you and your audience as you deliver what you have prepared.

8. Students, before taking that test, writing that paper or reading that difficult book, make yourself aware of God's presence. Your mind will be sharper, and a partnership with creative power awaits you.

---

[155] Based on notes taken from messages delivered by Bill Johnson.

[156] Bill Johnson.

CHAPTER 6

THE FIVE-FOLD EQUIPPING GIFTS

Jesus has given some amazing gifts to us. When we, the church, open our hearts to receive these gifts, our inadequacies disappear, and we are made ready to fulfill the works that God has ordained for us to do. Through these powerful gifts, we are built up, we become unified in faith, and we are drawn together around the common focus of knowing Jesus more intimately. In short, we get filled up with all that Jesus truly is.

This chapter's opening paragraph is another way of stating what Paul wrote to the Ephesians, saying,

> It was he who gave some to be apostles, some to be prophets, some to be evangelists, and some to be pastors and teachers, to prepare God's people[157] for works of service, so that the body of Christ may be built up until we all reach unity in the faith and in the knowledge of the Son of God and become mature, attaining to the whole measure of the fullness of Christ.[158]

What are the gifts that Jesus has given? They are the apostles, prophets, evangelists, pastors and teachers. Some refer to these five gifts as anointings, offices, leadership gifts or empowering gifts. Here we will primarily refer to them as equipping gifts. Whatever we want to call them, we must realize that these gifts are *not* mystical or spiritual impartations. Indeed, in other places in the New Testament there *are* gifts and manifestations that are essentially mystical, but something of a different nature is going on here. What is so different about this grouping of five gifts? The unavoidable truth is that these blessings to the church are real-life flesh-and-blood *people*—human beings.

---

[157] More literally, "the saints."

[158] Ephesians 4:11-13.

Who are these people—these apostles, prophets, evangelists, pastors and teachers? What do they do, and how does their function relate to everyone else in the church? There is a divine order to how these gifts function together. According to Paul's instruction to the Corinthians, the apostles and prophets lead in the ministry of the church; the teachers fulfill their ministry following the lead of the apostles and prophets; and everyone else proceeds in kingdom service in harmony with the leadership of these three (i.e., apostles, prophets and teachers).[159] A more in-depth study will be needed at another time to adequately define all five leadership gifts; however, for now let us consider how five-fold ministry functions on the basis of the following working definitions.

Apostles

Apostles are "sent ones"—sent by God to authoritatively fulfill a specific work in an assigned region or realm. For instance, Paul was an apostle to the Gentiles, and Peter was an apostle to the Jews.[160] One pre-Christian use of the word, apostle, signified an emissary who had been sent into a conquered area to establish the culture and government of the empire. The Christian use of the word carries a similar meaning. Apostles are sent by God to establish the culture and government of heaven in assigned regions and realms of the earth. Some are sent into geographic regions, and others are sent into sectors of society to bring kingdom influence.

Apostles are always concerned with the big picture of what God is doing, both in heaven and on earth. They are more attuned to the heartbeat of heaven than they are to any agenda that earth may try to dictate. They often desire to network with other apostolic leaders of like passion, reaching beyond their own immediate ministry contexts to build such relationships.

Following the biblical portrayal of apostles, they are noted for ministering supernaturally,[161] and they provide a model of leadership that motivates

---

[159] 1 Corinthians 12:28.

[160] Galatians 2:8.

[161] 2 Corinthians 12:12.

others to do the same. Often they are able to move in and out of the other four leadership anointings, and they have the ability to discern how all five can work together within the ministry context. As Peter Wagner states it, they are leaders of leaders.[162]

Attention needs to be given to the leading role of the apostle among the other four equipping gifts. 1 Corinthians 12:28 presents an order depicting a flow of authority and leadership:

> And in the church God has appointed first of all apostles, second prophets, third teachers, then workers of miracles, also those having gifts of healing, those able to help others, those with gifts of administration, and those speaking in different kinds of tongues.

On the basis of this passage and others, it appears that apostles in the New Testament functioned in authority over the other equipping gifts.

For those who may question forms of church government that allow one person to exercise the primary leadership role, Harold R. Eberle observes and states,

> After observing many, many churches, I can tell you that no matter what form of government a church claims to have, there is always one person who openly or quietly holds the greatest influence over the church. Setting up the proper government is never a matter of keeping it out of the hands of one person, but putting it into the hands of God's person.[163]

How prominent was the apostle in the New Testament? Obviously the original Twelve fulfilled a role of great significance, as they were the first to accept the commission to extend the kingdom of heaven into the earth. Beyond the original, there were others. Including the original Twelve, there are at least twenty-two apostles named in the New Testament.

---

[162] Wagner, 31.

[163] Harold R. Eberle, *The Complete Wineskin: Restructuring the Church for the Outpouring of the Holy Spirit* (Yakima, Washington: Winepress Publishing, 1993), 151.

The Original Twelve[164]

1. Simon (Peter)
2. Andrew
3. James, son of Zebedee
4. John
5. Philip
6. Bartholomew (Nathanael)
7. Thomas (Didymus)
8. Matthew (Levi)
9. James, son of Alphaeus
10. Thaddeus (Lebbaeus)[165]
11. Simon the Canaanite/Zealot
12. Judas Iscariot

Others

13. Matthias[166]
14. Barnabas[167]
15. Paul[168]
16. Andronicus[169]
17. Junias[170]
18. James, brother of Jesus[171]
19. Epaphroditus[172]
20. Apollos[173]
21. Silvanus[174]
22. Timothy[175]

---

[164] Matthew 10:2-4; Mark 3:13-19; Luke 6:12-16.

[165] It is widely accepted that Thaddeus is the same person as Jude, brother of James, who is listed in Luke 6:12-16. He is also referred to as Judas, not Iscariot in John 14:22.

[166] Acts 1:26.

[167] Acts 14:14.

[168] Acts 14:14.

[169] Romans 16:7.

[170] Romans 16:7.

[171] Galatians 1:19.

[172] Philippians 2:25.

[173] 1 Corinthians 4:6-9.

[174] 1 Thessalonians 1:1, 2:6.

[175] 1 Thessalonians 1:1, 2:6.

Recognizing a person as an apostle has nothing to do with elevating him or her to a place of lordship over a church or grouping of churches. Only Jesus is Lord. However, recognizing a person as an apostle is about acknowledging that Jesus has commissioned this individual to come into our midst to lead and to serve, and if we will allow him or her to fulfill that commission, we will all benefit from the deposit that the apostle carries. The kingdom will advance; the culture of heaven will be propagated in the earth; the church will become better established; a place will be made for the prophets, teachers, evangelists and pastors in our midst; and the saints will become equipped for works of service. The bottom line is that the work of the apostle is to lead the church into becoming apostolic—to authoritatively extend the kingdom of heaven into the earth. For the apostle, it is all about the kingdom and the big picture.

Prophets

Prophets see and hear the heart and mind of God, and they act and speak accordingly. At times they speak of what is to come; at other times they speak of what God reveals regarding the past or present. From a leadership standpoint, they know what God wants to accomplish, and together with the apostle, they work to lead the church in that direction. The prophet leads the way in helping the church become a prophetic church—a community of believers devoted to living their lives and fulfilling their mission on the basis of what God has revealed. For the prophet, it is all about what God is saying.

1. Characteristics of a prophet. True New Testament prophets have discernable characteristics:

a. **True prophets are people of godly character.** Their lives reflect the character of the One they represent. In Matthew 7:15-20, Jesus said that we would know true and false prophets by their fruit. Mike Bickle states, "These are people who diligently seek to cultivate holiness and deep passion for Jesus in their lives."[176]

---

[176] Mike Bickle, *Growing in the Prophetic* (Lake Mary, Florida: Creation House, 1996), 122.

b. True prophets improve the life of the faith community. Their ministry results in strength, encouragement and comfort,[177] and their prophetic gifts are ongoing and effective for the benefit of the body.[178]

c. True prophets are often intense in ministry. They are totally convinced of what they have seen and heard in the heavenlies, and they are committed to walk with God until that revelation has fulfilled its purpose. This intensity often translates into assertiveness. As a result of prophets frequently encountering resistance, many have developed a determined and assertive persona. The intensity of prophets serves the positive purpose of challenging those who are around them.[179] However, the caution here is that prophetic intensity not be taken as a license for rudeness or insensitivity.[180]

d. True prophets are often fixated on their message. Prophets are entrusted with a specific message, and they become fixated on it—as they should be. As a result, they may talk about the same topics repeatedly.[181]

e. True prophets are often perceived as unbalanced. Eberle is correct when he says of prophets that "they are *supposed* to be 'unbalanced,' at least through our natural eyes."[182] Disrupting[183] the status quo is a large part of what prophetic ministry is all about, in both the Old and New Testaments.

---

[177] 1 Corinthians 14:3.

[178] Bruce Yocum, *Prophecy: Exercising the Prophetic Gifts of the Spirit in the Church Today* (Ann Arbor, Michigan: Word of Life, 1976), 55.

[179] Eberle, 26.

[180] A review of 1 Corinthians 13 reveals that love should motivate and envelope the practice of all charismatic gifts.

[181] Eberle, 24.

[182] Ibid.

[183] The use of the word "disrupting" in this context should not be misconstrued as meaning that prophetic ministry should be rude, negative or condemning in nature. The intent here is to suggest that prophetic ministry does not leave things as they are found. When true prophetic ministry is received, something changes.

f. True prophets are sensitive to spiritual realities. They are more sensitive to spiritual forces and realities than the average Christian.[184] They are like people born before their time—thinking, acting and speaking on the basis of what will be and not necessarily on the basis of what already is. They typically conduct themselves in a way that does not make sense to people around them. What they have seen or heard in the heavenlies makes more sense to them than what their physical eyes can see or their physical ears can hear. Later others will likely see and hear what they see and hear, but initially they can come across as out of touch with immediate tangible realities.

g. True prophets are not easily swayed from their message. They know that they have heard from God, and they are convinced of what they have seen and heard. They are not influenced much by persecution or the opinions of others.[185] The caution here is that the prophet needs to remain open to the possibility that others may carry needed pieces of the prophetic picture. While the original revelation that the prophet had received may be undeniably a word from the Lord, the prophet's interpretation and application of what has been revealed may need additional prophetic input from others.

h. True prophets sometimes battle depression. The disparity between what *is* in the present and what *will be* in the prophetic future can be discouraging, especially when others *refuse* to see or believe what the prophet has seen. The persecution that often accompanies prophetic ministry can wear on the prophet and become disheartening. For this reason, it is critical that the prophet sustain a life centered in on hosting and stewarding the presence of God—the source of the prophet's joy and strength. It is also important for the prophet to not become isolated and insulated from other trusted believers who might be used of God to bring encouragement.

i. True prophets can be dramatic. They are inclined to dramatically emphasize the message God has placed on their hearts.[186]

---

[184] Eberle, 25.

[185] Ibid.

[186] Ibid.

j. True prophets value solitude. They are sometimes alone more than the average Christian.[187] The craving to hear from God consumes them.

2. The difference between Old and New Testament prophetic ministry. There are at least three misconceived differences between Old and New Testament prophetic ministry, and there are a few properly conceived differences as well.

The first misconceived difference relates to the issue of prophetic development. Some characterize the New Testament as lenient toward novice prophets who are still in development while the Old Testament does not make such an allowance. On the contrary, within the Old Testament there is evidence of many phases of prophetic development.[188]

The second misconceived difference relates to issues of relationship with the faith community. Some characterize Old Testament prophets as autonomous individuals in contrast to New Testament prophets who function within a community dynamic. While that perception may be accurate in many instances, Rickie Moore observes that there is one point in the Old Testament where there is a *community* of prophets—a situation that resembles the picture of New Testament prophetic ministry.[189]

The third misconceived difference relates to issues of intensity. Dr. Rickie Moore has stated, "What people are trying to avoid by drawing a line between the Old Testament prophet and the New Testament prophet is the intense demand of speaking for God."[190]

Rather than trying to distance itself from the intensity, the church is called to be just as intense and radical as the Old Testament prophets. The end

---

[187] Ibid.

[188] Rickie Moore, "The Prophetic Journey," a prophetic ministry conference, 2005, Westmore Church of God, Cleveland, Tennessee.

[189] Ibid.

[190] Floyd McClung, Jr., "The Prophetic Journey," a prophetic ministry conference, Westmore Church of God, Cleveland, Tennessee, 2005.

of the book of Revelation demonstrates the intensity of the prophetic gifting in the New Testament era.[191]

There are some properly conceived differences between prophetic ministry in the Old and New Testaments. The difference is not so much the result of a change in the relationship between God and the prophet, but in the relationship between God and his people as a whole. Bruce Yocum explains,

> The Old Testament prophet was a man unique among God's people because of the Holy Spirit's action in him. He was in direct communication with the Lord, while the people as a whole were not. But under the New Covenant, *all* of God's people receive the Holy Spirit, and *all* of God's people are in direct communication with God himself. In Old Testament Israel the prophet was thoroughly unique; in the 'new Israel' the prophet is one means among many by which God can speak directly to his people.[192]

The relationship of God to the prophet remains the same in the New Testament; he is the Lord's official spokesman, authorized to publicly declare His word.[193]

3. The prophet's role. What is the prophet's role from the biblical perspective? First, prophets are God's messengers;[194] they receive and proclaim the Word of the Lord.[195] Bruce Yocum says, "When the Christian community needs guidance, it can rightly look to its prophets for a word from the Lord.... Perhaps God will speak, perhaps he will not."[196]

Second, prophets are servants of God.[197] As His servants, they desire God's will to be done on earth, and they actively seek out God's will and

---

191 Ibid.

192 Yocum, 34-35.

193 Ibid., 35.

194 Ibid., 47. Isaiah 44:26, Haggai 1:13, Malachi 3:1.

195 Ibid., 49.

196 Yocum, 50.

197 Yocum, 47. Isaiah 20:3; Amos 3:7; Jeremiah 7:25; 24:4.

God's word[198] Once God has spoken, prophets are moved to obey the promptings of the Spirit.[199]

Finally, prophets are guardians,[200] and watchmen[201] and intercessors.[202] These aspects of the prophet's ministry clearly reflect God's heart of care for his people.

Teachers

Teachers have an extraordinary understanding of divine truth and have the anointed ability to communicate that truth in a way that transforms people. The teacher is first and always a student—a lifetime learner. He or she is a student of the Scriptures, a student of the Spirit and a student of the world around them. They are not just people who astound others with their amazing knowledge or intellect; they are gifted in the area of spiritual formation. They help people make the connection between cognitive knowledge and experiential knowledge. Their gifting is not limited to instruction in the Scriptures. The teacher is also gifted to impart understanding related to practical and even logistical aspects of ministry. Because they follow the lead of the apostle and the prophet,[203] their teaching is focused on making the church's apostolic direction and prophetic vision comprehensible and applicable to the life of the believer. Ultimately, the teacher empowers the church to be a community of disciples consumed with a passion for insight and understanding. The teacher also empowers God's people to be instructors of others—disciple-makers, in other words. For the teacher, it is all about the Scriptures, truth, insight, understanding and the making of disciples.

---

[198] Ibid., 50.

[199] Ibid., 49.

[200] Ibid., 47. Isaiah 62:6.

[201] Amos 3:4, Isaiah 56:10, Jeremiah 6:17, Ezekiel 3:17.

[202] Isaiah 62:6-7.

[203] 1 Corinthians 12:28.

Evangelists

Evangelists are consumed with a passion to release the kingdom of heaven to everyone on earth, and they are just as zealous about motivating every other believer to have the same passion. They carry both the message and the power of the cross. They lead people to faith in Christ, but they also demonstrate the power of the Good News through healings, miracles and deliverances. The mission of the evangelist is to prepare and empower the church to be an evangelistic church. For the evangelist, it is all about souls and the hope that the Good News brings.[204]

Pastors

Pastors[205] are devoted to the care of people. They are intimately involved with congregants, and they want to make sure that everyone's needs are met. People with a pastoral anointing and calling generate a church culture all around them that is characterized by care. Members of the congregation are supernaturally drawn together around that anointing,[206] just as sheep are drawn to their shepherd. For the pastor, ministry is all about care and the meeting of needs.

What can be confusing is that through the passing of time, the church world has settled into referring to the primary congregational leader as the "pastor." The term "pastor" is seldom used in the Scriptures to refer to congregational leaders. Floyd McClung is correct in saying, "'Pastor' is an overused term."[207] In many cases, the person holding the title, "pastor," does not function under the anointing of a pastor. He or she may be an apostle—a

---

[204] Eberle makes this insightful point: "God wants evangelists to be free. He left evangelists off the list of authority gifts [1 Cor. 12:28] because He does not want evangelists to be restricted to a rulership position. God's intention for evangelists is evangelism – not the supervision of a local church." Eberle, 66.

[205] Both the word, "pastor," and the ministry associated with the word call forth the imagery of a shepherd with his sheep.

[206] Eberle, 12.

[207] Floyd McClung, Jr., "The Prophetic Journey," a prophetic ministry conference, Westmore Church of God, Cleveland, Tennessee, 2005.

big picture kind of person who needs others on his team who are prophetic, evangelistic, pastoral and able to teach. Or the congregational leader may be an evangelist. In such cases, he or she may need to partner with apostolic and prophetic leaders, and a team of pastors and teachers may be needed as well. A congregational leader can be any one of the five within the five-fold model; he does not have to be a person who functions primarily in a pastoral anointing. In fact, Eberle goes so far as to say, "God's intention was that pastors work among the sheep, not rule over the local church."[208] More will be said along these lines as we consider the need to recognize all five of the equipping gifts.

Recognizing the Equipping Gifts

If we insist that our primary congregational leader be a pastor while he is actually a prophet, teacher, evangelist or apostle, we run the risk of stifling his or her ability to function in their true anointing, and we are shutting out a great gift that Jesus is trying to deliver to us. Understanding which of the five enabling or leadership anointings a congregational leader functions under is vitally important. Otherwise, it can be a very frustrating leadership situation.

If people are expecting their leader to be a pastor when he or she is actually an apostle, they might erroneously perceive that their "pastor" does not care about the needs of the people. "All he cares about is his vision or the next big city-wide project," they may say. Likewise, if they are expecting their "pastor" to be an evangelistic soul-winning leader just like their previous "pastor," while his or her true anointing is that of a teacher, they might erroneously think that their "pastor" does not care about souls. "All she does is study and conduct all of these classes and seminars. When are we going to reactivate our outreach ministries?" they may complain.

We need to consider how we are going to receive these equipping gifts with honor. The Bible teaches us to honor everyone,[209] and to honor one

---

[208] Eberle, 72. While I agree with what Eberle is suggesting from an administrative standpoint, I do recognize that even with pastoral ministry there is an aspect of "ruling," just as a shepherd has a responsibility to rule among his sheep.

[209] 1 Peter 2:17.

another above ourselves.[210] One aspect of honor is the acknowledgment of another person's value—receiving that person on the basis of what God has made them to be. Bill Johnson of Bethel Church (Redding, California) teaches that believers are truly functioning in a culture of honor when they are able to celebrate who people are without stumbling over what they are not. When a church is functioning in such a culture of honor, it strengthens the unity and reduces the likelihood that divisions will occur.[211]

Jesus taught us, "Anyone who receives a prophet because he is a prophet will receive a prophet's reward."[212] There is a principle here that helps us understand the function of honor in any relationship, but it especially speaks to how we receive people who come to us as one of Jesus' five leadership gifts. When we receive apostles, prophets, evangelists, pastors and teachers with honor, we open a door through which the rich deposit that these leaders carry may be imparted into our lives. If we do *not* receive a person on the basis of the anointing that he or she carries, we will miss out on the blessing that God intended to bring our way.

Consider this case study that illustrates how our receptivity to the five enabling gifts works. Jason[213] (not his real name) was a thirty-seven year old lead pastor recently appointed to serve a thriving New England congregation. Jason already knew many of the people in the church; he had grown up with a number of them and had actually attended this church when he was younger. One Sunday evening Jason and one of these friends met at a restaurant to get caught up with one another; it had been about seven years since they had last spent time together. While eating dinner, Jason's friend said, "It is great to have you back, I want you to know that. But I could never receive you as my pastor. You are my friend—not my pastor."

---

[210] Romans 12:10.

[211] 1 Corinthians 12:24-25.

[212] Matthew 10:41a.

[213] The names in this story are not the real names of the people who were involved, and some of the details have been altered as well.

While Jason was glad to hear the affirmation of friendship, he sensed that not being received on the basis of his leadership anointing could become problematic. About two years later, that gut-level feeling proved to be accurate. His friend encountered a personal crisis in which pastoral guidance was greatly needed, but there was no openness at all to receiving such assistance from Jason. Eventually his friend left the church.

A few months later Jason was ministering to a different friend from the past who had been struggling with a number of family issues. This friend said, "I know that we have been friends for a long time, but...." His friend choked up, trying to hold back the tears. He tried to continue, speaking with emphasis on each word, "You... are... my... pastor." In this second example, Jason had great freedom in ministering out of his place of anointing. In this case, a pastor had been received in the name of a pastor. This same principle carries over to all five of the equipping gifts.

Recognizing these enabling leadership gifts is important both for the leader and for the ones being led. Harold R. Eberle notes, "In the New Testament, we do not see Christian leaders being labeled as president, assistant pastor or superintendent or anything else short of their gifts."[214] When a person traditionally labeled as a "pastor" comes to recognize that he or she is actually an apostle and is able to say, "I am an apostle," that person is then able to move more fully in that calling. The same applies to recognizing any of the five leadership gifts.

Peter Wagner affirms this point when he applies it to the identifying of apostles in particular:

> When a given apostle knows for sure exactly what ministry or call God has given him or her, their self-confidence rises accordingly. This is not pride. Their confidence rests not in their own ability but in a deep assurance that they are obeying God and acting according to His will. To the degree that this happens, the apostle's authority increases.[215]

---

[214] Eberle, 36.

[215] C. Peter Wagner, *Apostles and Prophets: The Foundations of the Church* (Ventura, California: Regal Books, 2000), 28.

Others also need to recognize a leader's calling or anointing.[216] Each enabling gift needs to acknowledge and partner with the other enabling gifts. For instance, the apostolic needs the prophetic around it. It is the apostle who bears the responsibility for making a place for the prophet.[217] When we recognize which anointing or gifting is functioning through our leaders, as Eberle teaches, it is then that we will know what to expect from them.[218] If we will recognize all five leadership gifts, then the church will have a greater potential for seeing all five in operation.[219]

The Five-fold Versus Four-fold Debate

Many argue that Ephesians 4 is presenting us four leadership gifts and not five. According to the four-fold interpretation of Ephesians 4:11, "pastor" and "teacher" are two aspects of the same ministry gifting, making it more appropriate to refer to the gift as "pastor-teacher." Kelvin Page and others cite both exegetical and practical rationale for this position. For them, it would

---

216 Eberle, 36.

217 Kelvin Page, "The Prophetic Journey," a prophetic ministry conference, Westmore Church of God, Cleveland, Tennessee, 2005. In response to Page's presentation, when the apostolic proceeds to make a "roadway" for the prophetic, great care must be taken in this task. Apostolic leaders should not assume that they have the exclusive insight as to how this "roadway" is to be constructed. The very process of making the road should be prophetically informed. If the road is solely the product of human ideas, the functional relationship between the apostolic and the prophetic will not endure. The prophetic must be engaged in the very processes that define how it should function. This engagement requires a mutual exchange of insights between the two enabling gifts. It must be remembered that part of the nature of the prophetic is for God to come breaking in upon the church's predetermined models and methods. J. Randolph Turpin, Jr., "A Synthesis and Critique of 'The Prophetic Journey': The 2005 Prophetic Ministry Conference Conducted at Westmore Church of God" (an unpublished paper, Church of God Theological Seminary, 2005), 39.

218 Eberle, 37.

219 Ibid., 38.

appear that the text grammatically supports the four-fold position. Practically, they hold that it would almost be inconceivable for a person to be a true pastor and not also have the ability to teach the flock.[220]

Although grammatically a case can be made in either direction, the New Testament seems to most often present the pastoral and teaching roles separately.[221] Furthermore, if the enabling gift is truly a hyphenated pastor-teacher gifting, what is to be said about the anointed pastor who is not strong in the area of teaching? Likewise, what is to be said about the anointed teacher who is not strong in the care aspects of ministry? To force these two aspects of ministry together into one enabling or leadership gift may be taking the matter beyond the writer's intent in the Ephesians passage.[222]

---

[220] Kelvin Page, "The Prophetic Journey," a prophetic ministry conference, Westmore Church of God, Cleveland, Tennessee, 2005.

[221] In an Assemblies of God position paper addressing the issue of apostles and prophets, regarding the five-fold versus four-fold debate, they state, "Greek grammar would seem to dictate four, but the New Testament often discusses pastoral and teaching roles separately." "Apostles and Prophets," a position paper (Springfield, Missouri: General Council of the Assemblies of God, 2001), 1.

[222] Page.

CHAPTER 7

A BIBLICAL INTRODUCTION TO THE MANIFESTATION GIFTS

Paul's treatment of the *charismata* in 1 Corinthians 12-14, the Spirit-empowered ministry of Jesus in the Gospels and the anointed ministry of early believers in the Book of Acts will be the focus of this biblical overview. Insights gleaned from this survey will provide guiding principles for the practice of Spirit-empowered ministry in the church.

The entire Bible is the product of supernatural interaction between God and man. Every word is the result of some receptive person receiving revelation through the agency of the Holy Spirit.[223] From that point of view, the Bible as a whole is *the* source for this study. Here scripture selection will be limited to relevant New Testament passages that either make direct reference to the *charismata* or demonstrate by example the operation of the Spirit's power.

The *Charismata* in 1 Corinthians

First Corinthians 12-14 calls for the integrated exercise of nine manifestation gifts in a context of mutual love and respect. These gifts of the Spirit are given to individuals for the benefit of the body. Paul teaches the believer to earnestly desire spiritual gifts. He also teaches that they are necessary for the edification of the church.

---

[223] 2 Peter 1:21.

In what appears to be a response to a Corinthian question,[224] Paul states that he does not want his readers to be ignorant regarding spiritual matters. Realizing that as pagans they had been familiar with ecstatic utterances, here he may be trying to assure them that utterances and other gifts manifested through the Holy Spirit were not of evil origin.

After noting that there is a diversity of grace gifts (*charismata*), ministries and divine powers, operating by the "same Spirit," Paul states, "Now to each one the manifestation of the Spirit is given for the common good."[225] Have the gifts been given to *individuals* or to the *corporate church*? Paul's words imply that both are true. The gifts have been given "to each one" or to individuals, but they have been given to those individuals for the good of the faith community or the "common good."

Paul proceeds to list nine manifestations of the Spirit that are given to individuals for the common good: word of wisdom, word of knowledge, faith, gifts of healing, operations of miraculous powers, prophecy, distinguishing between spirits, various kinds of tongues, and interpretation of tongues. These gifts are not based in natural abilities; they are supernatural, for they are in fact manifestations of the Spirit.

The following is a concise overview of the nine manifestation gifts. Expanded descriptions and more detailed instructions will be covered later in the text.

1. The Word of Wisdom. While the word of wisdom may generally be a spontaneous manifestation of a God-given insight or perspective to the mind or spirit of the believer, references to God's secret wisdom in 1 Corinthians 2:6-10 and elsewhere in the letter may enhance the understanding of this gift. The secret wisdom pertains to the Gospel that Paul preached.[226] This wisdom relates to that which God had previously hidden and destined for the glory of

---

[224] "Now about" is used here in a way similar to its usage in 7:1.

[225] 1 Corinthians 12:7.

[226] 1 Corinthians 1:17, 21. In 1:24 and 30, the Apostle Paul states that Christ is the wisdom of God.

believers.[227] It is a wisdom that speaks of those things that God has prepared for those who love Him.[228] These emphases from the broader context of the Corinthian letter could imply that the gift known as the "word of wisdom" involves insight into God's plans and preparations for the believer. These things are not made known through human wisdom; they are revealed or manifested by the Holy Spirit.[229] As is the case with all of the manifestation gifts, the expectation is that the word of wisdom be exercised out of a heart of love.[230]

2. The Word of Knowledge. The word of knowledge is not defined in the Corinthian letter. However, 13:2 does indicate that a person is a "nobody," if he functions in this gift without having love. In 14:6, Paul implies that this gift is desirable for the edification of the church, yet according to 13:8, knowledge will one day pass away.

3. Faith. Faith as a manifestation gift is not given much definition in this context. However, 13:2 states, "If I have a faith that can move mountains, but have not love, I am nothing."[231] Paul's reference to "a faith that can move mountains" calls to remembrance Jesus' message about faith moving mountains when He said,

"Have faith in God," Jesus answered. "I tell you the truth, if anyone says to this mountain, 'Go, throw yourself into the sea,' and does not doubt in his heart but believes that what he says will happen, it will be done for him."[232]

---

[227] 1 Corinthians 2:7.

[228] 1 Corinthians 2:9.

[229] 1 Corinthians 2:10.

[230] In 1 Corinthians 13:2, Paul says, "If I... can fathom all mysteries [possibly implying the word of wisdom]..., but have not love, I am nothing."

[231] As is the case with the other gifts, it is not the gift of faith that is invalidated; it is the person functioning in the gift without love that is invalidated.

[232] Mark 11:22-23.

The words translated "have faith in God" might also be rendered, "Have the kind of faith that comes from God."[233] These words of the Lord could be a reference to the gift of faith.

4. Gifts of Healing. Gifts of healings may include a broad range of divine acts of restoration.[234] In addition to physical restoration, the biblical concept of healing even embraces forgiveness[235] and deliverance from demonic oppression.[236] The context of 12:28-29 suggests that God has appointed certain individuals in the church to function in "gifts of healing," but not all will function in such gifts.

5. Miraculous Powers. "Miraculous powers" is literally "operations of powers." According to 12:28, the Lord has appointed individuals in the church as "workers of miracles," but as verse 29 suggests, not all are "workers of miracles." Paul models the essential role of the miraculous in the proclamation of the Gospel, stating,

---

[233] The 1599 Geneva Bible notes the legitimacy of understanding πίστιν θεου to mean "faith of God." *Geneva Study Bible* [on-line Bible and commentary], accessed March 21, 2003, available from http://bible.crosswalk.com/Commentaries/GenevaStudyBible/.

[234] It is in keeping with the Greek tendency to think of this medical term and related words in the broader sense of "to restore" or "to make good." G. Kittel, G. W. Bromiley and G. Friedrich, eds., *Theological Dictionary of the New Testament*, vol. 3 (Grand Rapids, Michigan: Eerdmans, 1964-1976), 199.

[235] In the Old Testament, Yahweh heals by withdrawing His judgment, which may be manifested in the form of sickness or calamity (Genesis 20:17; Exodus 15:26; Hosea 6:1; 7:1; 11:3). The prerequisite of healing is the remission of sins, which is dependent on repentance. Healing and forgiveness are closely linked (Isaiah 6:10; 6:2; 29:2; 40:4). G. Kittel, G. W. Bromiley and G. Friedrich, eds., *Theological Dictionary of the New Testament*, vol. 3 (Grand Rapids, Michigan: Eerdmans, 1964-1976), 203.

[236] In the New Testament, affliction is associated with demonic activity (e.g., Matthew 12:22 and Luke 13:11). Ibid., 204.

> My message and my preaching were not with wise and persuasive words, but with a demonstration of the Spirit's power [literally, "in demonstration of Spirit and power"], so that your faith might not rest on men's wisdom, but on God's power.[237]

6. Prophecy. Compared to the other manifestation gifts, "prophecy" and tongues are addressed quite extensively in the Corinthian letter. Regarding prophecy, 1 Corinthians 13:2 says that without love, the one who prophesies is "nothing." Paul aims to keep prophetic gifting in perspective, noting that it will one day cease.[238] He also indicates that when one prophesies, he speaks only a portion of God's revelation.[239]

To this point it might appear that the Apostle is downplaying the gift. On the contrary, he elevates the gift of prophecy above the other manifestation gifts, stating in 14:1, "Eagerly desire spiritual gifts, especially the gift of prophecy."[240] Prophecy serves to strengthen, instruct, encourage, comfort and edify the church.[241] The gift also has potential to expose the secrets of men's hearts, causing them to repent and worship God.[242]

In contrast to speaking in tongues, which is a means of communication *to God*,[243] when one prophesies, he is speaking *to men*.[244] As much as Paul desires all believers to speak in tongues, prophecy is a greater gift, for it edifies the

---

[237] 1 Corinthians 2:4-5.

[238] 1 Corinthians 13:8.

[239] 1 Corinthians 13:9.

[240] Paul repeats his call for the earnest pursuit of the prophetic gift in 1 Corinthians 14:39, where he says, "Therefore, my brothers, be eager to prophesy, and do not forbid speaking in tongues."

[241] 1 Corinthians 14:3-4, 31.

[242] 1 Corinthians 14:24-25.

[243] 1 Corinthians 14:2.

[244] 1 Corinthians 14:3.

church. However, tongues are just as beneficial for mutual edification as prophecy when they are accompanied by an interpretation.[245]

The Apostle gives instructions for order in the exercise of the prophetic gift. No individual should monopolize the opportunity for prophesying. If a person is prophesying and someone else interrupts with another prophecy, then the first speaker should be quiet and allow the one who interrupted him to proceed.[246] Paul says, "You can all prophesy in turn so that everyone may be instructed and encouraged."[247] Two or three should prophesy, and then others who are prophetically gifted should "weigh carefully what is said."[248] A plurality of prophetic voices helps to confirm what God truly is saying. Once two or three prophecies have been delivered, time should be taken for other prophetically gifted individuals to carefully weigh what has been said. The people should consider the possibility that God may be speaking to them. The context suggests that dialogue and inquiry might even be desirable as each prophecy is weighed.[249]

7. Discerning of Spirits. The gift of discerning of spirits (also known as "distinguishing between spirits") is not defined in the context of the letter. However, in light of 12:2-3, it is evident that the Corinthian believers' worldview allowed for the existence of spirits of both holy and unholy origin.

---

[245] 1 Corinthians 14:5.

[246] 1 Corinthians 14:30.

[247] 1 Corinthians 14:31.

[248] 1 Corinthians 14:29. In 14:32, Paul states, "The spirits of prophets are subject to the control of prophets." Those who minister prophetically are to be accountable to other prophetically gifted people. Whenever prophets speak publicly, they need to have a submissive spirit to those in authority who might find it necessary to scrutinize those prophecies publicly. In light of 14:36-38, those who minister prophetically are not above the need for scrutiny; none of them individually are the final authority regarding the word of God.

[249] 1 Corinthians 14:33-35. In the Corinthian context, Paul found it necessary to instruct the women to not enter into the open inquiry related to weighing prophetic utterances. Should women have doubts regarding the legitimacy of a prophetic utterance, they should discuss it privately with their own husbands at home.

As the first century church encountered demonic forces, the need for this gift became apparent.[250]

8. Various Kinds of Tongues. The operation of various kinds of tongues is given detailed treatment in the Corinthian letter. These tongues are not the product of language studies; they are supernatural manifestations of the Spirit.[251] According to 12:28, God has appointed individuals in the church to be especially gifted in speaking in various kinds of tongues. Although Paul would desire all believers to speak in tongues,[252] he recognizes that not all will do so.[253] The Apostle notes that this gift will one day cease[254] and that love is crucial for it to function properly.[255]

Beginning in 14:2, although Paul does not condemn speaking in tongues in the gathering of believers,[256] he does teach that tongues are to be directed to God and not to men. One who speaks in tongues does well in that he strengthens himself, but when speaking in tongues to others, the hearers are not edified.[257] Apparently some among the Corinthians had thought that they could mystically instruct believers through tongues.[258] Paul points out that without the understanding of what is being said, the hearer does not benefit

---

250 Acts 5:16; 8:7; 16:16-18; 19:12-16; 2 Corinthians 11:4; 1 Timothy 4:1; James 2:19; 1 John 4:1-6.

251 1 Corinthians 12:7-11.

252 1 Corinthians 14:5.

253 1 Corinthians 12:30.

254 1 Corinthians 13:8.

255 1 Corinthians 13:1.

256 1 Corinthians 12:7; 14:5, 18.

257 1 Corinthians 14:4, 6-11.

258 A Corinthian attempt to instruct through speaking in tongues may be implied in 1 Corinthians 14:19.

from the utterance.[259] If one is to speak to the people, it is either prophecy or tongues accompanied by the gift of interpretation that should be exercised.[260]

What then is the benefit or purpose of speaking in tongues? First, outside of the Corinthian letter, tongues are at times depicted as an initial evidence of the baptism of the Holy Spirit.[261] Second, as previously noted, speaking in tongues accompanied by interpretation does edify those who hear.[262] Third, the manifestation of tongues enables the human spirit to express mysteries to God in prayer and worship.[263] Fourth, when a person prays or worships in tongues, his own spirit is built up.[264]

The fifth function of tongues is in 14:22. Tongues serve as a sign for unbelievers. If the unbeliever does not understand the tongues, it is a sign that he is not a part of the community of believers. The context may also suggest that the sign is one of eschatological significance. In light of 14:21, tongues are an evidence that the resources of the present age are insufficient to communicate the purposes of God; therefore, He has manifested the power of the age to come to convey His purposes. Such a manifestation is an indictment against the present order and serves as a sign of judgment.[265]

Paul gives instructions for order in the exercise of tongues in the context of the gathered believers. He states that if everyone tries to speak to one another in tongues while unbelievers or those without understanding are

---

[259] 1 Corinthians 14:9-11.

[260] 1 Corinthians 14:1-6, 13.

[261] Acts 1:13-15; 2:1,4; 8:5-19; 10:44-47; 19:1-6.

[262] 1 Corinthians 14:5, 13.

[263] 1 Corinthians 14:2, 14-17. In verse 15, the gift is manifested through song.

[264] 1 Corinthians 14:4.

[265] This interpretation rises out of Paul's use of Isaiah 28:11-12, where the prophet announces judgment to the people of Israel. Israel would not heed the warnings of prophets who spoke to them in Hebrew, so God sent them voices in tongues that they could not understand as a sign that He had exhausted the resources of language to speak to them, and yet they would not hear. Consequently, only judgment remained.

present, those onlookers will say that the speakers are out of their minds.[266] There is nothing wrong with everyone manifesting a gift when the church gathers, for "all of these must be done for the strengthening of the church."[267] However, those gifts should operate in a way that promotes understanding. If believers do speak out in tongues so as to address those who are gathered, they should speak one at a time. Once a person speaks in tongues, an interpretation should be anticipated. If a second or third message is delivered in tongues, and there has been no interpretation, then those who are speaking in tongues should assume that no interpreter is present, and they should cease to direct their tongues as a message to the church. If they do continue speaking in tongues, they should do so only as prayer or worship directed to God.[268] As a concluding remark regarding tongues, Paul raises the caution that in pursuing order, the church should be careful that it does not forbid the manifestation.[269]

9. The Interpretation of Tongues. The gift of interpretation of tongues is that which causes tongues to be beneficial for the edification of the church. It is one of the gifts that Paul says is necessary for the strengthening of the church.[270] If a person is already functioning in the gift of tongues, he should pray that he may also interpret tongues.[271] When Paul says, "I will pray with my spirit, but I will also pray with my mind,"[272] he may be implying that a person should give attention to the prayerful thoughts that are in his mind as he speaks in tongues. It could be that his thoughts in those moments may actually reflect the meaning of that which he is saying. If such is the case, the practice of giving heed to one's thoughts while speaking in tongues could have ramifications for training people to function in the gift of interpretation.

---

[266] 1 Corinthians 14:23.

[267] 1 Corinthians 14:26.

[268] 1 Corinthians 14:27-28.

[269] 1 Corinthians 14:39.

[270] 1 Corinthians 14:26.

[271] 1 Corinthians 14:13.

[272] 1 Corinthians 14:15.

In the corporate gathering, if an individual speaks out in tongues, the church should prayerfully and expectantly wait for an interpretation. As has been indicated in the discussion on tongues, if there is no interpretation to the first utterance, and yet a second or even a third utterance is given in tongues without an interpretation, at that point, with the obvious absence of an interpreter, those who speak in tongues should do so quietly. Evidently, either someone is not being responsive in giving the interpretation, or it is not God's intention to manifest a message through tongues and interpretation at this time.

The Spirit-Empowered Community

Although this biblical review is primarily concerned with defining the manifestation gifts, the main concern of 1 Corinthians 12-14 is to consider the manner in which the gifts work *together* in the context of a Spirit-empowered *community of faith*. Paul uses the physical body as a metaphor for the body of Christ, indicating that "God has arranged the parts in the body, every one of them, just as he wanted them to be."[273] Then he teaches about love, "the most excellent way" or the most excellent manner in which the gifts should operate. He is *not* speaking of a *gift* that is more excellent than those noted in chapter twelve. He is speaking of a *manner* or *way* of functioning in those gifts that is more excellent than a manner characterized by disregard for one another in the body.[274] In the corporate gathering, everyone has something to contribute, and all of it is necessary.[275] When the members have a motivation of love and a mutual regard for one another's gifts, the result is the strengthening of the church.

---

[273] 1 Corinthians 12:12-27.

[274] 1 Corinthians 13:1-13.

[275] 1 Corinthians 14:26.

The *Charismata* in the Gospels

Having introduced the charismatic gifts of 1 Corinthians 12-14, the Gospels will now be searched for parallels to the charismata in the ministry of Jesus and His disciples. In John 14:12 Jesus said, "I tell you the truth[276], anyone who has faith in me will do what I have been doing. He will do even greater things than these...." In light of the promise that believers would do the works that Jesus did, they should carefully study the things that Jesus did and how He went about doing those things. It is His work that believers are to emulate.

The purpose of this portion of the scriptural review is to identify in the Gospels the signs and wonders that foreshadow gifts previously surveyed in 1 Corinthians 12. Observations will be made on selected texts, and preliminary analyses will be offered. In some places, analyses will be accompanied by suggested applications relevant to the equipping of those who minister.

Matthew's Gospel

Matthew's Gospel shows that Jesus' teaching and preaching in Galilee was characteristically accompanied by the healing of "every disease and sickness among the people" and the delivering of the oppressed.[277] While there were those who responded in unbelief, these works usually caused many to believe and glorify God.[278] Several miraculous healings and deliverances are documented in Matthew 8:1-17. In those verses Jesus is seen

---

[276] Jesus' words, "I tell you the truth," signals the hearer that the words to follow are not common. Jesus is about to express an unexpected truth. J. H. Bernard, *A Critical and Exegetical Commentary on the Gospel According to St. John,* vol. 2, ed. A. H. McNeile (Edinburgh: T. & T. Clark, 1972), 542.

[277] Matthew 4:23-24. Other general and non-specific references to signs and wonders accompanying the ministry of Jesus include Matthew 9:35, Matthew 12:15, Matthew 14:14, Matthew 14:34-36, Matthew 15:29-31, Matthew 19:1, Matthew 21:12-16, John 2:23, Mark 1:32-34, Mark 1:39, Mark 3:9-10, Mark 6:53-56, and Luke 4:40-41.

[278] This belief motif will be seen more clearly in the review of passages from John's gospel.

cleansing a leper, healing a servant sick of the palsy, breaking a woman's fever, and restoring many other afflicted and oppressed people. These works were in fulfillment of Isaiah's prophecy: "He took our infirmities and carried our diseases."[279]

In this Gospel, Jesus' example serves as a model for Spirit-empowered ministry: (1) The integrity of His ministry was dependent upon the Spirit and the Word. (2) His ministry was not confined to predetermined patterns and methods. (3) Faith was the condition by which supernatural works were accomplished. (4) He responded to human faith-driven initiatives. (5) Unbelief was known to restrict His ability to work. (6) He often associated affliction with demonic oppression. (7) He endured persecution or religious backlash for ministering in the supernatural. (8) On occasion, His ministry followed observable sequential patterns. (9) He authorized His disciples to do the works that He had been doing.

The integrity of Jesus' ministry was dependent upon the Spirit and the Word. Prior to His Galilean ministry, the Holy Spirit and the Scriptures guided Jesus through an intense temptation experience.[280] When the devil tempted Jesus to turn stones into bread, He responded, "It is written, Man does not live on bread alone, but on every word that comes from the mouth of God."[281] Jesus in effect was saying, "My life depends on heeding God's voice: Man shall live 'on every word that comes from the mouth of God.'"[282] He resisted any motivation to work miracles that did not originate out of His Father's will. In application, when supernatural power is entrusted to a Spirit-filled believer, he too is responsible for the disciplined use of those gifts. He must guard against presumptuous use. Dependence on the voice of God is critical to the proper exercise of the spiritual gifts.

---

[279] Here Matthew quotes from Isaiah 53:4. Parallel accounts of these miracles are found in Mark 1:29-34, Mark 1:40-45, Luke 4:38-41, Luke 5:12-15 and Luke 7:1-10.

[280] Matthew 3:11-12, 16-17; 4:1-11.

[281] Matthew 4:4.

[282] This dependence on the voice of God is foundational to the understanding of the revelatory gifts.

Matthew 14:22-33 demonstrates that Jesus' disciples learned to live by this same sense of dependence. This text is the account of Peter's brief miracle of walking on the stormy sea. After Jesus had calmed His disciples' fears by saying, "It is I; don't be afraid,"[283] Peter said, "Lord, if it's you, tell me to come to you on the water." Jesus responded, "Come." Peter obeyed the Master's call, and he walked on the water to go to Jesus. Of course, the miracle did not last long, for fear overtook this disciple, and he began to sink.

Several observations here hold potential implications for Spirit-filled believers: (1) Peter recognized that he could not presumptuously start walking on the water. He could do so, only if the Lord Himself would so command. (2) Obedience to the word of the Lord was the key to the release of God's power.[284] (3) Once Peter started walking on the water, the distraction of contrary circumstances, fear, lack of faith and doubt interfered with the successful operation of the miraculous.

Jesus employed diverse and even unpredictable methods in healing and deliverance. This fact may actually demonstrate that ministering in the supernatural cannot be reduced to the following of predetermined formulas and methods. Nevertheless, His methods are worth noting. In response to faith,[285] He often healed with a touch and a spoken word.[286] He once healed a woman's fever by rebuking it,[287] touching the woman and lifting her up by the

---

[283] John 6:20. Mark 6:45-51 and John 6:15-21 are parallel passages. This example may suggest that the calming of fear is the first task in ministering to people in the power of the Spirit. Calvin Rogers, interview by the author, Scarborough, Maine, 1998.

[284] Luke 5:4-11 tells of another occasion when Simon Peter experienced the power of obedience. Simon had fished all night long, yet Jesus said to him, "Launch out into the deep, and let down your nets for a draught." Simon heeded the Lord's word, and they caught more fish than they could handle. This miracle so impacted the faith of Simon and the others that they left their nets to follow Jesus. The lesson is one of obedience.

[285] Matthew 8:13.

[286] Matthew 8:3.

[287] Luke 4:38-39.

hand.[288] When delivering numerous oppressed people, "he drove out the spirits with a word…."[289] Physical touch and the spoken word are reoccurring factors in acts of healing and deliverance.[290]

In the Lord's ministry, faith was the condition by which supernatural works were accomplished. He responded to faith, and He ministered in full faith that His Father would honor His work. Likewise, He instructed His disciples to function in such faith. In Matthew 21:18-22, Jesus states the conditions for the working of miracles. In this passage, He had just cursed a fruitless fig tree, and it withered away. When the disciples marveled at the miracle, Jesus said to them,

> I tell you the truth, if you have faith and do not doubt, not only can you do what was done to the fig tree, but also you can say to this mountain, "Go throw yourself into the sea," and it will be done. If you believe, you will receive whatever you ask for in prayer.[291]

Mark's account[292] introduces this teaching with Jesus saying, "Have faith in God,"[293] or "Have the faith that comes from God" – a statement that may be pointing to a kind of faith synonymous with the gift of faith noted in 1 Corinthians 12:9.[294] If such an understanding of Jesus' words is correct, then

---

288 Mark 1:29-34.

289 Matthew 8:16.

290 Other general references to Jesus healing or ministering deliverance in direct response to expressed faith include Matthew 9:27-31, Matthew 15:21-28, Matthew 20:29-34, Mark 5:34, Mark 7:24-30, Luke 7:1-10, and Luke 18:42. Additional general references to Jesus healing or delivering through a spoken word include Matthew 8:16, Matthew 9:27-31, Mark 2:11, and Luke 7:1-10.

291 This passage parallels Mark 11:12-14, 20-24.

292 Mark 11:12-14, 20-24.

293 Mark 11:22.

294 The 1599 Geneva Bible notes the legitimacy of understanding πίστ@ν θεου to mean "faith of God." *Geneva Study Bible* [on-line Bible and commentary], accessed March 21, 2003, available from http://bible.crosswalk.com/Commentaries/GenevaStudyBible/.

the implication would be that the gift of faith conditions the believer for the working of miracles.

Several observations may be drawn from this passage. (1) The presence of faith and the absence of doubt are necessary for the working of miracles. (2) There is a correlation between the spoken authoritative word and the working of miracles. (3) There are times when the spoken authoritative word may be spoken to inanimate objects to affect God's appointed outcome.

Jesus had the ability to discern when faith was present. In Matthew 9:2-7, four men brought another man who was sick of the palsy to Jesus. The four had made their faith visible through their actions. When Jesus "saw their faith," He spoke a word forgiving the afflicted man of his sins. Within moments Jesus spoke another word affecting healing.[295] Key lessons for prayer ministry are these: (1) it is important to discern the presence of faith, and (2) at times faith needs to be made visible through corresponding action.[296]

On some occasions, Jesus did call for action on the part of the afflicted to demonstrate their faith. In Matthew 12:9-15, when He met a man with a withered hand, He said to him, "Stretch out your hand." The man stretched out his hand, and it was restored.

While acknowledging that supernatural works are subject to the sovereignty of God, it should also be noted that Jesus responded to human faith-driven initiatives. Many healings and deliverances in the Gospels clearly followed the initiative of some individual or group of people to approach the Lord for divine assistance. Matthew 9:18-34 presents four healing incidents that were precipitated out of apparent human initiative. First, a woman who had suffered from an issue of blood for twelve years said within herself, "If I only touch his cloak, I will be healed." She touched the hem of Jesus' garment,

---

[295] Luke 5:17 lends support to the thought that Jesus only healed under certain conditions. Luke says that "the power of the Lord was present to heal." Were there times when God's power was not present to heal? Is there a possibility that Jesus only ministered healing at special times when God sovereignly chose to manifest His presence and power?

[296] Mark 2:1-12 and Luke 5:17-26 are parallel passages.

power went out from Him,[297] and He responded by saying, "Take heart, daughter,... your faith has healed you."[298] In days that would follow, others would purpose to touch His garment in hope of receiving healing.[299]

Second, a ruler came to Jesus, worshipped him, and said, "My daughter has just died. But come and put your hand on her, and she will live." Jesus made it to the ruler's home, took the girl by the hand, and she arose.[300]

Third, two blind men cried out to Jesus for mercy. Jesus heard their cry and asked them if they believed that He was able to heal them. They answered, "Yes, Lord." Then He touched their eyes and said, "According to your faith will it be done to you." They were healed.[301] In addition to the noted human initiative, there is a sequence of events here worthy of consideration: (1) The afflicted ones prayed, (2) Jesus interviewed them, asking if they believed, (3) He touched them, and (4) He spoke the healing word.

Fourth, Matthew 9:32-34 presents a case of human initiative being taken on behalf of someone else. Some people brought a demonized man to Jesus who could not speak. When the devil was cast out, the man was able to speak.

Those searching Matthew's Gospel for lessons in Spirit-empowered ministry will find the negative role of unbelief to be an item with which they must grapple. Unbelief was known to restrict the Lord's ability to work. In Matthew 13:54-58, even Jesus could not do many mighty works in His home territory due to the unbelief of the people.[302] Mark's parallel account states, "He could not do any miracles there, except lay his hands on a few sick

---

[297] Mark 5:30.

[298] Matthew 9:20-22.

[299] Matthew 14:34-36.

[300] Matthew 9:18-26. See parallel accounts in Mark 5:22-43 and Luke 8:41-56.

[301] Matthew 9:27-30.

[302] Matthew 13:54-58 is also the place where Jesus taught that prophets are not typically received with honor in their own country, among their own relatives, or in their own house.

people and heal them."[303] Hindrance to supernatural power is seen again in Matthew 17:14-21.[304] In this case, unbelief and perhaps even prayerlessness on the part of Christ's disciples disabled an attempt at deliverance.[305] As Jesus corrected this situation, He taught that the authoritative word spoken in faith has the power to even remove mountains. However, some forms of demonic oppression cannot be removed apart from prayer.[306]

Jesus often associated affliction with demonic oppression. Healing encounters such as the one documented in Matthew 12:22-32 are examples of the connection between physical problems and demonic oppression.[307] In Matthew 12:28, Jesus said, "If I drive out demons by the Spirit of God, then the kingdom of God has come upon you." Signs and wonders were evidence that the kingdom of God had come.[308]

---

303 Mark 6:1-6.

304 Mark 9:14-28 and Luke 9:37-42 provide parallel accounts. Mark's account gives additional details that will be reviewed later.

305 Mark 9:14-29 sheds additional light. The issue here is not whether or not Jesus was able or willing to deliver the boy. The issue was whether or not anyone would believe. The father of the child confessed his struggle with unbelief while at the same time acknowledging faith in Jesus' ability to help. Jesus then issued the authoritative command that liberated the child.

306 Mark 9:29. The portion of the passage that is sometimes rendered "and fasting" has been omitted in some versions; this item of textual criticism needs to be studied before a strong case can be made for a call to fast on the basis of this text.

307 Physical illness or disability was often associated with demonic activity. In Matthew 12:22-32 Jesus delivered a demoniac, and in that moment the person was healed of severe speech and vision disorders. Parallel accounts are given in Mark 3:23-27 and Luke 11:17-22.

308 When offering evidence that He was indeed the Messiah, in Matthew 11:2-5 Jesus summarized His works in these words, "The blind receive sight, the lame walk, those who have leprosy are cured, the deaf hear, the dead are raised, and the good news is preached to the poor." According to Luke 7:21, in the same hour, Jesus healed many infirmities and plagues, cast out evil spirits and restored sight to the blind. His

Jesus endured persecution or religious backlash for ministering in the supernatural. The healing incident in Matthew 12:9-15 portrays the religious backlash that often followed Jesus' works of power. After the healing of the withered hand, the Pharisees went out, and held a council to determine how they might destroy Him. Jesus, operating in an ability that parallels the gift of "the discerning of spirits," knew their thoughts.[309] Upon receiving revelation of the plot, Jesus withdrew from that place. Religious backlash as a reaction to manifestations of the Spirit is not uncommon in the Scriptures.[310]

On occasion, Jesus' ministry followed observable sequential patterns. One of the most noteworthy sequences occurs in Matthew 14:14 – a sequence that highlights heart-motivation in Spirit-empowered ministry. This passage gives the account of Jesus healing a large number of people just prior to the feeding of the five thousand. His work of healing proceeded in this manner: (1) Jesus saw the people, (2) He was moved with compassion, and (3) He healed.[311] The lesson gleaned here relates to the necessity of (1) awareness of need, (2) compassion as the motivating factor for the healing and (3) an act of faith to affect the healing.

The sequence of actions in Christ's healing encounters continues to be informative. Matthew 20:29-34 records a second time[312] in Jesus' ministry when two blind men cried out to Him for mercy. Although the need would have been obvious to anyone, Jesus still asked, "What do you want me to do for you?" They answered, "Lord,... we want our sight." Jesus had compassion on them, touched their eyes and said, "Receive your sight; your

---

supernatural works were confirmations that the kingdom of God had come. Luke 7:18-35 is a parallel passage to Matthew 11:2-5.

[309] Luke 6:8.

[310] Mark 3:1-5 and Luke 6:6-11 are parallel accounts.

[311] Luke 7:11-17 provides one other instance of this sequence.

[312] Matthew's first account of Jesus responding to two blind men is found in 9:27-34.

faith has healed you."[313] The sequence is instructive. (1) The afflicted ones persistently prayed. (2) Jesus asked a question. (3) Answering the Lord's question, the afflicted expressed their faith. (4) Jesus had compassion. (5) He touched the afflicted. (6) Finally, He spoke the healing word.[314]

Jesus authorized His disciples to do the works that He had been doing. Matthew 10:1-8 marks the point where Jesus authorized His twelve disciples to cast out demons and to heal "every disease and sickness." He also commissioned them to raise the dead.[315] Throughout His ministry, Jesus gave as much emphasis to the demonstration of the kingdom's power as He gave to the proclamation of its message.[316]

Mark's Gospel

Mark portrays the mission of Christ and His disciples as one of great power against demonic forces. His Gospel suggests that there is a correlation between intimacy with God and one's ability to function in the supernatural. This truth would be an important lesson for the disciples to learn, but it is first seen in Jesus' own relationship with the Father. It would follow that the Master would summon His disciples to a similar depth of friendship with Himself.

---

[313] Matthew 20:29-34 and Luke 18:42. Mark 10:46-52 and Luke 18:35-43 are parallel passages. (Luke refers to only one of the two blind men. Mark recalls the name of one of the men: "Bartimaeus.")

[314] A portion of the sequence in Matthew 20:29-30 is similar to the one seen in Mark 1:40-45: (1) a leper in need comes to Jesus in worship and prayer: "beseeching him, and kneeling down to him," (2) Jesus is "moved with compassion," (3) Jesus touches the leper, and (4) Jesus speaks the healing word: "Be thou clean." This account demonstrates five elements relevant to a ministry of healing: (1) an attitude of worship on the part of the recipient, (2) the petition of the one in need, (3) compassion on the part of the one ministering to the one in need, (4) a physical touch, and (5) a spoken word that affects healing. Matthew 8:2-4 and Luke 5:12-14 are parallel passages to Mark 1:40-45.

[315] Matthew 10:8.

[316] Mark 6:7-11 and Luke 9:1, 3-5 are parallel passages.

In the light of Mark's account, how did Jesus' relationship with the Father impact His ministry? The Scriptures present a pattern of engagement and disengagement in the Lord's ministry – engagement in ministry followed by disengagement for the sake of communion with His Father. Jesus frequently retreated into solitary places to pray immediately after great manifestations of His power or just prior to taking on a new or difficult phase of ministry.[317] Out of one such time of prayer, Jesus emerged in Mark 1:35-38 with a clear sense of what He needed to do next. He announced to his disciples a transition: "Let us go somewhere else – to the nearby villages – so I can preach there also. That is why I have come."[318]

Just as Jesus' ministry was dependent upon His relationship with the Father, so would the work of His disciples be influenced and empowered by their relationship with the Master. Jesus called His disciples to intimate friendship with Himself. The Master would eventually send forth His closest companions to proclaim the Gospel and demonstrate its power. To prepare them for such a mission, Mark 3:13-15 shows that these men needed to be *with* Him.[319] They would live every moment in His company, absorbing His words and coming to know His heart. There was a mystical dimension to this relationship; although they would one day be physically separated, in reality, Jesus would never leave His disciples. Whatever spiritual work they might do, it would actually be the Lord working in and through them by the agency of the Spirit.

---

[317] In Mark 6:30-32, after Jesus' disciples had been engaged in an intense season of ministry, He had them draw aside to rest for awhile. Spirit-empowered ministers need to rest and be refreshed after intensive spiritual engagements. For the disciples, rest and renewal was found in spending this time with Jesus. Again in Mark 6:45-46, after intensive ministry and just prior to the miracle of walking on the water, Jesus drew aside to a solitary place of prayer. Other references to Jesus drawing aside to pray include Luke 5:16 and Luke 6:12-13. Here is a pattern: (1) Spirit-empowered ministry, (2) solitude and prayer, (3) Spirit-empowered ministry, (4) solitude and prayer, and so forth.

[318] Mark 1:38. Luke 4:42-43 parallels this text.

[319] Intimate communion with Jesus should be regarded as a prerequisite to effectiveness and integrity in charismatic anointing.

The authority of Christ over demonic force emerges as a prominent theme in the Gospel of Mark. This gospel shows that the sound of God's Word and the presence of the Lord are enough to stir demons from their places of hiding, even if no other intentional action is taken to confront them.[320] In Mark 1:21-28, while Jesus taught authoritatively in the synagogue at Capernaum, a man in attendance began to manifest a demon. The man cried out, and Jesus rebuked him, saying, "Hold thy peace, and come out of him." The unclean spirit tore the man, cried out with a loud voice, and came out. Here is an example of demons being exposed simply by their host being under the sound of the authoritative Word and in the presence of Jesus.[321]

Several lessons regarding deliverance ministry can be learned from Jesus' encounter with demonic forces in Mark 5:1-20.[322] Upon His arrival, a demoniac immediately met Him. Why did he respond so quickly to the presence of Christ? Could it be that the demons quickly reacted because they felt threatened by the Lord's arrival? On the other hand, maybe the man had momentary control of himself and perceived that Jesus might be able to

---

320 While this statement is made on the basis of the biblical text, its truth has been part of the author's experience as well. In 1999 while ministering in Brazil, a demon began to manifest through a man in the congregation as the preaching was in progress. Ushers, who had been trained in how to respond in such situations, discreetly escorted the man out of the sanctuary and ministered to him until he was delivered. At the close of the service his testimony revealed that he was a leader in a well-known gang and occultic group in the city.

321 Luke 4:31-37 provides a parallel account. Mark 3:11-12 also speaks of the demonized crying out simply because Jesus was present. His very presence upset evil spirits and mandated submission to His will.

322 The review of Matthew 8:28-34 has already given the account of Jesus delivering the demoniacs in the land of the Gadarenes. Mark 5:1-20 brings out some additional details; however, Mark speaks of only one demoniac while Matthew speaks of two. This account demonstrates some of the effects of demonization. According to Mark 5:3-5, this demoniac had unusual physical strength; he could not be restrained—not even with chains. He had suicidal tendencies and lived a life of torment.

deliver him. The text does say, "When he saw Jesus from a distance, he ran and fell on his knees in front of him."[323]

Jesus commanded, "Come out of this man, you evil spirit!"[324] Jesus addressed one single unclean spirit. The man was not immediately delivered. Moments later, Jesus addressed a plurality of demons; the spirits had collectively identified themselves as "Legion," for they were many.

At least five implications for deliverance ministry may be drawn from this account: (1) Demons can operate in clusters or groups. (2) The person conducting the deliverance may need to deal with one dominant spirit first before other associated spirits can be exorcised. (3) Violent behavior, self-destructive tendencies, unusual and supernatural physical strength and excessive crying as though in torment may all be indications of demonic oppression. (4) While conversation with demons is not normative, should conversation with them become necessary, the one conducting the deliverance should remain in control of the dialogue.[325] (5) Finally, the result of deliverance is that the kingdom of God is advanced. At the close of this passage, as the man told the story of his deliverance throughout Decapolis, "all the people were amazed."[326]

Mark's Gospel also contains some interesting portrayals of Jesus' methods. Mark 7:31-37 contains unique elements not seen in other healing incidents of Jesus' ministry. A man was brought to Jesus who had both a speech and hearing impairment. His friends asked Jesus to place His hand on the man. Jesus took him aside and away from the crowd, He put his fingers in the man's ears, He spit, and He touched His tongue.[327] It may be that the Lord

---

[323] Mark 5:6.

[324] Mark 5:8.

[325] Jesus rarely engaged evil spirits in conversation; he merely commanded them to depart.

[326] Mark 5:20.

[327] These unusual actions demonstrate that the exercise of the *charismata* is often unpredictable and spontaneous. Each incident of need is unique; therefore, those who minister must follow the Spirit's leading in addressing each situation's uniqueness.

took these symbolic actions for the purpose of communicating with this man who could hear nothing that had been said. By seeing and feeling Jesus touching his ears and tongue, the man was receiving a message to which his faith might respond.[328] Looking up to heaven, Jesus sighed and said, "Be opened," and the man received healing.[329]

Mark 8:22-26 demonstrates a healing in two phases. Jesus took a blind man by the hand, led him out of the town, spit on his eyes, and put his hands upon him. Then Jesus asked him if he could see anything. He looked up and said, "I see people; they look like trees walking around."[330] Jesus put His hands on the man's eyes again and had him look up. The text says, "His sight was restored, and he saw everything clearly."[331]

This case raises questions supporting the notion that healing encounters cannot be reduced to formulas, patterns and outcomes that man can predict. Why did Jesus spit? Why was the man not totally healed the first time Jesus placed His hands on him? Is there any significance to the fact that on some occasions[332] Jesus drew the afflicted aside and out of the view of the crowd before He would heal them? This case encourages persistence in those times when favorable results are not immediately achieved.

At the close of Mark's Gospel, Jesus commissions His disciples to preach the gospel to every creature, saying,

---

Unique and spontaneous response is in order. Unprecedented methods are not necessarily out of order. No one should interpret these insights as an "anything goes" license. The qualifying factor is the genuine leading of the Holy Spirit.

[328] R. Jamieson, A. R. Fausset, and D. Brown, "Mark 7:33," *A Commentary, Critical and Explanatory on the Old and New Testaments* [CD-ROM] (Oak Harbor, Washington: Logos Research Systems, Inc., 1997).

[329] Matthew 15:19-31 parallels this account.

[330] Mark 8:24.

[331] Mark 8:25.

[332] Mark 7:31-37 and Mark 8:22-26 in particular.

"And these signs will accompany those who believe: In my name they will drive out demons; they will speak in new tongues; they will pick up snakes with their hands; and when they drink deadly poison, it will not hurt them at all; they will place their hands on sick people, and they will get well." [333]

After Jesus ascended into heaven, Mark reports that the disciples obeyed the command: "Then the disciples went out and preached everywhere, and the Lord worked with them and confirmed his word by the signs that accompanied it."[334]

Luke's Gospel

There are conditions attached to Spirit-empowered ministry. Numerous conditions have already been mentioned, but Luke's Gospel reveals several other qualifications. Furthermore, this account of the Lord's mission portrays methods and patterns not previously noted in the other Gospels. What are the conditions to a ministry of signs and wonders according to Luke? The anointing of the Holy Spirit, a heart of humility, a life of intimacy with Christ and the aptitude for compassion are all necessary for a ministry characterized by supernatural manifestations.

Jesus was powerful in ministry because of the Holy Spirit's anointing that was upon Him. This truth is evident in Luke 4:16-30, where Jesus issued His personal mission statement:

> The Spirit of the Sovereign LORD is on me, because the LORD has anointed me to preach good news to the poor. He has sent me to bind up the brokenhearted, to proclaim freedom for the captives and release from darkness for the prisoners, to proclaim the year of the LORD's favor and the day of vengeance of our God, to comfort all who mourn....[335]

In addition to identifying "the Spirit of the Sovereign Lord" as the source of His power, these words also present the priorities of the Lord's ministry on the earth. Later in Luke 9:1-6, 10-11, Jesus commissioned the Twelve to fulfill

---

[333] Mark 16:17-18. Whether or not Mark 16:9-20 was part of the original text is in dispute.

[334] Mark 16:20.

[335] Isaiah 61:1-2.

the same mission, giving them power and authority over all devils and giving them power to cure diseases. If the church is to represent and continue with Christ's ministry, then identification with the mission statement of Luke 4:16-30 is necessary.[336]

Once when a group of seventy-two disciples returned from a mission excited that demons had submitted to them in Jesus' name,[337] the Master took the opportunity to teach them regarding spiritual warfare, especially underscoring the necessity of maintaining a humble heart when victories have been won. Jesus said,

> "I saw Satan fall like lightning from heaven. I have given you authority to trample on snakes and scorpions and to overcome all the power of the enemy; nothing will harm you. However, do not rejoice that the spirits submit to you, but rejoice that your names are written in heaven."[338]

Several observations are worthy of note: (1) Devils are subject to authorized believers in Jesus' name. (2) Satan's status is that he has fallen from his position in heaven. (3) Jesus promises protection for those who engage in this spiritual warfare. (4) It is implied that the motive for the believer's rejoicing is the mercy of God and not the powerful things the believer has done in Jesus' name. Here the Spirit-empowered minister is reminded to maintain an attitude of humility whenever the Lord works through him in signs and wonders.

Although the story of Mary and Martha in Luke 10:38-42 does not directly relate to the theme of Spirit-empowered ministry, it does profoundly illustrate the intimacy with Christ to which Spirit-filled ministers should aspire. The opposing dispositions of Mary and Martha demonstrate the

---

[336] Since the ministry of the church is the continuation of the ministry of Jesus, that which the Spirit accomplished through Jesus has implications for the ongoing work of the church. In other words, when the Spirit of the Lord is upon God's people, they too will sense that they have been sent to the poor, the brokenhearted, the captive, the blind and the bruised. It is through the agency of the Spirit that the church preaches, heals, and delivers.

[337] Luke 10:17-20.

[338] Luke 10:18-20.

contrast between preoccupation with doing works of service for the Lord and preoccupation with sitting at His feet in intimate communion, listening for His voice. Neither is condemned; however, Jesus elevates intimacy and listening as a high priority for the believer. The "being" precedes the "doing." Passion for Jesus precedes passion for engagement in His work. To practically apply the concept: prayer, meditation and worship should be primary disciplines of those who would desire to function in ministry.

While the methods of the Master are worth mentioning, it is His compassion that emerges as the most consistent feature of His ministry. Observations of the Lord's methods in Luke reveal the same recurring patterns found in the other Gospels. One instance, Luke 7:11-17, finds Jesus at Nain, where He saw a mother whose only son had died. He had compassion on her and comforted her saying, "Don't cry."[339] Jesus then touched the bier and said, "Young man, I say to you, get up!" The young man sat up alive. This miracle included these elements: (1) Jesus saw the need, (2) He was moved with compassion, (3) He ministered comfort, (4) He touched, and (5) He spoke the word which affected the miracle.

A number of miracles recorded in Luke are not covered in this portion of the review because they have already been touched upon in the survey of the other Gospels. However, the healing documented in Luke 13:11-17 must be noted. The way this miracle was initiated deviates from Jesus' usual pattern. Here was a woman that had a spirit of infirmity eighteen years. She had been bowed down and could not lift herself up. The text gives no indication that she was asking for help; neither is anyone interceding for her. Jesus does not even ask her what she would like Him to do for her. The Bibles indicates that Jesus simply saw her, called her to Him and spoke these words to her: "Woman, you are set free from your infirmity."[340] Then He laid his hands on her, and immediately she was made straight, and glorified God.

---

[339] Luke 7:13.

[340] Luke 13:12.

While the Lord's usual pattern was to respond to expressed need or faith, here He breaks that pattern. There is no indication that she was requesting healing. Jesus just stepped in and took authority in the situation.

The story of Jesus healing the ten lepers in Luke 17:11-19 contains some observations regarding methodology not yet mentioned. Ten lepers lifted their voices saying, "Jesus, Master, have pity on us!"[341] When Jesus saw them, He said to them, "Go, show yourselves to the priests."[342] As they started on their way to obey Christ's instructions, they were cleansed of their leprosy. One of them turned back, glorified God with a loud voice and fell on his face at Jesus' feet giving him thanks. He was a Samaritan.

Herein are lessons regarding gratitude, cross-cultural ministry, racial discrimination, obedience and healing. It is also interesting to note Jesus' varied methods. While on other occasions Jesus *touched* lepers as He administered healing, in this case, He did not. Neither did He pray for them. He did not even issue the usual command, "Be cleansed!" What does Jesus do? He commands them to go to the priests. It is as they respond in obedience that they are healed. Once again, Jesus cannot be restricted to clearly defined methods. His tendency is to spontaneously move in the Spirit in unpredictable ways.

John's Gospel

Many miracle stories found in John's Gospel have already been told in previous sections of this review. In this section, additional incidents have been selected that demonstrate (1) how Jesus was guided in the working of miracles, (2) how Jesus viewed the relationship between sin and affliction and (3) how the impact of signs and wonders resulted in the salvation of souls.

Did Jesus work signs and wonders by His own initiative, or did He rely upon guidance? In response to His critics, in John 5:17, 19 Jesus stated,

---

[341] Luke 17:13.

[342] Luke 17:14.

> My Father is always at his work to this very day, and I, too, am working.... I tell you the truth, the Son can do nothing by himself; he can do only what he sees his Father doing, because whatever the Father does the Son also does.[343]

Jesus did not move presumptuously in signs and wonders. He discerned what the Father was doing or desired to do and then aligned His actions accordingly. In similar fashion, the believer is to discern what the Father is doing or desires to do in each unique ministry context and then align his actions accordingly.[344]

How did Jesus view the relationship between sin and affliction? John 5:1-21 implies that there may be a connection between sin and affliction. After Jesus healed the man at the pool of Bethesda in Jerusalem, He found him in the temple. Jesus warned him saying, "See, you are well again. Stop sinning or something worse may happen to you."[345]

Clearly, had this man continued in his sinful behavior, he could have opened the door for further calamity in his life. Some afflictions may be the direct result of personal sin; however, that is not to say that all affliction is the result of sins that a person may have committed. Such seems to be Jesus' point in John 9:1-41. Here when Jesus encountered a man blind from birth, his disciples immediately assumed that this affliction was the result of sin. They asked, "Rabbi, who sinned, this man or his parents, that he was born blind?" Although the general association between sin and affliction was not necessarily incorrect, in this case Jesus answered, "Neither this man nor his parents sinned,... but this happened so that the works of God might be displayed in his life."[346] Then Jesus spit on the ground, made clay, put it on

---

[343] John 5:17, 19. A similar emphasis is seen in John 8:28-29, 38.

[344] It is important to determine what needs to be done, how it is to be done, and when it is to be done. Such guidance, knowledge and wisdom are provided through the anointing that the Lord has given to His church.

[345] John 5:14.

[346] John 9:3.

the blind man's eyes and told him to wash in the pool of Siloam. In obedience, the man washed himself and came seeing.[347]

In Jesus' ministry, manifestations of God's power had a profound impact upon the hearts of people. As a result of signs and wonders, many souls were saved as they placed their faith in Christ. For instance, John 4:1-42 shows Jesus moving in prophetic gifting as He converses with the Samaritan woman at Jacob's well. Here the equivalent of the "word of knowledge" coupled with prophecy is observed as Jesus reveals the secrets of the woman's heart and life. These signs and wonders caused the woman to believe, and her faith led to the preaching of the Gospel to the whole community.

Another example of evangelistic signs and wonders is seen in John 4:43-54, where a nobleman asked Jesus to come and heal his son who was at the point of death. Jesus said to him, "You may go. Your son will live."[348] The man believed the word of Jesus, went on his way and learned that his son was healed in the same hour that Jesus had spoken the word that had affected the healing. Because of this healing, the nobleman and his whole household placed their faith in Jesus.

John 10:37-42 indicates that the miracles of Jesus were intended to prompt faith in the hearts of the people so that they might believe. Although the miracles made no difference for many of the Jews, others did recognize that Christ's supernatural works testified to the truth of His claims. Miracles serve to open men's hearts to the revelation of Christ.

Several aspects of Spirit-empowered ministry are represented in the dramatic story of Jesus raising Lazarus from the dead. In John 11:1-45, Mary and Martha sent a message to Jesus informing Him that Lazarus was sick. The Lord delayed two days before departing for Lazarus' home. When Jesus finally started toward Lazarus' home, by revelation[349] He already knew that Lazarus had died. By the time Jesus came near to the scene, Lazarus had

---

[347] John 9:13-34.

[348] John 4:50.

[349] The revelatory power in which Jesus is functioning appears to be the equivalent of the gift of the "word of knowledge."

already been in the grave four days. The atmosphere was filled with grief and disillusionment. Jesus Himself empathized with the family's sorrow and wept.

The Lord Jesus approached the grave, instructed that the stone be removed from its opening, and began to pray. As He concluded His prayer, He cried with a loud voice, "Lazarus, come out!"[350] Lazarus came forth alive, and many believed on Jesus because of this miracle.

This dramatic story demonstrates the following: (1) A delayed response to need might be divinely ordered. (2) Revelatory guidance enables confident and effective ministry, especially when natural circumstances appear contrary to such guidance. (3) When grief and disillusionment surround adverse situations, the focus needs to be brought back to faith in Jesus. (4) Empathy accompanies faithful and effective ministry. (5) Passionate prayer may precede great miracles. (6) A vocal command may affect miraculous results.[351]

As is the case in the other Gospels, in this Gospel Jesus commissioned His disciples to do the things that He had been doing. In John 14:12-14, Jesus gave this promise to believers:

> I tell you the truth, anyone who has faith in me will do what I have been doing. He will do even greater things than these, because I am going to the Father. And I will do whatever you ask in my name, so that the Son may bring glory to the Father. You may ask me for anything in my name, and I will do it.[352]

In light of the promise that believers would do the works that Jesus did, those aspiring to engage in a ministry characterized by signs and wonders would be wise to include in their curriculum a study of the things that Jesus did and a survey of how He went about doing those things. It is His work that believers are to emulate.

---

[350] John 11:43.

[351] These observations only should not be interpreted as a formula for producing miracles. Everything noted here is the result of clear divine guidance.

[352] John 14:12-14.

The *Charismata* in the Book of Acts

The book of Acts demonstrates that the movement and experience of the church were the result of the Holy Spirit's work. At nearly every turn the reader is met with manifestations of the Spirit's power. This account of the church's earliest days elevates the expectation that demonstrations of God's power should be normative for the church. This portion of the review is presented chronologically, following the progression of the Acts narrative.

In Acts 1:4-8, Jesus promised that the gift of the Holy Spirit would soon come. He instructed His followers to wait for that promise. The coming endument of power would enable believers to be witnesses unto Christ throughout the whole world.

Acts 2:1-41 reports the fulfillment of the prophecy. With the Holy Spirit's arrival came manifestations of a sound like a mighty wind, something that looked like flames resting on the seekers, and supernatural tongues. Onlookers had mixed responses and reactions: some mocked, some doubted, and others believed. Peter preached a sermon identifying this outpouring as a partial fulfillment of a prophecy given by the prophet Joel:

> "I will pour out of my Spirit upon all flesh: and your sons and your daughters shall prophesy, and your young men shall see visions, and your old men shall dream dreams. And on my servants and on my handmaidens I will pour out in those days of my Spirit; and they shall prophesy."[353]

Peter went on to preach the Gospel, and three thousand souls were added to the church that day.

This passage is important in this study, for it demonstrates (1) that manifestations of the Spirit's power create mixed responses, (2) that the receiving of the Spirit is not just for an elite few, (3) that prophecy and revelatory dreams and visions are to be anticipated,[354] and (4) that the Holy Spirit's power produces evangelistic results.

---

[353] Acts 2:17-21. This passage is a quotation from Joel 2:28-32.

[354] See Acts 7:55-56.

The context for supernatural ministry in the Jerusalem church is described in Acts 2:42-47. This passage provides a detailed picture of the faith community's life. The normative life of the church carried the following features: (1) They devoted themselves to the apostles' doctrine. (2) They devoted themselves to the fellowship. (3) They devoted themselves to the breaking of bread from house to house, eating together with glad and sincere hearts. (4) They devoted themselves to prayer. (5) Everyone was filled with awe. (6) The apostles did many wonders and signs. (7) All that believed were together, and had all things common, even to the point of selling possessions and goods and distributing to those in need. (8) Every day they assembled at the temple. (9) They were characterized as people who praised God. (10) They enjoyed favor with all the people. (11) The Lord added to their numbers daily as people were being saved.

Acts 3 reports the first recorded miraculous healing of the newly empowered faith community. Peter, being with John, fastened his eyes on a lame man who had been begging at the temple gate and said, "Look at us!" The man looked at them expectantly. Peter said, "Silver or gold I do not have, but what I have I give you. In the name of Jesus Christ of Nazareth, walk." He lifted the man by the hand, and immediately his feet and ankle bones received strength.[355]

This miracle precipitated a reaction from religious authorities. They locked up Peter and John until the next day. The following day the two apostles were interrogated: "By what power or what name did you do this?" Peter, filled with the Holy Ghost, responded, "It is by the name of Jesus Christ of Nazareth whom you crucified but whom God raised from the dead, that this man stands before you healed." When the authorities saw the boldness of Peter and John, they marveled and noted that these men had been with Jesus. Being ordered to no longer speak in Jesus' name, they answered, "We cannot help speaking about what we have seen and heard."[356]

---

[355] Acts 3:1-10.

[356] Acts 4:1-20. As the church seeks the reviving of the *charismata* in this generation, the question must be asked, "What observable models for ministering in the power of the Spirit does the church have?" Are emerging ministers seeing and

The following observations from this account may be of value to a study of the manifestation gifts. (1) The disciples did not pray for healing; they commanded healing in the name of Jesus. (2) They took the man by the hand and lifted him to his feet even though healing had not yet been manifested. There was no outward evidence of the healing until they had taken this faith-motivated action. (3) Ministry in signs and wonders stirred up a backlash. (4) Peter's response to religious authorities was enabled by the Holy Spirit. (5) These apostles were regarded by some to be unlearned and ignorant, yet the dynamic of the Spirit affected what education and refinement could have never brought about. God worked through them. (6) The ministry that had flowed from these men was the result of their close relationship with Jesus. (7) The ministry which Peter and John displayed was the result of what they had seen and heard.

In Acts 4:24-31, the Lord hears the cry of His people for boldness, healings and the manifestation of signs and wonders. Their place of assembly was shaken, they were all filled with the Holy Ghost, and they spoke the word of God with boldness. By example, this incident of answered prayer encourages believers to ask God for the supernatural in their midst.

Acts 5:1-10 presents a sobering scene. Ananias and Sapphira lied to the Holy Spirit, Peter supernaturally perceived their sin, and consequently, the apostle rebuked them. As a result, each of them dropped dead. The Lord's requirement of holiness was accentuated, and the fear of the Lord came upon the whole church. Here the church learns to take the Holy Spirit seriously. Furthermore, this passage serves as an example for gifts of revelation.

After this incident, great fear came upon the church, many signs and wonders were performed, they gained the respect of the populace, and multitudes of people were added to the church. People even brought their

---

hearing the wonders of God? Those who would hope to operate in signs and wonders should keep themselves in association with those who are already moving in the power of the Spirit, for seeing and hearing what God has already done motivates faith to advance further in the things of the Spirit. Furthermore, those who would desire to be used by the Spirit would do well to keep themselves in the presence of God—in a place where they can both see and hear what God is doing and desires to do.

sick into the streets in hopes that Peter's shadow might fall on them affecting healing. Every person vexed with unclean spirits was healed.[357]

Acts 8:5-25 reports how the gifts of the Spirit powerfully advanced the church's mission in Samaria. In that region, Philip worked miracles, delivered the oppressed and healed the afflicted. The result was great joy among the people. Later, Peter and John went to Samaria, placing their hands on believers, and many received the Holy Spirit.

In Acts 9:10-22, a disciple in Damascus received a revelation that would ultimately assist the mission to the Gentile world. The disciple's name was Ananias, and he had a vision in which the Lord prepared him for ministry to Saul -- a persecutor of the church. The Lord sent Ananias to administer the healing of Saul's blindness and to impart to him an infilling of the Holy Spirit.

Acts 9:32-35 finds Peter traveling about the country and ministering in the power of the Spirit. In Lydda, Peter ministers healing to Aeneas, a man sick of the palsy, saying, "Aeneas, Jesus Christ heals you. Get up and take care of your mat." He arose immediately. All who lived at Lydda and Sharon saw him and turned to the Lord.[358]

Peter then went to Joppa. There a disciple named Dorcas (also known as "Tabitha") had died. He knelt down, prayed, turned toward her body, and said, "Tabitha, arise." She came back to life, and many believed in the Lord.[359]

One day in Lystra while Paul was speaking, he saw a man in the crowd who had been crippled from the time of his birth. Paul discerned the man's spirit: the man had faith to be healed. With a loud voice Paul then said, "Stand up on your feet!" In that moment the man leaped and walked. Here might be observed (1) the discerning of spirits, (2) the word of knowledge, (3) the word of wisdom, (4) prophecy, (5) a gift of faith, (6) a gift of healing, and (7) the working of a miracle.[360]

---

[357] Acts 5:11-16. In this context, affliction is associated with demonic oppression.

[358] Acts 9:32-35.

[359] Acts 9:36-42.

[360] Acts 14:8-11.

Once in awhile in the Gospels, Jesus would minister in a way that would break the pattern of what He normally would do. Something similar happened with Paul. In Acts 19:11-12, God worked extraordinary miracles through Paul in Ephesus. Handkerchiefs or aprons from his body were even taken to the afflicted and the oppressed, and they were healed and delivered. No explanation is offered for this unusual act. It is just one more indication that the work of the Holy Spirit cannot be reduced to predetermined formulas and patterns.

CHAPTER 8

THE REVELATORY GIFTS

God still speaks to His people. In 1 Corinthians 12, Paul notes three revelatory gifts given through the Spirit: the word of wisdom, the word of knowledge and the discerning of spirits. In addition to these three means of revelation, elsewhere in the New Testament we learn that God also brings revelation through dreams and visions.

The Word of Wisdom

To the Corinthians, Paul wrote, "To one there is given through the Spirit a message [word] of wisdom."[361] Here I want to present two possibilities for understanding what the gift called "the word of wisdom" truly is. First, the word of wisdom is generally regarded as a spontaneous manifestation of supernatural insight or perspective to the mind or spirit of the believer. It is a revelation of God's view of what should happen in a particular situation. This gift is *not* an impartation of a huge quantity of wisdom causing a person to become an all-wise individual. Rather, it is the manifestation of a single word or message of wisdom—the precise golden nugget needed for the matters at hand.

Another possible understanding of this gift requires a consideration of how the word "wisdom" is used elsewhere in 1 Corinthians. God's secret wisdom noted in 1 Corinthians 2:6-10 and elsewhere pertains to the Gospel that Paul preached.[362] If the writer intended us to make a connection between

---

[361] 1 Corinthians 12:8.

[362] 1 Corinthians 1:17, 21. In 1:24 and 30, the Apostle Paul states that Christ is the wisdom of God.

the "word of wisdom" and the concept of God's "secret wisdom," then these two points may further define the gift:

1. A word of wisdom will deliver a revelation relating to that which God had previously hidden and destined for the glory of believers.[363]
2. A word of wisdom will deliver a revelation that speaks of those things that God has prepared for those who love Him.[364]

These emphases could imply that the gift known as the "word of wisdom" involves insight into God's plans and preparations for the believer. These things are not made known through human wisdom; they are revealed or manifested by the Holy Spirit.[365]

I remember the first time that I sensed the Spirit wanting to manifest this gift in me. The incident occurred during my college years while I was traveling with a campus organization known as the Pioneers for Christ. We were ministering at a small mission, and the altar call had been given. Singers were singing, and the altar workers were ministering to seekers who had come forward. Being one of the guest ministers, I was certainly welcome to minister in the altar, but for some reason I chose to stand to the side offering supportive prayer.

Then I noticed a young lady kneeling alone. She was obviously very intense in her praying, but no one was praying with her. Suddenly words came into my mind seemingly from nowhere related the Lord's purpose for this woman's life. I knew exactly what the Lord wanted to speak to her. However, I doubted. Nothing like this had ever happened with me before. Was this God, or was it just me imagining that God was speaking?

I began to feel deep stirrings inside as I could not shake what I was hearing in my spiritual ear. It was like a fire shut up inside that just had to come out; however, I resisted. I was afraid. What if it was not God?

---

[363] 1 Corinthians 2:7.

[364] 1 Corinthians 2:9.

[365] 1 Corinthians 2:10.

Suddenly, I felt the burden of that message lift from me, and the deep burning of the Spirit stopped. At that very moment I saw another person kneel beside that young lady, and I heard him speak to her the exact same message that the Lord tried to get me to speak. She began to cry and experienced a great breakthrough that night. At the same time, I fell to my knees in tears, asking God to forgive me for not obeying the prompting of His Spirit. It was a long time before I experienced the same kind of manifestation again. I do believe that the manifestation that the Spirit was trying to bring forth through me that night was that which Paul refers to as "the word of wisdom."

The Word of Knowledge

Paul instructed the Corinthians saying that the Spirit gives "to another a message [word] of knowledge by means of the same Spirit."[366] The gift identified as the "word of knowledge" is not defined in the Corinthian letter. However it is generally regarded among charismatic believers as a supernatural revelation of knowledge to the mind or spirit of the believer. It is *not* an impartation of an immense body of knowledge, and neither is it an anointing to be a super-learner. It is the revelation of a single word, message or piece of knowledge about a person or situation.

When a word of knowledge is received, the Holy Spirit is not aiming to publicly uncover every hidden detail of a person's life. Imagine a room full of file cabinets containing comprehensive information about a person. When the gift of the word of knowledge is at work, it is as though the Holy Spirit walks into that room full of cabinets, approaches only one of those cabinets, opens one drawer of that one cabinet, pulls out one file folder, removes one sheet of paper from the folder and covers everything up on that page except one single word or phrase. Revealing that one piece of knowledge for redemptive purposes is what the Spirit is after. That is basically how it works.

Those who function in this gift experience its work in numerous ways. At times a word of knowledge manifests simply as a supernatural burst of knowing something that was not previously known by the person operating

---

[366] 1 Corinthians 12:8.

in the gift. This is the way that I first experienced this gift the year after I graduated from college.

I was on a summer ministry trip in upper state New York with my good friend, Leland Smelser. We had just finished a revival service at a church located outside of Syracuse. Departing from the church premises, I drove my car back to the pastor's home while Leland and the pastor remained at the church to take care of a few matters. While I waited in the pastor's driveway for him and Leland to arrive, I suddenly received my first word of knowledge. I instantly knew that the pastor's car battery was dead and that he and Leland were praying for me to return to the church to assist them!

I was awestruck that God would speak to me in that way. My heart pounded as I drove back to the church, pulled into the parking lot and found those two guys sitting there in the car awaiting my arrival. They got out of the vehicle and said, "We were praying for you to come back."

I pulled out my jumper cables, we jump-started the car, and we made our way home. It was an amazing experience that brought assistance into a real-life situation, and it made me more aware of the dynamic of the Holy Spirit in my life.

There are other ways in which this manifestation gift occurs. At times, a single word or a short phrase may visibly or almost visibly appear before a person's eyes. This gift manifests in this manner with me on occasion. I will be looking at a person, and almost visibly in three-dimensional letters, a word will float in front of me. Typically the word will convey a message of affirmation or encouragement. On one occasion it was a date, "March 24th," with flames leaping off of the letters. It turned out to be the very date on which a major revival breakthrough would take place several weeks later among the group of ministers with which I was working at the time.

On other occasions, the word of knowledge may come as a physical sensation in the body. I think the year was 1995. My wife and I were hosting a camp meeting service at our church in Scarborough, Maine. While prayer ministry was going on at the altar, my wife, Kerry, suddenly went partially blind in one eye. She came to me, told me what had happened and said, "I don't think that this is my blindness. I believe that the Lord is showing me that someone here tonight is experiencing partial blindness in their left eye."

We put it to the test. Kerry went to the microphone and said, "I believe that there is someone here who is experiencing partial blindness in the left eye. If that is you, if you will come forward, I believe that the Lord will heal you."

A man stepped forward confirming that the word of knowledge was for him; he was experiencing partial blindness in his left eye. Kerry then prayed for his healing. We do not recall whether or not the man was instantly healed, but the important thing to note is that God spoke, Kerry heard His voice, and she took the risk to act on what He said. This was the first time that she had ever received a word of knowledge.

Discerning of Spirits

Paul taught that the Spirit gives "to another distinguishing between spirits."[367] The gift of discerning of spirits (also known as, "distinguishing between spirits") is not defined in the context of the Corinthian letter. However, in light of 12:2-3, it is evident that the Corinthian believers' worldview allowed for the existence of spirits of both holy and unholy origin. As the first century church encountered demonic forces, the need for this gift became apparent.[368]

Please note that this gift is not exactly the same thing as spiritual discernment. Spiritual discernment is generally understood to be the ability of the believer to make sound spiritual judgments in his or her own life. What is right, and what is wrong? Is this of God, or is it not? Although there may be a relationship between the two to a degree, the gift of the discerning of spirits or distinguishing between spirits has to do with receiving revelation regarding underlying spiritual forces.

---

[367] 1 Corinthians 12:10.

[368] Acts 5:16; 8:7; 16:16-18; 19:12-16; 2 Corinthians 11:4; 1 Timothy 4:1; James 2:19; 1 John 4:1-6.

In ministry encounters it is very important to know what kind of spirit is at work. Is the Holy Spirit driving the things that are happening? If so, what is He doing? Is there a demonic spirit at work? Is there an angelic presence? If so, what is their assignment? What is the state of the human spirit of the person to whom ministry is being offered? The gift even helps the church in knowing other believers in terms of who they are in spirit. It includes knowing what grace or gift they carry for the benefit of the church.

All of these factors can be very complex to the human mind, but the Holy Spirit knows exactly the nature of the spirit or spirits involved, and He knows precisely what the one ministering needs to know about the situation. Thus, the Spirit of God is ready to deliver the needed discernment. The one ministering just needs to be listening for the Holy Spirit's voice.

Certainly there are many who are far more experienced with casting out demons than I, but my wife and I have witnessed several dramatic deliverances over the years. On one occasion while ministering in a Southeastern church, I saw a young woman coming forward for prayer during an altar service. I will call her Sue (not her real name). I had spoken with Sue on other occasions and knew that she had been suffering from panic attacks. For some reason, I had never made the connection between her sufferings and any demonic cause. However, on this night it did not take long before I would realize what was really going on, and as I describe this incident you will clearly see that my actions in this case were not the result of any acquired skill.

As Sue came within twelve feet of the prayer ministry area at the altar, she suddenly bent over holding her stomach as though she were in pain. People standing nearby thought she was simply physically sick and started praying for her healing. Remember that prior to this occasion, the thought of demonic activity would have never entered my mind in this situation; nevertheless, in this moment I instantly knew that a demon had a hold on her. I just knew it. How did I know? It was simply a manifestation of the gift of distinguishing between spirits.

I drew aside a couple of Spirit-filled people and told them that we were dealing with a demon in this woman's situation. One of the prayer ministers issued the authoritative command, "Go in Jesus' name!" and instantly Sue was delivered. She collapsed to the floor, and two or three believers began ministering to her further until her whole countenance lit up. She started laughing joyfully. Sue left that service a free woman, and the panic attacks did not reoccur. Glory to God!

Dreams and Visions

Although dreams and visions are not explicitly listed among the gifts of 1 Corinthians 12-14, the New Testament record does legitimize these manifestations as means by which God speaks. [369] The Scriptures provide little direct instruction regarding how they are to be interpreted; however, experience in this area qualifies some to suggest guidance.

The following guidelines for understanding dreams and visions are based in part on insights offered by prophetic intercessor, Cindy Jacobs:

1. Record the details of the dream or vision in your journal.
2. Ask the Lord if the dream or vision was from him. Listen for his response.
3. If you sense that the dream or vision was from the Lord, ask him for the interpretation. Listen for his response, and write down what he says.
4. If no interpretation comes, hold on to your notes; do not discard them. The understanding may come at another time.
5. Be careful with whom you share the revelation. Hold it close. Not everyone values the prophetic as you do.
6. If the revelation is calling for a major change of personal direction, ask the Lord for confirmation through other prophetically gifted people.
7. If the dream does not seem relevant to your own immediate context, bear in mind that it may be for someone else.[370]
8. Allow the guidelines for the other prophetic gifts to inform the way that you process the dream or vision.

---

[369] Acts 2:17.

[370] Based in part on insights offered by Cindy Jacobs in *The Voice of God: How God Speaks Personally and Corporately to His Children Today* (Ventura, California: Regal Books, 1995), 216.

Not all dreams are intended to be revelatory, but I do wonder if perhaps the Lord would be pleased to speak to us much more frequently through dreams. Ask Him to do so, and see what happens.

Visions are similar to dreams, except for the fact that they occur while a person is awake. *Open visions* are vivid revelations that are as real to the eye as any other thing that can be seen in the room. Some describe these visions to appear like a projection on the wall or in the space in front of them. Others have described visions in which they seemed to be translated to another place; their perception was that they became present as a participant within the revelation. *Internal visions* appear vividly in the spiritual mind of a person. Sometimes a complete internal vision can come in a split second, but it may take weeks or months to unpack everything that was revealed in that moment.

Ministry Precision

A lot of ministry takes place these days through what I have called a "shot gun" approach. We will try one thing to help a person, and if that does not work, we will try something else. Maybe we will even try several potential solutions at one time in hopes that at least something will hit the bull's eye and meet the need. It's like shooting at a target with a shot gun, scattering shot all over the place with the hope that a least one piece of shot will hit the target.

Wouldn't it be better to be a sharp shooter and to hit that target's bull's eye with one single bullet from a highly precise rifle? Similarly, wouldn't it be better in ministry stop guessing our way through to answers and to have precisely what is needed for a person's given situation? The revelatory gifts fulfill this very need. Whether it is the word of wisdom, the word of knowledge or distinguishing between spirits, these gifts give the prayer minister the precise guidance needed for the ministry at hand.

Suggested Assignments

A helpful resource for going further in this portion of the study would be the following book by Jack Deere: *Surprised by the Voice of God: How God Speaks*

Today through Prophecies, Dreams, and Visions. Grand Rapids, Michigan: Zondervan, 1996.

The essential role of listening for the voice of God should be assumed when considering the revelatory gifts. Meditation is a discipline that sharpens the believer's ability to hear God's voice. During this next week, set aside time for meditative prayer, and allow the Lord time and space to speak to you. Ask Him to reveal to you what is on His heart. If He begins to impress images on your mind, take note of them. Even if they do not make sense, jot down a description of what you are seeing or hearing. You may be receiving one piece of a much larger revelatory puzzle. Maybe you will receive the other pieces at a later time, or maybe the Lord will reveal the other parts to others so that the body of Christ can share in the revelatory event together.

CHAPTER 9

THE VOCAL GIFTS

From the beginning, God has used the human voice as a means for making His purposes known. Through the Holy Spirit, three vocal gifts have been given to the church for the purpose of speaking as the oracle of God: prophecy, various kinds of tongues and the interpretation of tongues.

Prophecy

In 1 Corinthians 12:10, Paul says that the Sprit gives "to another prophecy." The verb "prophesy" means "to speak before" or "to speak forth." In other words, it can be a divinely inspired foretelling of things to come, or it can be a matter of speaking on God's behalf—speaking forth things that are on His heart and mind.

Prophecy is not necessarily the same thing as the preaching of the Word. The preaching of the Word may at times be prophetic; however, one should not equate all preaching as prophecy. In short, prophecy is the supernatural ability to speak forth a message from God. It can be a predictive word, a directive word or even a corrective word; however, Paul shows us in 1 Corinthians 14:3 that prophecy should always be redemptive in nature, ultimately bringing strength, encouragement and comfort.

How much emphasis should be placed upon this gift? How important is it? In contrast to speaking in tongues, which is a means of communication *to God*,[371] when one prophesies, he is speaking *to men*.[372] As much as Paul desires all believers to speak in tongues, prophecy is a greater gift, for it edifies the

---

[371] 1 Corinthians 14:2.

[372] 1 Corinthians 14:3.

church.[373] He further indicates that revelatory ministry is *necessary* for the strengthening of the church.[374] Paul elevates the gift of prophecy above the other manifestation gifts, stating in 14:1, "Eagerly desire spiritual gifts, especially the gift of prophecy."[375]

God's order for the function of prophecy in the church is detailed in 1 Corinthians 12-14. Paul indicates that when a person prophesies, he or she speaks only a partial revelation: "we know in part and we prophesy in part."[376] Imagine a single piece of a one-thousand piece jig-saw picture puzzle. When we prophesy, we deliver a single puzzle piece of a larger revelatory picture. This realization should cause all who prophecy to take on an attitude of humility and interdependence with other members of the faith community. No individual has the exclusive word from God; we all need to be willing to hear what He may be saying through others. Often it is not until we receive a number of prophetic insights from various individuals that the full picture of what God wants to communicate comes into view.

No individual should monopolize the opportunity for prophesying. If a person is prophesying and someone interrupts with another prophecy, then the first speaker should be quiet and allow the other to proceed.[377] I realize that this guideline does not line up with common etiquette in Western culture, but it is what the Bible says. Paul says, "You can all prophesy in turn so that everyone may be instructed and encouraged."[378] Two or three should

---

[373] However, tongues are just as beneficial for mutual edification as prophecy when they are accompanied by an interpretation. See 1 Corinthians 14:5.

[374] 1 Corinthians 14:26.

[375] Paul repeats his call for the earnest pursuit of the prophetic gift in 1 Corinthians 14:39, where he says, "Therefore, my brothers, be eager to prophesy, and do not forbid speaking in tongues."

[376] 1 Corinthians 13:9.

[377] 1 Corinthians 14:30.

[378] 1 Corinthians 14:31.

prophesy, and then others should "weigh carefully what is said."[379] A plurality of prophetic voices helps to confirm the message.

Once two or three prophecies have been delivered, time should be taken for other prophetically gifted individuals to carefully weigh what has been said. The people should consider the possibility that God may be speaking to them. The context suggests that dialogue and inquiry might even be desirable as each prophecy is weighed.[380]

Prophecy is spontaneous and unpredictable in nature. Therefore, a great responsibility rests upon pastoral authority to help maintain an atmosphere of divine order. At the same time, leadership needs to sense when it is appropriate to allow room for the Spirit to do the unusual whenever He needs to do so. The Spirit must be Lord of His own operations.

Compared to the other manifestation gifts, prophecy and tongues are addressed quite extensively in the Corinthian letter. Regarding prophecy, 1 Corinthians 13:2 says that without love, the one who prophesies is "nothing." Paul aims to keep prophetic gifting in perspective, noting that it will one day cease.[381] Further instruction concerning this gift is a major focus of this text.

Various Kinds of Tongues

The Holy Spirit gives "to another speaking in different kinds of tongues."[382] Speaking in various kinds of tongues is the second of the vocal

---

[379] 1 Corinthians 14:29. In 14:32, Paul states, "The spirits of prophets are subject to the control of prophets." Those who minister prophetically are to be accountable to others. Whenever prophets speak publicly, they need to have a submissive spirit to those in authority who might find it necessary to scrutinize those prophecies publicly. In light of 14:36-38, those who minister prophetically are not above the need for scrutiny; none of them individually are the final authority regarding the word of God.

[380] 1 Corinthians 14:33-35. In the Corinthian context, Paul found it necessary to instruct the women to not enter into the open inquiry related to weighing prophetic utterances. Should women have doubts regarding the legitimacy of a prophetic utterance, they should discuss it privately with their own husbands at home.

[381] 1 Corinthians 13:8.

[382] 1 Corinthians 12:10.

gifts. These tongues are not the result of language studies. They are utterances enabled by the Holy Spirit. When speaking in tongues, a person does not need to fear that he might be babbling some blasphemous thing, for 1 Corinthians 12:3 says that "no one who is speaking by the Spirit of God says, 'Jesus is cursed.'"

The city Corinth was known for its "every man for himself" mentality. Unfortunately, when people of that culture came to faith in Christ, many carried the baggage of that ego-centric mindset into the life of the church. Evidently, this distorted concept of relationships produced a congregational environment where there was little regard for how one's exercise of spiritual gifts was connected to the overall good of the faith community. Even in the church, it was "every man for himself." This dysfunction became especially apparent in the way the Corinthians were prophesying and speaking in tongues. Paul provided the needed instruction for divine order.

Paul desired that all believers speak in tongues,[383] but he did recognize that not all would do so.[384] The absence of this manifestation gift in a believer's life does not relegate that person to a lower spiritual classification. Prophecy is elevated above speaking in tongues, as far as the benefit to the church body is concerned; however, speaking in tongues yet remains as one of the gifts that the Corinthians were encouraged to earnestly desire.[385]

Beginning in 14:2, although Paul does not condemn speaking in tongues in the gathering of believers,[386] he does teach that tongues are to be directed to God and not to men. One who speaks in tongues does well in that he strengthens himself, but when speaking in tongues to others, the hearers are not edified.[387] Apparently some among the Corinthians had thought that they

---

[383] 1 Corinthians 14:5.

[384] 1 Corinthians 12:30.

[385] 1 Corinthians 14:1.

[386] 1 Corinthians 12:7; 14:5, 18.

[387] 1 Corinthians 14:4, 6-11.

could mystically instruct believers through tongues.[388] Paul points out that without the understanding of what is being said, the hearer does not benefit from the utterance.[389] If one is to speak to the people, it is either prophecy or tongues accompanied by the gift of interpretation that should be exercised.[390]

What is the benefit or purpose of speaking in tongues? First, outside of the Corinthian letter, tongues are at times depicted as an initial evidence of the baptism of the Holy Spirit.[391] Second, as previously noted, speaking in tongues accompanied by interpretation does edify those who hear.[392] Third, the manifestation of tongues enables the human spirit to express mysteries to God in prayer and worship.[393] Fourth, when a person prays or worships in tongues, his own spirit is built up.[394] Fifth, tongues serve as a sign for unbelievers.[395]

What does Paul mean when he says that tongues serve as a sign for unbelievers? Some have suggested that if the unbeliever does not understand the tongues, it is a sign that he is not a part of the faith community. Such may be true; however, the context may also suggest that the sign is one of eschatological significance. In light of 14:21, tongues are an evidence that the resources of the present age are insufficient to communicate the purposes of God; therefore, He has manifested the power of the age to come to convey His

---

[388] A Corinthian attempt to instruct through speaking in tongues may be implied in 1 Corinthians 14:19.

[389] 1 Corinthians 14:9-11.

[390] 1 Corinthians 14:1-6, 13.

[391] Acts 1:13-15; 2:1,4; 8:5-19; 10:44-47; 19:1-6.

[392] 1 Corinthians 14:5, 13.

[393] 1 Corinthians 14:2, 14-17. In verse 15, the gift is manifested through song.

[394] 1 Corinthians 14:4.

[395] 1 Corinthians 14:22.

purposes. Such a manifestation is an indictment against the present order and serves as a sign of judgment.[396]

Paul gives instructions for order in the exercise of tongues in the assembly. If everyone tries to speak to one another in tongues while unbelievers or those without understanding are present, those onlookers will say that the speakers are out of their minds.[397] There is nothing wrong with everyone manifesting a gift when the church gathers, for "all of these must be done for the strengthening of the church."[398] However, those gifts should operate in a way that promotes understanding.

If believers do speak out in tongues so as to address those who are gathered, they should speak one at a time. Once a person speaks in tongues, an interpretation should be anticipated. If a second or third message is delivered in tongues, and there has been no interpretation, then those who are speaking in tongues should assume that no interpreter is present, and they should cease to direct their tongues as a message to the church. If they do continue speaking in tongues, they should do so only as prayer or worship directed to God.[399]

In the midst of the Apostle's detailed guidelines regarding tongues and the other manifestations, it appears that he might have been concerned that some would misinterpret his directives as restrictions. Paul raises the caution that in pursuing order, the church should be careful to not forbid tongues.[400]

---

[396] This interpretation rises out of Paul's use of Isaiah 28:11-12, where the prophet announces judgment to the people of Israel. Israel would not heed the warnings of prophets who spoke to them in Hebrew, so God sent them voices in tongues that they could not understand as a sign that He had exhausted the resources of language to speak to them, and yet they would not hear. Consequently, only judgment remained.

[397] 1 Corinthians 14:23.

[398] 1 Corinthians 14:26.

[399] 1 Corinthians 14:27-28.

[400] 1 Corinthians 14:39.

The Interpretation of Tongues

The Holy Spirit gives "to still another the interpretation of tongues."[401] The gift of interpretation of tongues is that which causes tongues to be beneficial for the edification of the church. It is one of the gifts that Paul says is necessary for the strengthening of the church.[402] If a person is already functioning in the gift of tongues, he should pray that he may also interpret tongues.[403] When Paul says, "I will pray with my spirit, but I will also pray with my mind,"[404] he may be implying that a person should give attention to the prayerful thoughts that are in his mind as he speaks in tongues. It could be that his thoughts in those moments may actually reflect the meaning of that which he is saying. If such is the case, the practice of giving heed to one's thoughts while speaking in tongues could have ramifications for training people to function in the gift of interpretation.

In the corporate gathering, if an individual speaks out in tongues, the church should prayerfully and expectantly wait for an interpretation. As has been indicated in the discussion on tongues, if there is no interpretation to the first utterance, and yet a second or even a third utterance is given in tongues without an interpretation, at that point, with the obvious absence of an interpreter, those who speak in tongues should do so quietly. Evidently, either someone is not being responsive in giving the interpretation, or it is not God's intention to manifest a message through tongues and interpretation at this time.

---

401 1 Corinthians 12:10.

402 1 Corinthians 14:26.

403 1 Corinthians 14:13.

404 1 Corinthians 14:15.

CHAPTER 10

THE POWER GIFTS

Jesus gave His disciples power and authority over all demons, and He gave them power and authority to cure diseases.[405] This same empowerment has come to us. When the Holy Spirit was poured out on the Day of Pentecost, the church received power to do everything that Jesus did when He walked the earth. This power has manifested in a number of ways, and nine of those ways are noted in 1 Corinthians 12:8-10 as gifts of the Spirit. Out of those nine gifts, three specifically manifest God's power in ways that changes things: faith, the gifts of healing and the working of miracles. A number of scholars refer to these three as power gifts.

Faith

Faith as a manifestation gift is not given much definition in this context. However, 13:2 states, "If I have a faith that can move mountains, but have not love, I am nothing."[406] Paul's reference to "a faith that can move mountains" calls to remembrance Jesus' message about faith moving mountains when He said,

"Have faith in God," Jesus answered. "I tell you the truth, if anyone says to this mountain, 'Go, throw yourself into the sea,' and does not doubt in his heart but believes that what he says will happen, it will be done for him."[407]

---

[405] Luke 9:1.

[406] As is the case with the other gifts, it is not the gift of faith that is invalidated; it is the person functioning in the gift without love that is invalidated.

[407] Mark 11:22-23.

The words translated "have faith in God" might also be rendered, "Have the kind of faith that comes from God."[408] These words of the Lord could be a reference to the gift of faith.

In 1988 my wife and I were at a place in our ministry where we did not know which way to turn. I had been serving as an associate pastor in a congregation that had just severed its ties with the denomination with which I was credentialed. I was in a dilemma of conflicting loyalties. Should I remain with this congregation, or should I remain with the denomination? After three days of fasting and praying on the rocky coast of Maine, it became a settled matter in my heart: I knew that the Lord had called me to remain with the denomination and to return to seminary in Tennessee to pursue a Masters of Divinity program.

With that decision being made, at that point I knew that I was without a job, without a home and without a circle of friends to stand with me. All I had was my pregnant wife, my first-born daughter, forty dollars in my pocket and a word from the Lord: "I am giving you a gift of faith for the things through which I am about to take you."

In most cases where I have known the gift of faith to be manifested, it has been in the context of praying for a specific need or taking a specific action at a particular point in time. However, in this instance the Lord was manifesting a gift of faith that would be manifested through a season of my life that would extend for about seven years. I left that place of prayer on that day with an absolute confidence that the Lord was ordering my steps and that every need would be met.

For seven years that supernaturally sustained faith did not wane. It was a gift from God; it was not of my own making. Through many trials and financial tests, the Lord guided us in wisdom and provided for every need. Two years into this season of uncommon faith, I completed my M.Div. work and went to pastor a rural church of twelve people, simply because I heard

---

[408] The 1599 Geneva Bible notes the legitimacy of understanding πίστ@ν θεου to mean "faith of God." *Geneva Study Bible* [on-line Bible and commentary], accessed March 21, 2003, available from http://bible.crosswalk.com/Commentaries/GenevaStudyBible/.

the Spirit's call to do it. Again, the gift of faith continued to drive us forward until that small church had become a strong self-supporting congregation. To God be the glory!

This story may seem a bit dramatic, but it does illustrate how the gift of faith enables believers to pursue things that otherwise they would be unable to do. When engaged in your next prayer encounter, you may want to ask the Lord to manifest a gift of faith in you regarding the matter. Should He choose to grant that gift, it will be with you for as long as it is needed for that specific situation. Remember, the gift of faith is a temporary manifestation of the Spirit given for something specific. Once the situation or prayer encounter has passed, that same strong sense of faith might not continue.

The gift of faith is listed as a power gift for it is the key to the releasing of the gifts of healing and the working of miracles. Too often believers rush into asking God for healings and miracles without understanding the critical need for a gift of faith in the matter at hand. If you can grasp what I am about to convey here, it will save you a lot of disillusionment in prayer ministry.

Allow me to illustrate by going back to my story. Faith comes by hearing and hearing by the Word of God. When I was sitting on those rocks on the coast of Maine in 1988, a word from God came to me. It was not audible, but it was unmistakably my Father's voice. He told me what to do, and He manifested the faith needed to obey. Faith came by hearing. While I have not shared the details of all that happened in those seven years, suffice it to say that on many occasions the way that the Lord worked was irrefutably miraculous. I heard His voice, I believed in my heart, a gift of faith was manifested, obedience followed, and miracles resulted from it all. Do you see the progression toward the miraculous in this illustration? It all starts with hearing the voice of the Lord and allowing the hearing of His voice to cause faith to come.

Let us apply this progression to a prayer encounter in which a miracle might be needed. Do we just rush in commanding tumors to be removed and backs to be straightened? No. We wait and listen for the Father's voice. If we hear nothing, we simply present a petition to the Lord according to whatever knowledge we may have about the situation. I have seen many prayers answered even when there was no supernatural revelation to guide me. However, I am very reluctant to authoritatively command things to happen apart from a word from the Lord. It is for this reason that we listen for the Father's voice, and when He speaks, we believe what He says, and we act accordingly. When we act on what He shows us or speaks to us, we must be thorough and precise in our obedience; we must do it exactly as He says. It is through such faith-driven obedience that miraculous manifestations can begin to occur. The gift of faith is the key to the other two power gifts.

Gifts of Healing

Gifts of healings may include a broad range of divine acts of restoration. In addition to physical restoration, the biblical concept of healing even embraces forgiveness[409] and deliverance from demonic oppression.[410] The context of 1 Corinthians 12:28-29 suggests that God has appointed certain individuals in the church to function in "gifts of healing," but not all will function in such gifts. That is not to say that the ministry of healing is restricted only to those who have a gift of healing; rather, it may suggest that some will have such consistent and frequent incidents of healing breakthrough in their ministry that it can be said of them that they possess gifts of healing. In other words, in the body of Christ, they are known for having power to heal the afflicted in Jesus' name.

The chapter entitled, "A Biblical Introduction to the Manifestation Gifts," provides a detailed survey of gifts of healing in the Gospels and the Book of Acts. At this point in your study, it would be advisable to review those pages with an eye for how the example of Jesus and His disciples should influence our approach to healing ministry.

---

[409] In the Old Testament, Yahweh heals by withdrawing His judgment, which may be manifested in the form of sickness or calamity (Genesis 20:17; Exodus 15:26; Hosea 6:1; 7:1; 11:3). The prerequisite of healing is the remission of sins, which is dependent on repentance. Healing and forgiveness are closely linked (Isaiah 6:10; 6:2; 29:2; 40:4). G. Kittel, G. W. Bromiley and G. Friedrich, eds., *Theological Dictionary of the New Testament*, vol. 3 (Grand Rapids, Michigan: Eerdmans, 1964-1976), 203.

[410] In the New Testament, affliction is associated with demonic activity (e.g., Matthew 12:22 and Luke 13:11). Ibid., 204.

The Working of Miracles

The Holy Spirit gives "to another miraculous powers."[411] "Miraculous powers" can also be rendered, "the working of miracles." The words in the original language literally mean, "operations of powers." According to 12:28, the Lord has appointed individuals in the church as "workers of miracles," but as verse 29 suggests, not all are "workers of miracles." Paul models the essential role of the miraculous in the proclamation of the Gospel, stating,

> My message and my preaching were not with wise and persuasive words, but with a demonstration of the Spirit's power [literally, "in demonstration of Spirit and power"], so that your faith might not rest on men's wisdom, but on God's power.[412]

What is the distinction between the working of miracles and the gifts of healing? Miracles can include the gifts of healing, but they are not limited to acts of healing. The multiplying of loaves of bread and fish to feed the multitude would be an example of a miracle that was not an act of healing. Jesus and Peter walking on the water would be another example.

The story of Jesus and Peter walking on water is a good case study for us to learn how to work miracles in Jesus' name. When I teach this lesson, I like to entitle it, "How to Walk on Water."

Jesus' miracle on the water[413] immediately followed the incident of Him multiplying five loaves and two fish to feed a crowd of over five thousand.[414] After they had been fed, Jesus sent the crowd away. He also commanded His disciples to get into their boat and cross over to the other side of the lake while he went up on a mountainside by himself to pray. While he was there, a storm arose on the lake, placing his disciples in danger. It was then that Jesus went out to them, walking on the water.

---

[411] 1 Corinthians 12:10.

[412] 1 Corinthians 2:4-5.

[413] Matthew 14:22-33.

[414] Matthew 14:15-21.

When the disciples saw Jesus approaching, they were terrified. They thought they were seeing a ghost. Jesus quickly assured them, saying, "Take courage! It is I. Do not be afraid."

Peter replied, "Lord, if it's you, tell me to come to you on the water."

Have you ever wondered why Peter said this? I have wondered. Someone has suggested that Peter recognized that being with Jesus was safer than being in the boat, so he asked Jesus to invite him to join Him on the water.

Jesus responded and said, "Come."

Now, if this were a ghost or an evil spirit trying to deceive them, how would asking this person on the water to speak this invitation make any difference? Wouldn't a deceiving spirit also respond by saying "Come"? It certainly would be a good way to drown and eliminate one of Jesus' key disciples.

There was something about hearing the Lord speak a command that would make a difference for Peter. Peter had come to recognize the command of Christ in his spirit. Faith comes by hearing, and hearing by the word.

Jesus said, "Come." Peter immediately swung himself over the side of the boat, stepped down onto the water and walked on the water toward Jesus. As Reinhard Bonnke says, Peter stepped out of the boat and started walking on the "c" ("sea"), and then the "o," and then the "m," and then the "e." He stepped out onto the very word that Jesus had spoken.

The only constant and stable element in this story is Jesus. He is the constant. You cannot walk on water apart from the presence of Jesus. You cannot walk in miracles apart from Jesus. What is making this work? It was the presence of Jesus. Jesus was already walking on the water. All Peter was doing was aligning his actions with Jesus' actions.

Peter's faith was fixed on Jesus. Peter's faith was not in his spiritual gift of water-walking. Similarly our faith should not be in our gift of working miracles. Peter was rightly captivated with the presence of Jesus, and so should we.

We know the rest of the story. After a few steps, Peter got distracted by the wind, became fearful and started to sink. People like to criticize Peter for doubting, but at least he got out of the boat. Like Bill Johnson and others say, "Faith is spelled r-i-s-k." But some object, "What if I fail while taking the risk?" What if you do? Just like He did with Peter, Jesus will catch you.

So, how can we work miracles? First, have faith in the One who is already in the middle of your impossible situation; He is already walking on the water. Second, ask Him for a word, and when He speaks, get out of your comfort zone—your boat, and start walking. Start acting on the basis of what He has said. Finally, keep your eyes on Jesus, and do not doubt.

The chapter entitled, "A Biblical Introduction to the Manifestation Gifts," provides a detailed survey of the working of miracles in the Gospels and the Book of Acts. A notable feature of the working of miracles in the ministry of Jesus and His disciples is that miracles seemed to always happen in response to an authoritative word that had been spoken, either by Jesus or one of His disciples. There are even cases where the person in need of a miracle spoke an authoritative prophetic word over themselves, and the miracle manifested.[415] Miracles often occur in a context of obedient response. At this point in your study, it would be advisable to review those pages with an eye for how other examples from the ministry of Jesus and His disciples should influence our approach to the working of miracles.

Suggested Assignments

On the basis of these teachings and God's sovereign work in your life, expect the Holy Spirit to start manifesting revelatory, vocal and power gifts through you. As you begin to experience the release of God's power in your times of ministry, take note of what is accomplished. Take time to write down your testimonies, and if you are working through this text in the context of coursework, submit your testimonies to your instructor.

---

[415] See the story of the woman with an issue of blood who said to herself, "If only I touch his cloak, I will be healed" (Matthew 9:21).

CHAPTER 11

THE INTERRELATIONSHIP OF THE GIFTS

There appears to be a functional interrelationship between the gifts of the Spirit. We have already addressed this matter in part in the section dealing with the gift of faith; however, here we will take a broader perspective that embraces more of the gifts.

How do the gifts interrelate? The revelatory gifts enable those who minister to either act or speak on the basis of that which has been received by revelation. Once the revelation has been received, it is at that point that the vocal gifts can be engaged. When the word from the Lord has been authoritatively verbalized, faith is generated in the hearts of those who hear; "faith comes by hearing, and hearing by the word of God."[416] With the power gift of faith activated, the other two power gifts become operative: i.e., gifts of healing and the working of miracles.

When this inter-relationship is considered, it is not difficult to imagine how members of the church body can work together as a ministry team as they engage the charismatic gifts. For instance, John, Mary and Paul are ministering to a seeker by the name of Jack who is experiencing back problems. Paul is the primary one-on-one prayer minister in this case, and he is ministering directly to Jack, but initially it does not seem that they are making much progress in the ministry encounter.

John and Mary are part of the team, and they are offering supportive prayer. However, while Paul is ministering to Jack, Mary receives a very strong impression that Jack has a kidney infection. She leans over to Paul and says, "I think that the Lord just showed me that he has a kidney infection."

---

[416] Romans 10:17

With that word from the Lord, Paul then proceeds to pray a very strong and authoritative prophetic prayer. The anointing of the Spirit is strong. While Paul is still praying out loud, John, who has stood by relatively quiet up to this point, starts feeling a hot burning sensation in his right hand. He gets a strong sense that he should place that hand on Jack's lower back. He quickly obeys the prompting, and when he does, all of them are nearly overwhelmed by the sudden surge of God's power that they feel. Within a few minutes, Jack reports that the pain in his back is gone.

This hypothetical case study illustrates how members of a prayer team might function as the gifts manifest through each of them in unique ways. Mary received a word of knowledge, Paul prophesied, and the Holy Spirit manifested a gift of healing through John.

Chapter 12

The Power of Testimony

Out of your life-story, a powerful testimony is emerging. In every instance where you have encountered God, an empowering grace has been deposited into your life that has left you forever changed. The grace that you experience today can remain upon you for years to come; you actually carry it for the benefit of others. The telling of your testimony is a way of stewarding that grace.

The Hebrew word for "testimony" or "witness" comes from a word meaning "to give evidence." At its primitive root, the word means "to repeat, to do again." Testimony brings that past event into the present as though it were happening again—as though it were being reenacted in full view of your hearers.

Testimony increases the likelihood that the encounter or miracle will happen again. When you share your testimony, you are *inviting* God to do it again. You are announcing that God is present to do it again. When you hear a testimony, recognize that it is an invitation from God for you to step into the realm of His goodness in that same area in your life. For instance, if another student shares a testimony of how God restored his or her self-confidence, believe that God can do the same thing for you. In a sense, when you hear a testimony, you can reach out and take it. It is for you.

When a person shares a testimony about a particular outcome, God actually allows you to imitate that person's faith! Consider these words from the book of Hebrews: "Remember your leaders, who spoke the word of God to you. Consider the outcome of their way of life and imitate their faith. Jesus Christ is the same yesterday and today and forever."[417]

Can one person actually imitate another person's faith? When I hear another person tell their story about how faith in Christ has made a difference in their life, I want to imitate their faith. When I imitate their faith, I can expect Jesus to be just as faithful in my situation as He was in the situation of the person whose testimony I have heard. Why do I have that expectation? I have that expectation because of Hebrews 13:8: "Jesus Christ is the same yesterday and today and forever." What He has done before, He can do again. Another person's testimony of faith inspires me to have faith, and Jesus will respond to my faith just like He responded to the other person's faith.

When I was ten years old I heard another ten-year-old boy deliver a testimony of how he gave his life to Jesus. I said in my heart, "If he can give his life to Jesus, I can give my life to Jesus too." The altar call was given, I went forward, and I gave my life to Jesus that night. I was imitating the faith of that other ten-year-old child. His testimony was simple, yet powerful.

A few years ago in an evening service at the church I was pastoring in Maine, a teenage girl experienced an instantaneous healing of a severe eyesight disorder. She shared her testimony with the congregation the following Sunday. Immediately after the testimony, a middle-age woman stood to her feet believing that God could heal her eyes too. Jesus instantly delivered her from a similar eyesight condition! Several months later I shared both of those accounts with a group of pastors at a seminary in Haiti, and while hearing those testimonies one pastor exercised his faith believing that God could do the same for him. Within moments he came forward having just received the ability to read the small print in his Bible for the first time! Glory to God!

The Bible contains numerous examples of the power of testimony. Consider the account in Mark 5 of the man whom Jesus delivered from a legion of demons: "As Jesus was getting into the boat, the man who had been

---

[417] Hebrews 13:7-8.

demon-possessed [possessed with a legion of demons] begged to go with him."[418]

The newly delivered man wanted to go with Jesus, but Jesus had another thought in mind. He said to the man, "Go home to your own people and tell them how much the Lord has done for you, and how he has had mercy on you."[419]

The story continues. The man went away into a region of ten cities—the Decapolis—and began to broadcast what Jesus had done for him. Regarding the impact of his testimony, the Bible reports, "And all the people were amazed."[420] His amazing transformation affected amazing results in the lives of others as he shared his story.

I also love the example found in the story of the woman healed from twelve years of bleeding. She said to herself, "If I could just touch his cloak, I will be healed."[421] The woman pressed through the crowd, came up behind Jesus and did just as she had purposed in her heart to do. She touched the edge of his cloak, and she was instantly healed![422] This miracle occurred in Matthew 9.

Between Matthew 9 and 14, something significant happened. Matthew 14:34-36 reads,

> When they had crossed over, they landed at Gennesaret. And when the men of that place recognized Jesus, they sent word to all the surrounding country. People brought all their sick to him and begged him to *let the sick just touch the edge of his cloak, and all who touched it were healed* [emphasis mine].[423]

---

[418] Mark 5:18.

[419] Mark 5:19.

[420] Mark 5:20.

[421] Matthew 9:21 (paraphrased).

[422] Matthew 9:20-22.

[423] Matthew 14:34-36.

Why were these people asking for the sick to be allowed to touch the edge of Jesus' cloak? They had heard the story of the woman who touched the edge of His cloak! They had heard what had been done before. How did they hear of what had been done before? In all likelihood, the woman had been sharing her testimony. She had been telling her story. Testifying is what the Holy Spirit does. Concerning the Holy Spirit, Jesus said, "He will testify about me."[424] Then He said, "You also must testify."[425] When you testify, you are partnering with the Holy Spirit.

There is more to the Holy Spirit's role in this matter of testifying. Before His ascension into heaven, Jesus said to His followers, "You will receive power when the Holy Spirit comes on you, and you will be witnesses unto me."[426]

What does it mean to be "witnesses" unto Jesus? What is a witness? A witness is a person who has seen or heard something and then tells about it. Consider the account of Peter and John standing before the Sanhedrin in Acts 4. These two apostles said, "As for us, we cannot help speaking about what we have seen and heard."[427] As a witness, you have seen and heard some things, and now you live to tell about them.

Summary

In summary, remember that when you testify, you glorify God. You strengthen your own faith. You remind yourself of what God has done. You strengthen the faith of others. You deliver grace into the present situation and greatly increase the likelihood that God will do it again.[428]

---

[424] John 15:26.

[425] John 15:27.

[426] Acts 1:8.

[427] Acts 4:20. See also 1 John 1:1-4.

[428] Most of this chapter has been adapted from J. Randolph Turpin, Jr., *Gateway to the Christian College Experience* (Canal Winchester, Ohio: Declaration Press, 2015), 12-16.

CHAPTER 13

DEFINITIONS FOR PROPHETIC MINISTRY AND LEADERSHIP

God has something that He wants to say, do and reveal in the earth. He has made His intentions known through Jesus, and He continues to make them known through an amazing partnership that exists between the Holy Spirit and the church. He truly delights in revealing His heart and purposes to those who are leaning in to listen.

The definitions that follow will help the reader understand concepts conveyed throughout the rest of this text. Some of the terms may be unique to the way that I teach on this subject; however, most are commonly used by other teachers in the prophetic movement.

Spirit-Empowered Ministry

Spirit-empowered ministry is an approach that intentionally includes the presence and work of the Holy Spirit in the conduct of ministry. It most notably involves the charismatic gifts of the word of knowledge, the word of wisdom, the discerning of spirits, prophecy, tongues, the interpretation of tongues, faith, gifts of healing and the working of miracles. Proponents of Spirit-empowered ministry hold that biblically this is the normative model for the ministry of the church.

A synonym for the term "Spirit-empowered ministry" might be the term "supernatural ministry," as made popular by Bethel School of Supernatural Ministry in Redding, California. Prophetic ministry and prophetic leadership are concepts that come under the larger heading of Spirit-empowered ministry.

The Prophetic

Floyd McClung defines the prophetic as "that realm of life where the natural interfaces with the supernatural. It is God communicating with human beings."[429] The prophetic is that realm of spiritual activity characterized by the manifestation of dreams, visions and the following revelatory and vocal charismatic gifts: word of knowledge, word of wisdom, discerning of spirits, tongues, interpretation of tongues and prophecy. I refer to this grouping of gifts as "the prophetic cluster."

Prophecy

Prophecy is the spoken manifestation of a revelation from God. It is the speaking forth of heaven's perspective and the Father's heart on a matter. It is also the charismatic gift that enables such a spoken communication to be delivered.

According to 1 Corinthians, New Testament prophecy strengthens, encourages and comforts.[430] At times it also contains an element of instruction.[431] Some are inclined to think that prophecy must have a critical element—exposing sin and pronouncing judgment. Such is not the prevailing focus of New Testament prophecy. It is always redemptive in nature. If it does address sin and the possibility of judgment, the final word will be one of hope.

Prophetic Gifting

While all believers may be empowered to prophesy, some are especially gifted to do so. Mike Bickle explains, "Believers who regularly receive impressions, dreams, visions or other types of revelation have prophetic

---

[429] Floyd McClung, Jr., "The Prophetic Journey," a prophetic ministry conference, Westmore Church of God, Cleveland, Tennessee, 2005.

[430] 1 Corinthians 14:3.

[431] 1 Corinthians 14:31.

gifting."[432] Believers may eagerly desire and pray for this level of prophecy, but ultimately the Spirit sovereignly determines to whom the gifting is given.

Prophet

A prophet is a spokesperson for God.[433] Not everyone who prophesies is necessarily a prophet, but when the faith community recognizes frequent and authentic prophecies coming forth from particular individuals, those people may possibly be prophets.

According to Ephesians 4:11-12, prophets serve together with apostles, pastors, teachers and evangelists to prepare God's people for ministry and to build them up until they take on the traits of Jesus Christ. Prophets, in particular, serve to equip and empower God's people to be a prophetic people. When prophets are fully functioning in their appointed role, there should be an increase in the number of people under their influence who are being released to function prophetically. Not all are prophets, but all can prophesy.

If the title "prophet" is used, it should be used cautiously and sparingly because of experience, maturity and credibility concerns.[434] The ministry of a prophet is given only by the sovereign call of God,[435] and if a person is a true prophet, it will be confirmed by the empowering influence that he or she will have upon the church body.

Prophetic Ministry

Depending upon the context, the term "prophetic ministry" can mean one of two things. First, it may reference the exercise of prophetic gifts in direct ministry engagement with people. Mike Bickle suggests when the label

---

[432] Floyd McClung, Jr., "The Prophetic Journey," a prophetic ministry conference, Westmore Church of God, Cleveland, Tennessee, 2005.

[433] Bruce Yocum, *Prophecy: Exercising the Prophetic Gifts of the Spirit in the Church Today* (Ann Arbor, Michigan: Word of Life, 1976), 33.

[434] Bickle, 116.

[435] Sullivant, 187.

"prophetic ministry" may be used: "Believers whose gifting has been recognized, nurtured and commissioned for regular ministry in the local church are in prophetic ministry."[436] According to Michael Sullivant, this level of prophecy is available to fewer people, but the Lord may possibly give it to those who seek for it.[437]

Second, "prophetic ministry" may be a reference to ministry involving non-prophetic functions (e.g., teaching, leading, evangelizing) that operate in a *mode* characterized by its reliance upon prophetic revelation. Often such ministries are given labels like "prophetic teaching," "prophetic leadership" or "prophetic evangelism."

Prophetic Leadership

Prophetic leadership is a mode of leadership that intentionally embraces and relies upon the prophetic leading of the Holy Spirit. Simply stated, God speaks, and leaders lead in direct obedience to what God has said. Prophetic leaders may lead individually or they may lead as a team through a process of shared discernment, honoring the prophetic insights of one another as they seek divine guidance together. [438]

Allow me walk through the rationale that undergirds the concept of prophetic leadership. The essence of leadership is to influence others to conduct themselves toward a desired destination or objective. In other words, a leader leads people from where they are to where they are not. In order to lead in such a manner, the leader must have some level of knowledge of the place or objective to which he is leading others.

How is a leader to know where to lead his or her followers? Knowledge of the desired destination or objective can be pursued in two ways: a leader may lead by reason, or a leader may lead by revelation.

---

[436] Bickle.

[437] Sullivant, 187.

[438] J. Randolph Turpin, *Shared Discernment: A Workbook for Ministry Planning Teams* (Scarborough, Maine: DrawNear, 2011).

By reason, leaders can appraise a situation and make a judgment call based that appraisal. However, while the engaging of reason is a vital aspect of a leader's thinking, it does have limitations. Reason cannot access knowledge of the future. Reason cannot access knowledge of the spiritual forces and realities at work. Reason alone cannot always rightly discern the will of God. Reason alone does not engage the leader in relational communion with God. Reason alone does not suffice; something more is needed.

Revelation is needed because the agenda for ministry is not set by natural factors; only God Himself determines that agenda. The ongoing and ultimate question for leadership in Christian ministry is this: "What is the will of God?"

God greatly desires to reveal His will, and He delights in doing so through both objective and subjective means. The objective means for the delivery of revelation is through the Scriptures—the already-written Word of God. The subjective means is through the prophetic.

Prophetic Leader

A prophetic leader is a leader who functions within the prophetic leadership model. A prophetic leader does not necessarily have to be a prophet, but he or she does value and rely upon the prophetic.

The prophetic leader carries a weighty responsibility, for once a directional revelation has been received from God, stewarding that prophetic word is absolutely required. Although the prophetic leader may need further wisdom to accompany a revelation prior to taking action, ignoring the leading of the Spirit is not an option.

Prophetic leaders take risks. They are willing to act in faith and authority solely on the basis of what God has said, even when such actions are not popular. A prophetic leader does not necessarily wait for God to show outward evidence that a particular action is going to produce something favorable. Often the will of God will not be done in a situation until after the prophetic leader has acted.

Chapter 14

The Purpose and Benefits of the Prophetic

What is the purpose and benefits of the prophetic? Michael Sullivant states, "The prophetic is basic to genuine Christianity simply because it relates to the Word of God being made alive in people's experiences."[439] All Christians have experienced the prophetic to some degree. New Testament prophecy is on a graduated spectrum, ranging from the call to salvation to the prediction of future events.

The Call to Salvation

Occasionally I run into Christians who say they have never heard God's voice. That is not true. If they are true believers, they have heard God's voice. At some point, something from the heart of the heavenly Father pierced through every barrier and made its way into their hearts. They sensed the tug of His love and responded in faith. They may not have heard an audible voice, but that moment of conviction resulting in their salvation was actually an encounter with God's voice—a call to salvation. Michael Sullivant states, "The fact is that no one can even become a true Christian without receiving a direct personal revelation from the Holy Spirit. In other words, no one comes to Jesus to be saved without 'hearing' from God."[440] All believers have experienced this level of prophecy.

---

[439] Sullivant, 55.

[440] Ibid., 54.

Passion

Revelation 19:10 records the words of an angel who said, "Worship God! For the testimony of Jesus is the spirit of prophecy." What do these words mean? The words, "the testimony of Jesus is the spirit of prophecy," could first mean, as Michael Sullivant suggests, that "the essence or 'spirit' of prophecy is the testimony—or the spoken words—*of* the risen Christ Himself *to* His people"[441] Second, it could mean, as Floyd McClung suggests, that the ultimate purpose of prophecy is to testify *of* Jesus. Floyd McClung states, "It is *about* Jesus." Then he continues with a statement that I think gets at the very heart of what prophetic ministry is all about: "The purpose of prophecy is to win the hearts of God's people to Jesus."[442]

McClung's words are thought-provoking. Think about it. He is suggesting that the purpose of prophecy among a people *already belonging to* Jesus is to win their hearts *to* Jesus. Could it be as simple as this: that the primary purpose and benefit of prophecy is that Jesus wants to talk to us, and he wants us to know his heart? We can get so caught up in the ministry implications of the prophetic that we can miss the fact that at the heart of all of this there is passion—a desire on the part of Jesus to have a heart to heart friendship with us. He is passionate in his affections toward us, and he so desires that we would be passionate in our affections toward him.

Floyd McClung offers further comment to emphasize what he believes Jesus is really after:

> Jesus is not committed to or interested in programs. In fact, He is willing to take away such things that may separate the church from its infatuation with Him. The less the church is impressed with itself, the more the Lord can use the church. It is as though the Lord would say, "My people are more important to me than anything they will ever do for me."[443]

The first purpose and benefit of the prophetic is *passion*.

---

[441] Sullivant, 70.

[442] Floyd McClung, Jr., "The Prophetic Journey," a prophetic ministry conference, Westmore Church of God, Cleveland, Tennessee, 2005.

[443] Ibid.

Strength, Encouragement and Comfort

In 1 Corinthians 14:3, Paul instructed the church, writing, "Everyone who prophesies speaks to men for their strengthening, encouragement and comfort."[444] Strength, encouragement and comfort are almost inseparable concepts and experiences. It is difficult to imagine having one without the others. Just one word delivered supernaturally from the Lord can raise a believer out of weakness, instill courage in one who has lost all courage, and console the person whose hopes and dreams have been shattered. When God speaks, it is a reminder of the fact that he has not left the scene, and he is still in charge. That's the power of prophecy.

Many believers function at this simple level of prophecy without even realizing they are prophesying. Mike Bickle explains,

> A simple prophecy is given when any believer speaks something God has brought to mind. This is usually within the scope of encouragement, comfort and exhortation explained in 1 Corinthians 14:3, and it doesn't include correction, new direction or predictive elements of prophetic words.[445]

According to 1 Corinthians 14, all believers can and should seek after this level of prophecy.[446] This mode and application of prophetic ministry is what I often call "Level One Prophecy." It is entry level, and it is always where I encourage my students to start when I am teaching on this subject.

Edification

The Bible says, "He who prophesies edifies the church."[447] When I see the way that some people approach prophecy, it makes me cringe. By listening to some, one would think that prophecy is all about criticizing, tearing down,

---

444 The same purpose and benefit for prophecy is suggested in Acts 15:32, where it is recorded, "Judas and Silas, who themselves were prophets, said much to encourage and strengthen the brothers."

445 Bickle, 120.

446 1 Corinthians 14:1 and 5.

447 1 Corinthians 14:4b.

pronouncing condemning judgment and declaring a message that says, "It is too late for anything of a redemptive nature to happen in the earth; all hope is gone!" Some people mistakenly think that their proclivity toward criticism is a spiritual gift; they call it discernment, or they think that they are a "prophet." True prophetic ministry always delivers a sense of hope, for it is always aligned with truth, and the truth always brings freedom and hope. True prophetic ministry builds up and does not tear down. It edifies.

Instruction

Paul taught the Corinthians, "You can all prophesy in turn so that everyone may be instructed and encouraged."[448] I can almost hear someone right now saying, "Ah ha! There it is! It says 'instructed'! See there, prophecy isn't all about making people feel better about themselves! There is some correction involved too!" Actually the Greek word for "instructed" simply speaks of learning or becoming informed; there is not a corrective aspect to it. The Lord often manifests prophecy because he wants us to know something that we otherwise would not have known apart from the prophecy. It could be a word concerning life or ministry direction, or it could be something as personal as letting us in on what he has been thinking about us. Whatever the prophetic word might be, it will be something that is encouraging; that is why "instructed and encouraged" are joined together as they are in the passage.

Conviction of Sin and Awareness of God's Presence

Although New Testament prophecy is primarily a ministry of strength, encouragement, comfort and edification, there are times when God does reveal sins and destructive behaviors. Such revelations are not for the purpose of humiliating or condemning the person; rather, the intent is to summon the person to a place of mercy, grace, safety and wholeness. Even while the Holy Spirit is manifesting encouraging and edifying words, the holiness of his presence can cause a sense of remorse over unresolved sin issues. Paul states this function of prophecy in these words:

---

[448] 1 Corinthians 14:31.

But if an unbeliever or someone who does not understand comes in while everybody is prophesying, he will be convinced by all that he is a sinner and will be judged by all, and the secrets of his heart will be laid bare. So he will fall down and worship God, exclaiming, "God is really among you!"[449]

In Acts 5, one prophetic encounter resulted in an exposure of sin that awakened the fear of God in an entire city. In this account, Ananias and Sapphira lied against the Holy Spirit. Their sin was prophetically pointed out, and they dropped dead. In this instance, the exposing of sin did not result in repentance. However, the revelation of sin and the punishment that followed brought a heightened awareness of God's holiness to the community.[450] Heavy prophecy of this nature is the exception and not the norm.

The Ananias and Sapphira story should never be taken as a license to publicly shame people for the sins they have committed. Upon careful examination of the story, you will see that the sin that this couple committed was a sin committed publicly; therefore, it had to be confronted publicly. The guidelines for when, where and how to confront sin were given to us by Jesus in Matthew 18:

> If your brother or sister sins, go and point out their fault, just between the two of you. If they listen to you, you have won them over. But if they will not listen, take one or two others along, so that "every matter may be established by the testimony of two or three witnesses." If they still refuse to listen, tell it to the church; and if they refuse to listen even to the church, treat them as you would a pagan or a tax collector.[451]

Just because a person is speaking prophetically—acting as God's spokesperson, it does not give the prophetic person a license to violate Jesus' teaching on this matter. If God reveals a person's sin to you, deal with it privately, just as Jesus instructed. If that person will not receive what you are saying, then you are to responsibly take the other steps according to Jesus' instructions.

---

[449] 1 Corinthians 14:24-25.

[450] Acts 5:1-10.

[451] Matthew 18:15-17.

A Reminder of Identity

We need to know who we are in order to function on the basis of who we are. Who are we? Biblically and theologically, we know that we are the children of God, but people need to know that truth deeply on a personal level. Every believer needs to live with a sense that God is their Father, and they are his child.

Romans 8:16 says, "The Spirit himself testifies with our spirit that we are God's children." Those words speak of the internal witness of the Spirit, but they also remind us that the Holy Spirit likes to speak revelations of identity to God's people. When we prophetically call out a person's identity as a son or daughter, it brings great encouragement.

The Recognition and Impartation of Anointings

Harold Eberle draws attention to the fact that the prophetic sometimes functions to highlight the anointing or calling upon another person's life.[452] In Acts 9, the Lord spoke to Ananias regarding Saul of Tarsus, saying, "This man is my chosen instrument to proclaim my name to the Gentiles and their kings and to the people of Israel."[453] The Lord then sent Ananias to heal Saul's blindness and to impart to him an infilling of the Holy Spirit.[454] As the result of Ananias' prophetic encounter, Saul began his journey toward becoming Paul—the great Apostle to the Gentiles.

The prophetic recognition and impartation of anointings occurs elsewhere in Scripture as well. In the Old Testament, God sent prophets to pour oil upon chosen individuals before those individuals occupied seats of authority. In the New Testament, Jesus was guided prophetically when he called Nathaniel to be one of his disciples,[455] and the church at Antioch was guided prophetically when they commissioned Barnabas and Saul to initiate

---

[452] Eberle, 25.

[453] Acts 9:15.

[454] Acts 9:10-22.

[455] John 1:47-51.

their mission to the Gentiles.[456] To cite yet another example, in one of Paul's letters, he noted an occasion when Timothy received an impartation accompanied by a prophetic declaration. Paul said to Timothy, "Do not neglect your gift, which was given you through prophecy when the body of elders laid their hands on you."[457]

Sustenance for Spiritual Life

Jesus spoke of God's word—every word that comes from the mouth of God—as a necessity for sustaining spiritual life. In my book, *Gateway to the Christian College Experience,* I speak to this point:

> Our very life depends on hearing and heeding the voice of God. When Jesus was tempted by the devil to turn stones into bread, Jesus said, "It is written, 'Man does not live on bread alone, but on every word that comes from the mouth of God.'"
>
> What lesson can we learn from these words? A spiritual life cannot be sustained by natural means. A spiritual life can only be sustained by "every word that comes from the mouth of God." When Jesus said, "every word that comes from the mouth of God," He was not just talking about Scripture as God's Word. He meant everything that God has to say, whatever way He may choose to say it—whether it be through the Bible or some other means.
>
> Cultivate a hunger for this kind of bread—"every word that comes from the mouth of God." Stir up a hunger for the sound of His voice. Have an attitude that says, "I can't wait to hear the next thing that He has to say. I can't wait to take the next thing that He says, devour it, embrace it, integrate it into my life, and act upon it."[458]

---

[456] Acts 13:1-3.

[457] 1 Timothy 4:14.

[458] J. Randolph Turpin, Jr., *Gateway to the Christian College Experience* (Canal Winchester, Ohio: Declaration Press, 2015), 52-53.

We know that knowledge of Scripture contributes to spiritual vitality, but the point here is that everything originating from the mouth of God—including a prophetic word—has the potential to revive and sustain the human soul.

Insight for Spiritual Warfare[459]

Prophecies spoken over a person's life can become useful in spiritual warfare. Against all odds, Christian warriors can remain steadfast when they stand confidently in the knowledge of what God has said about their purpose, destination and future. Paul once instructed Timothy to recall prophetic words. Although we are not told the specifics, there was something about the things that had been spoken over Timothy that would enable the young minister to "fight the good fight."[460]

Knowledge of Timing and Guidance[461]

Knowledge of God's timing and guidance can come through the prophetic. By the Spirit, Peter prophetically received his divine release to minister to Gentiles.[462] Barnabas and Saul were set forth to fulfill a mission that was already burning in their hearts when the church at Antioch corporately received a prophetic word that the time had come.[463] Church history tells us that prior to the destruction of Jerusalem in 70 A.D., a timely prophetic word came to the church, instructing believers to flee and resettle in Pella.[464]

---

[459] Sullivant, 84.

[460] 1 Timothy 1:18.

[461] Sullivant, 90.

[462] Acts 10:9-16.

[463] Acts 13:2-3.

[464] Mike Bickle cites a statement made by Eusebius (Book III, 5:4): "The members of the Jerusalem church by means of an oracle, given by revelation to acceptable persons there, were ordered to leave the city before the war began and settle in a town in Peraea called Pella." Bickle, 49.

Activation of Other Supernatural Works[465]

Prophecy is a supernatural manifestation. At times the prophetic simply delivers *information* received by revelation. At other times the prophetic affects change and *activates* other supernatural works—things that would not happen apart from a prophetic voice. For instance, Paul once spoke prophetically to a cripple in Lystra, saying, "Stand up on your feet!" and the man jumped up and started walking.[466] When a prophet speaks from the heart of God, the authority of heaven stands behind those words, and when the authority of heaven is realized, something is going to change. Harold R. Eberle states, "The purpose of the prophet's words is not simply to provide knowledge or understanding, but to change the structure or nature of that which is being spoken to."[467]

Prophetic Praying

The prophetic can inform prayer, in the sense that it can give intercessors insight regarding how and what they should pray, but the prophetic can also become a mode in which prayer is conducted. The exercise of the prophetic as a "mode" for prayer will require some explanation, so let us first touch on the prophetic as a means by which prayer is informed.

The prophetic *informs* praying. God speaks in advance so that believers will pray into things. When a person receives a revelation, it may be solely for the purpose of prompting prophetic intercession. The rewarding aspect of receiving foreknowledge of what God has willed is that the believer is blessed with the opportunity to partner with God, helping to bring the matter into being through prayer.

The prophetic is a *mode* in which prayer can be conducted. When a prophetic anointing comes upon intercessors, their praying shifts from petition to declaration. No longer are they asking God for anything. They are declaring the purposes of heaven into the earth.

---

[465] Sullivant, 92.

[466] Acts 14:9b-10.

[467] Eberle, 22.

CHAPTER 15

THE PROPHETIC COMMUNITY

Charismatic gifts work *together* in the *community of faith.* In fact, the *number one concern* of 1 Corinthians 12-14 is to consider how the charismatic gifts work *together* among believers. The Apostle Paul uses the physical body as a metaphor for the body of Christ, indicating that "God has arranged the parts in the body, every one of them, just as he wanted them to be."[468]

The Most Excellent Way

After presenting this truth in the imagery of the human body, Paul then teaches about love, "the most excellent way" or the most excellent manner in which the gifts should operate. He is *not* speaking of a *gift* that is more excellent than those noted in chapter twelve. He is speaking of a *manner* or *way* of functioning in those gifts that is more excellent than a manner characterized by disregard for one another in the body.[469]

Mutual Honor

In the corporate gathering, everyone has something to contribute, and all of it is necessary.[470] When the members have a motivation of love and a mutual regard for one another's gifts, the result is the strengthening of the church.

---

[468] 1 Corinthians 12:12-27.

[469] 1 Corinthians 13:1-13.

[470] 1 Corinthians 14:26.

Mutual honor between a prophetic minister and leaders functioning in a different equipping gift is vital. The significance of the five-fold equipping gifts is noted in Ephesians 4:

> It was he [Jesus] who gave some to be apostles, some to be prophets, some to be evangelists, and some to be pastors and teachers, to prepare God's people for works of service, so that the body of Christ may be built up until we all reach unity in the faith and in the knowledge of the Son of God and become mature, attaining to the whole measure of the fullness of Christ.[471]

The five equipping or leadership gifts that contribute to the church's maturity, unity and readiness for ministry are apostles, prophets, evangelists, pastors and teachers. In 1 Corinthians 12, three of these gifts are prioritized:

> And in the church God has appointed first of all apostles, second prophets, third teachers, then workers of miracles, also those having gifts of healing, those able to help others, those with gifts of administration, and those speaking in different kinds of tongues.[472]

The flow of authority follows this order: apostles are first; prophets are second; teachers are third. Apostles are sent by God as emissaries of His kingdom to establish the culture of that kingdom in the earth. Prophets serve that apostolic mission by perceiving and acting upon revelations of the heart and mind of God. Following the lead of the apostolic and the prophetic, teachers then align their teaching with the leadership established by the apostolic and prophetic leaders.

Ephesians 2 further demonstrates the need for honoring the place that apostles and prophets hold in God's household:

> Consequently, you are no longer foreigners and aliens, but fellow citizens with God's people and members of God's household, built on the foundation of the apostles and prophets, with Christ Jesus himself as the chief cornerstone. In him the whole building is joined together and rises to

---

[471] Ephesians 4:11-13.

[472] 1 Corinthians 12:28.

> become a holy temple in the Lord. And in him you too are being built together to become a dwelling in which God lives by his Spirit.[473]

The contribution of the apostolic and the prophetic is foundational to everything else involved in the building up of the church.

A relationship of mutual honor, submission and deference is required for this to work properly. No single Christian carries the full deposit. The natural inclination of any individual is for that person to think that he or she is always right; however, the corporate nature of charismatic gifts requires the preferring of one another.

How Prophecy Builds Up the Church

Prophecy equips and builds up the church by joining people's lives together.[474] Floyd McClung suggests the following line of thought that demonstrates the practical outworking of this truth:

1. A revelation comes to one person.
2. Church leaders discern the accuracy of the revelation and introduce that person to others who have received a similar revelation.
3. Connections are made, the church is built up, and kingdom life advances.[475]

According to Ephesians 4:12, the edifying role of the prophet is also about *equipping* or *perfecting* the saints so that they become effective in their life and work together. Expanding upon the meaning of the Greek word translated "equipping" or "perfecting," it could be said that when the prophetic functions together with the other four equipping gifts, the result is multi-faceted:

- The saints are completed; they are made into what they ought to be.
- They are mended or repaired.

---

[473] Ephesians 2:19-22.

[474] Floyd McClung, Jr., "The Prophetic Journey," a prophetic ministry conference, Westmore Church of God, Cleveland, Tennessee, 2005.

[475] Ibid.

- They are adjusted or arranged into order.
- They are strengthened.

Participation in the Faith Community

Due to the relational way in which the five-fold equipping gifts function, the prophetic minister must resist the tendency to become a loner. Prophetic ministers are validated by their involvement with the faith community, not by their separateness. They are catalysts to the community to learn to hear God together, and they serve within the church to help it fulfill its prophetic function. Bruce Yocum states, "In his service to the Lord, the prophet is subject to the community. But in its service to God, the community is subject to the authority of the word which the prophet brings."[476]

The Normative Life of the Faith Community

Acts 2:42-47 provides a detailed picture of the faith community's life:

1. They devoted themselves to the apostles' teaching (2:42).
2. They devoted themselves to fellowship (2:42).
3. They devoted themselves to having meals together—the breaking of bread (2:42).
4. They devoted themselves to prayer (2:42).
5. Everyone was filled with awe at the many wonders and signs performed by the apostles (2:43).
6. All the believers were together and had everything in common (2:44).
7. They sold property and possessions to give to anyone who had need (2:45).
8. Every day they continued to meet together in the temple courts (2:46).

---

[476] Yocum, 59.

9. They shared meals together in their homes and ate together with glad and sincere hearts, praising God (2:46-47).
10. They enjoyed the favor of all the people (2:47).
11. They welcomed newcomers into the faith community. The Lord added to their number daily those who were being saved (2:47).

Nothing in this description sounds very prophetic, so why consider it in our discussion? It is important to remember that New Testament prophetic ministry takes place in the context of normal everyday Christian living. The prophetic is not an anomaly in that divine culture. It flows as part of a corporate life characterized by devotion to teaching, fellowship, prayer, miracles, gladness, sincerity, worship, favor with outsiders, mutual concern for one another and a desire to be inclusive—welcoming new people into the family of faith. Those qualities are not pushed aside when the operation of the prophetic is taking place.

CHAPTER 16

REVELATION, INTERPRETATION AND APPLICATION

Whenever a personal prophecy is given and received, it is important to distinguish between the actual revelation, the interpretation and the application.[477] Many have found themselves disillusioned when a particular interpretation or application of a personal prophecy has proven to be inaccurate or in error. The inclination is to dismiss the entire revelation as not being from God in such cases. Could it be that the original revelation was truly God speaking and that only the interpretation and application are amiss? Understanding these three components of prophetic ministry—revelation, interpretation and application—may help to bring clarity to this matter.

Revelation

The revelation is the part that comes from God. If the Holy Spirit releases that word to be shared, then generally only the revelation itself should be shared. Generally the one who has received the revelation should not try to interpret it for the person to whom the message is directed.[478]

---

[477] David Pytches, *Some Said It Thundered: a Personal Encounter with the Kansas City Prophets* (Nashville, Tennessee: Oliver-Nelson, 1991), 121.

[478] Floyd McClung, Jr., "The Prophetic Journey," a prophetic ministry conference, Westmore Church of God, Cleveland, Tennessee, 2005.

Interpretation and Application

Interpretation takes place in the heart and mind of the person to whom the message is directed or in the context of a group process—confirmed in the mouth of two or three witnesses.[479] Interpretation and application are typically the human components of the process, and those parts should not be held as absolute. The church runs into problems when interpretation and application are esteemed to the same degree that the revelation is esteemed. Interpretation and application should not be held as absolute.[480]

Floyd McClung issues a warning about adding personal interpretation to the revelation that the Lord has given. One of the reasons that prophetic people get into trouble is that they sometimes get into too much speculation about what the revelation means.[481] A good example would be the way many interpreted the repeated revelations that Paul would suffer in Jerusalem. How is Paul's apparent refusal to heed prophetic warning[482] to be understood? When the believers in Caesarea heard the prophetic warning, they pleaded with Paul to not proceed to Jerusalem.[483] Acts 20:22-23 indicates that both the repeated warning and the compelling sense of guidance to proceed to Jerusalem came from the Holy Spirit. The implication is that the warning served to reassure Paul of the Lord's providence. It was not the Spirit's intention to dissuade Paul from going to Jerusalem.[484]

---

[479] Floyd McClung, Jr., "The Prophetic Journey," a prophetic ministry conference, Westmore Church of God, Cleveland, Tennessee, 2005.

[480] Ibid.

[481] Ibid.

[482] Acts 20:22-23; 21:4, 10-14.

[483] Acts 21:12.

[484] Floyd McClung, Jr., "The Prophetic Journey," a prophetic ministry conference, Westmore Church of God, Cleveland, Tennessee, 2005.

The Example of Jesus

David Pytches makes four observations from the ministry of Jesus regarding the processing and communication of revelations:

1. Jesus only did and said *what* he heard the Father saying and doing (John 5:19).[485]
2. Jesus only said what the Father said and only said it *how* the Father wanted him to say it (John 12:49). There are certainly counterproductive ways of saying what we sense God is saying. Paul had this in mind, I think, when he wrote about 'speaking the truth in love' (Eph. 4:15).[486]
3. Jesus only said and did things *when* the Father told him, and not before (John 16:12). Even though Mary was his own mother, Jesus resisted her pressing appeal for instant intervention at the wedding in Cana of Galilee (John 2:3,4); and He delayed after the urgent emotional pleas of his two friends, Martha and Mary, on the occasion of Lazarus' terminal sickness (John 11:3-6), because the time was not yet right.[487]
4. At times, it seems, things were revealed to Jesus that he never shared (John 16:12). It is not always necessary to communicate a revelation from God. Its purpose may simply be a pointer for prayer or a guide for helping someone in need.[488]

---

[485] Pytches, 123.

[486] Pytches, 124.

[487] Ibid.

[488] Ibid.

CHAPTER 17

CORPORATE PROPHECY

When prophetic ministry moves from the private environment into the public corporate environment, the potential benefit to the body dramatically increases. The need for spiritual oversight becomes greater as well. The Bible says, "Be eager to prophesy.... But everything should be done in a fitting and orderly way" (1 Corinthians 14:39-40).

The Sovereignty of the Holy Spirit

Before plunging into guidelines for order, we must first highlight the sovereignty of the Holy Spirit. One cannot predict, administrate or control the moving of the Holy Spirit. Programs, preconceived expectations and man's requirements cannot be forced upon the sovereignty of God.[489] With that point being made, the issue here is not that the Holy Spirit needs to be controlled. God forbid. The issue is that the human component needs guidance. How we facilitate the sovereign work of the Holy Spirit is the real matter at hand.

Spiritual Authority and Leadership

Spiritual authority and leadership are necessary for the proper functioning of corporate prophecy. Cindy Jacobs states, "Without proper spiritual authority, anarchy will occur. Where a leadership vacuum occurs, someone will fill the void."[490] The absence of leadership presents an unfavorable opportunity for random individuals to take the lead. Obviously, that kind of situation should be precluded by congregational leaders fulfilling

---

[489] Bickle, 74.

[490] Jacobs, 144.

their God-appointed role of leadership whenever the Holy Spirit is moving. Once again, the point here is not that leaders need to control the Holy Spirit; rather, they need to properly facilitate the congregation's movements with the Holy Spirit. In assemblies where the congregational leader cannot be present, properly authorized individuals should be placed in the lead as facilitators of prophetic ministry.

Administration is a gift of the Spirit. Michael Sullivant notes, "In the midst of cataloging the supernatural manifestations and ministries within the church in 1 Corinthians 12:28, Paul speaks of the charismatic gift of *administrations*."[491] The disciplined oversight and exercise of the prophetic maximizes its benefit to the church. Michael Sullivant notes,

> Paul cautions the Corinthians to discipline, temper and restrain themselves properly in order to channel their spiritual gifts in such a way that they will maximize the helpfulness of their anointings to the whole Christian community.[492]

Models for Facilitating Corporate Prophecy

The manner in which corporate prophecy is facilitated may vary from congregation to congregation and even from denomination to denomination. If you are worshiping in a setting other than your home church, it is important to honor the culture of that particular house. Here we will consider two models for facilitating corporate prophecy.

The Open Floor Model

Some Pentecostal churches have traditionally taken an open floor or open microphone approach to facilitating prophecies. This procedure consists of two basic parts: (1) Prophecies may be spoken spontaneously from the floor or at the microphone without being screened in advance. (2) Once the prophecy has been publicly presented, the officiating minister determines the appropriate response.

---

[491] Sullivant, 131.

[492] Ibid., 121.

Churches using this approach need to be aware of its potential problems. Jack Deere and others are careful to point out that the potential for disorder increases with the open floor or open microphone approach.[493] Without forewarning, someone could speak out a directional or correctional word, necessitating a potentially awkward process to judge the item openly before the whole congregation. If a church is taking the open floor approach, the congregation should be instructed to not deliver spontaneous words of a directional or correctional nature. Directional or correctional items should be taken to pastoral leaders who are gifted at processing and dealing with such matters. Spontaneous words should be edifying heart-impacting messages.[494]

Another potential problem with the "open floor" model is that it may convey the idea that anyone, whether known by congregational leaders or not, has the right to speak from the floor. Churches experiencing problems with this approach may want to consider alternative ways of facilitating corporate prophecy.

The Screening Model

An alternative procedure developed by Neocharismatics provides a screening or preview process prior to the delivery of the prophetic utterance. Whereas the open floor approach requires prophecies to be judged after they are publicly delivered, this preview approach judges revelations before they are publicly delivered. This procedure consists of three basic parts.

1. Present the revelation to a designated leader. As individuals receive revelations that they feel should be shared during the corporate gathering, they come forward to one of the designated facilitators (e.g., elders, pastors, other prophetically gifted leaders) seated on the front row and share with the facilitator the gist of the revelation. Cindy Jacobs even suggests, "If a

---

493 Deere, 196.

494 Floyd McClung, Jr., "The Prophetic Journey," a prophetic ministry conference, Westmore Church of God, Cleveland, Tennessee, 2005.

prophecy is for the church congregation as a whole, and you receive it before the service, write it down and give it to an elder whom you trust."[495]

Some may wonder, "What if God has truly given me a word, and the leader or elder does not recognize it as such?' Michael Sullivant appropriately states, "Trust God's providence working through worship leaders, pastoral leaders and other prophetic people—even if they may miss providing you an opportunity. God is bigger than these kinds of errors."[496] If a person is denied the opportunity to publicly deliver a word, he or she should remember that authority and liberty in prophetic ministry grow as a person develops a proven track record. Sullivant instructs, "Don't demand titles and microphones. Wait upon God to raise you up and back you up."[497]

2. Allow the designated leader to evaluate the revelation. The leader or elder will evaluate the content and timing of the prophecy to determine the timeliness or appropriateness of the message. The leader will determine if and when it will be presented in the service. The following are a few of the possible judgments that a leader may make regarding a word that has been brought to his or her attention:

i. The word is a timely word that should be publicly delivered by the person in that assembly at that time.

ii. The word is a timely word, but it should be delivered publicly by someone in authority and not by the person who received the revelation.

iii. The word is a timely word concerning those assembled, but it should not be delivered publicly. Rather, the word is esteemed as informative for prayer or for actions to be taken by those who are in authority.

iv. The word is a timely word, but it should be delivered privately to those for whom the message affects. The private delivery of the word

---

[495] Jacobs, 161-162.

[496] Sullivant, 191.

[497] Ibid., 193.

will be made either by the person who received the revelation or by someone with recognized authority in that setting.

v. The word may be from God, but it may not be for this time and place. It is to be held close to the heart until such time that God determines its release.

vi. The word is not from God. The person bringing the revelation forward may be well-intentioned, but the proposed message has originated from the person's own imagination and not from the Holy Spirit.

3. If approved, the leader will signal the person to speak at the appropriate time. It is best to have the person speak the prophetic word over the microphone. Doing so allows the entire congregation to adequately hear, and it enables sound technicians to record the word.

Critical Reflection on the Two Approaches

Let us critically reflect on these two approaches to facilitating corporate prophecy. While I personally favor the screening model, I cannot responsibly ignore the positive aspects of the open floor model.

When Pentecostals use the screening model, they may want to be careful to not categorically forbid spontaneous words from the floor. In biblical times, were prophecies submitted privately for review and interpretation before they were presented publicly? In the instructions of the Apostle Paul, it appears as though prophecies were typically spoken publicly and then judged publicly as well.[498] The public nature of the manifestation is implied in the lessons conveyed in the text:

i. No individual is to monopolize the opportunity for prophesying.[499]

ii. If a person is prophesying and someone else interrupts with another prophecy, then the first speaker should be quiet and allow the one who interrupted him to proceed.[500]

---

[498] Floyd McClung, Jr., "The Prophetic Journey," a prophetic ministry conference, Westmore Church of God, Cleveland, Tennessee, 2005.

[499] 1 Corinthians 14:29-31.

iii. In a gathering, opportunity should be given for multiple charismatic gifts to be manifested.[501]

Paul said, "You can all prophesy in turn so that everyone may be instructed and encouraged."[502] The Apostle went further stating that unbelievers even benefit when there is freedom for open spontaneous utterances at times when the "whole church"[503] is gathered:

> If an unbeliever or someone who does not understand comes in while everybody is prophesying, he will be convinced by all that he is a sinner and will be judged by all, and the secrets of his heart will be laid bare. So he will fall down and worship God, exclaiming, "God is really among you!"[504]

No matter which of the two approaches are used, after two or three people have prophesied, those who have heard the utterances should then "weigh carefully what is said."[505] A plurality of prophetic voices helps to

---

500 1 Corinthians 14:30. This allowance for interruptions should not be taken as a license to interrupt the speaker.

501 1 Corinthians 14:26 says, "What then shall we say brothers? When you come together, everyone has a hymn, or a word of instruction, a revelation, a tongue or an interpretation. All of these must be done for the strengthening of the church."

502 1 Corinthians 14:31.

503 1 Corinthians 14:23.

504 1 Corinthians 14:24-25.

505 1 Corinthians 14:29. In 14:32, Paul states, "The spirits of prophets are subject to the control of prophets." This statement can be interpreted in two ways. First, those who manifest a gift have control over how that gift is used. In other words, they are able to exercise discipline in their stewardship over the gift. The second possible interpretation is that those who minister prophetically are to be accountable to other prophetically gifted people. Whenever prophets speak publicly, they need to have a submissive spirit to those in authority who might find it necessary to scrutinize those prophecies publicly. In light of 14:36-38, those who minister prophetically are not above the need for scrutiny; none of them individually are the final authority regarding the word of God.

confirm what God truly is saying. The context suggests that dialogue and inquiry might even be desirable as each prophecy is weighed.[506]

Should prophecies be filtered through elders and prophetic teams before they are delivered? Often it is the spontaneous nature of supernatural revelation that convinces the heart that God is truly in the midst of His people.[507] Naturally, this freedom of prophetic expression adds a component of potential tension to the corporate worship experience, but it can be a beneficial component. In the prophetic moment, the entire church is thrust into both an opportunity and a responsibility to hear the voice of the Lord. The process of discerning the revelation is formative for the whole body. Therefore, whatever policies are placed upon the function of the prophetic in the corporate setting, they need to be both flexible and few.[508]

You may be accustomed to flowing in the Spirit one way, but the church you are visiting may have an entirely different approach. Restrain yourself. Watch and observe. Learn from how others in that environment are responding to the Holy Spirit. If necessary, discreetly ask someone, "If I receive a prophetic word for the congregation, how is that handled here?"

Further Instruction on Corporate Prophecy

The following suggestions and instructions are offered to further assist in the facilitation of corporate prophecy.

1. **When prophesying, speak in your normal language.** Most often culture influences the way individuals manifest charismatic gifts. Due to the diversity of cultures, the church may have to wrestle with the issue of diverse prophetic delivery styles.[509]

---

[506] 1 Corinthians 14:33-35.

[507] Floyd McClung, Jr., "The Prophetic Journey," a prophetic ministry conference, Westmore Church of God, Cleveland, Tennessee, 2005.

[508] Ibid.

[509] Ibid.

For instance, for some people, prophesying in King James English may seem like a good way to underscore the sacredness of a prophetic utterance, yet for others, it may come across as unnecessary, strange and distracting. I usually instruct people to avoid prophesying in King James English. However, if prophetic people do regress to King James English, they should not be stigmatized.

Also avoid saying "Thus saith the Lord." Those words are not necessary. If it is indeed the Lord speaking through you, the prophetic word will carry its own weight of authority. Besides, when you say, "Thus saith the Lord," it leaves hearers feeling like they have no other choice but to receive your words as an absolute message from God. Of course, New Testament prophecy is supposed to leave room for hearers to weigh and test prophetic words. If you feel that you *must* preface your words in a way that designates your prophecy as a word from God, it may be better to say, "I believe the Lord is saying…."[510]

On a related note, increasing your volume or changing the tone of your voice is unnecessary. Michael Sullivant states, "Genuine prophecy will still make its impact even if the style of delivery is 'dialed down'."[511] He also says, "We encourage people who prophesy first to try to relax and calm themselves."[512]

Some feel that they do not have control over the words that come out of their mouths when they are in prophetic mode. It is true that the explosive fire of the Spirit sometimes erupts in a way that causes self-awareness to nearly disappear, but as much as is possible, the speaker should still take responsibility for the manner in which the prophetic word is delivered. I agree with Bruce Yocum who notes, "The language we use in prophecy is under our control."[513] Speaking in the normal vernacular of the people is preferred.

---

[510] Sullivant, 192.

[511] Sullivant, 147.

[512] Ibid., 176.

[513] Yocum, 83.

2. Utilize Scripture. Live a lifestyle of storing up the already-written word of God in your heart and mind. By doing so, you are giving the Holy Spirit something to draw upon. A prophetic revelation will drop into your spirit, and your anointed mind will then quickly associate a passage of Scripture with the revelation. A prophetic word coupled with the declaring of the written world is powerful.

3. Be concise. Deliver the revelation that God has given you, and then stop. Far too often, people keep speaking beyond what God has actually given them to say, resulting in the prophetic impact of their words being diluted.

4. In faith, speak boldly and confidently. The Bible says that if a person's gift is prophesying, then that person should exercise prophesy in proportion to his or her faith.[514] The message should also be delivered boldly and confidently, for it is the very word of God.[515]

5. Speak in love. Christians are to always be held accountable for the words they speak. That requirement is not lifted just because a person may be under the anointing. The anointing must never become an excuse for speaking harshly or in any manner that does not edify. In fact, believers speaking under the unction of the Holy Spirit are held to a higher standard. The Apostle Paul clearly stated the standard when he wrote to the Corinthians, saying, "If I have the gift of prophecy and can fathom all mysteries and all knowledge,... but do not have love, I am nothing."[516] Love is the standard.

Correcting Public Prophetic Disorders

When a church decides to be open to the public manifestation of prophetic gifts, along with the great corporate blessing of supernatural revelation also comes the potential for prophetic disorders to occur. When prophetic disorders happen privately, they can be addressed privately. When they happen publicly, that complicates matters.

---

[514] Romans 12:6.

[515] 1 Peter 4:11.

[516] 1 Corinthians 13:2.

1. New Testament Guidelines. Public prophetic disorders are to be corrected according to New Testament guidelines and not Old Testament guidelines. In New Testament prophetic ministry, *people* are not stoned when they make mistakes; the *words* that they speak are judged.[517]

In speaking of words being "judged," we are not to assume that skepticism is in order. No. The expectation is that God will speak frequently to the church through prophecy and that prophetic utterances in a healthy congregation will normally be deemed worthy of careful consideration. Paul instructed the Corinthians, saying, "Two or three prophets should speak, and the others should weigh carefully what is said."[518] We should not be quick to assume that "should weigh carefully" means that the weighing is about judging whether the prophecy is true or false. The careful weighing of prophecy primarily has to do with the careful consideration of how the prophetic things being spoken should be interpreted and applied. Interpretation includes weighing what has been spoken by one prophet in comparison or contrast with what the other prophets have spoken as well as other things that God has been speaking to the church through various means. The point is that judging is not always about focusing on that which is potentially false and in need of correction.

On the other hand, the judging or weighing of prophecies is important when dealing with dubious prophecies. The plurality of prophetic voices (e.g., "two or three prophets") working together in mutual accountability helps to authenticate the message. When a person speaks prophetically to the gathered church, the other prophetic people should listen carefully to discern the validity of the message. If the person speaking is someone not normally authorized to speak prophetically to the church, it becomes especially important for someone in leadership to respond publicly to the prophetic message. The leader can either confirm the message's validity or kindly bring correction. The correction should first be directed to the word that has been delivered. If correction to the person bringing the erroneous word is needed, then discernment is needed to determine whether that correction should be

---

[517] Bickle, 97.

[518] 1 Corinthians 14:29.

made publicly or privately. Many times public correction can be kindly administered in the form of instruction benefitting the whole congregation.

2. Suggested Procedures for Correction. Mike Bickle has outlined the procedure for the correction of public prophetic disorders used at Metro Christian Fellowship during his tenure as pastor:

> i. If someone prophesies something that we discern is fleshly, we will let it pass the first time unless it is clearly unbiblical or destructive in nature. People need to have room to make mistakes without the fear of being too quickly corrected.
>
> ii. If the problem happens again, then we talk with them very gently and suggest that they need to be a little more restrained.
>
> iii. If they do it a third time, then we tell them privately to stop it and warn them that we will publicly stop them the next time.
>
> iv. If they do it again, we will confront the issue publicly.... We will then publicly explain the entire process we have gone through.[519]

3. Types of Prophetic Words to Publicly Correct. There are three specific types of prophetic words that must be corrected. First, words of *rebuke* or *correction* delivered publicly that did not first go through the leadership team must be addressed correctively.[520] Second, the unauthorized public proclamation of a *new direction* for the church must be corrected. [521] Third, public prophecy containing *unorthodox doctrine* must be corrected.[522] The responsibility for correction, direction and the establishing of doctrine officially rests upon the five-fold leaders of the church. Prophetic people who are not recognized five-fold leaders in the congregation must follow the protocol and the order of authority for that house.

---

519 Bickle, 73.

520 Ibid., 156.

521 Ibid., 157.

522 Ibid.

CHAPTER 18

PERSONAL PROPHECY

There is a great need for instruction in the church regarding the giving and receiving of personal prophetic words. The spontaneous nature of prophecy could lead one to think that nearly anything goes in the practice of prophetic ministry, but such is not the case. The Scriptures, the Spirit's leading and God-ordained gifts in ministry provide the necessary guidance and parameters to assure the integrity of personal prophecy.

Giving Prophetic Words

Carefully consider the following guidelines for delivering personal prophecies. Many of these guidelines are applicable to the delivery of corporate prophecies as well.

1. Wait for God's permission to speak.[523] Do not assume that every word of knowledge and every word of wisdom is a signal for you to say something. The revelation may have come to you for some purpose other than to vocalize it. The development of prophetic gifting requires developing one's ability to wait.

2. Speak only the part that the Spirit has clearly revealed. If the Holy Spirit gives you what seems to be an incomplete revelation, do not try to fill in the blanks for Him. Often the speaking of revelatory fragments has greater impact on the hearer than messages we have tried to make more complete through the addition of our interpretations. Speak only the part that the Spirit has clearly revealed, "For we know in part and we prophesy in part…."[524]

---

[523] Deere, 191.

[524] 1 Corinthians 13:9.

3. Do not fear God's strategy of silence.[525] Silence tends to put pressure on the prophetic minister, tempting him or her to produce an uninspired "prophecy" out of human imagination. Isaiah 50:10-11 serves as a warning to those who might be tempted to manufacture their own prophetic words at a time when God is not speaking.

Remaining silent when God is silent is important.[526] We should not presume that we know what God should say or do.[527] At times God may speak to the prophetic minister, but He will require the prophetic minister to remain silent. Such occurrences may be a test of maturity and security in God.[528] The ability to remain silent and the previously described ability to wait are closely related.

God may require silence from a developing prophetic minister during seasons of divinely-ordered training. Mike Bickle suggests,

> People who are immature in the prophetic ministry may also need to restrain themselves for a season from sharing their insight in order to watch how their word comes to pass. This will help them learn how to interpret and apply what they are receiving.[529]

4. Refrain from modifying the message so that it suits your understanding or what you think the person *really* needs to hear. The Bible warns against changing what God has said.[530]

5. Revelations can be communicated effectively with the "interview method"[531] –a method that involves asking questions regarding the revealed matters rather than making indicative statements.

---

[525] Bickle, 104.

[526] Bickle, 105.

[527] Ibid., 110.

[528] Ibid., 114.

[529] Ibid., 115.

[530] Jeremiah 23.

[531] Jacobs, 184.

6. Leave the results in God's hands. Once you share the prophetic word, leave it there. When it seems that the recipient of the word is not "getting it," the prophetic minister can find himself or herself wanting to back-peddle and modify or over-interpret the message hoping that the hearer will respond in the affirmative. Just leave it.

7. Pray for those to whom you are prophesying. Declare over them the blessing implied by the word you have received. The prayer does not need to be long, and it does not need to sound impressive. Often a one-word or one-phrase prayer or declaration may be all that is needed.

8. Do not deliver negative messages in personal prophetic ministry times. If a supernatural insight comes to you of a negative nature, ask the Spirit for a redemptive word for the negative situation. Remember that New Testament prophetic ministry always aims for "strengthening, encouragement and comfort."[532] If you still feel that the person needs correction, please take the matter to whoever may have pastoral authority in the person's life. Let someone under a pastoral anointing deal with the matter in a spirit of gentleness.

9. Do not deliver major directive words in personal prophetic ministry times. A major directive word, as I would define it, would be a message calling for a significant shift in life direction: "Do this..." or "Go there..." or "Marry this person...." If you are sure that you are receiving a revelation that is of a major directive nature, once again, you should involve a pastoral person.

10. If you miss it, admit it, and apologize. Cindy Jacobs instructs,

> If you do miss His word, apologize and admit that you must not have been hearing correctly. This will keep you clean with the Lord and in your relationships; don't let pride get in the way.[533]

---

[532] 1 Corinthians 14:3.

[533] Jacobs, 185.

Responding to Prophetic Words

How should you process a prophetic word that someone has spoken to you? Here are a few suggestions:

1. Receive it as a *potential* word from God. If you are in doubt, you are not required to make a decision right there on the spot to determine whether you should accept or reject the word. Hold the message close, and ponder it for awhile to see if God is speaking to you through it. If He is speaking, receive what He is saying gladly. If it is not His voice, just do as our friends at Bethel Church in Redding, California say: "flush it."

You will typically recognize a word as a genuine message from God when it addresses a matter with which you are currently dealing. However, if it does not immediately resonate with your spirit, it does not necessarily mean that it is not from God. The purpose for that word may not yet be apparent. Pray into it, write it down in your journal, and trust that the Spirit will highlight it in a moment in which it is needed in your life.

2. If the word is a major directional message, ask God for confirmation. Do not assume that you should sell all of your earthly possessions and move to Antarctica just because a prophetic person said that you should. It is okay to seek confirmation directly from God or even from other trusted prophetic people in the church.

Mike Bickle emphasizes this point, stating,

> When you receive a prophetic word from someone, you must hold it at arm's length until God *Himself* confirms it in your heart. If a prophetic minister receives accurate and authentic revelation from God that, for example, you are going to have a street ministry, all they are doing is giving you an advance warning that *you* personally are going to hear a new direction from God about a street ministry. This prophetic notification is sometimes God's way of confirming ahead of time what you will hear for yourself later on.[534]

---

[534] Bickle, 174.

3. Use the prophecy as a "springboard" for diving into prayer and the Scriptures. What does the Father want to speak to you personally about the prophetic message? What do the Scriptures have to say about the matter?

4. Be aware of timing issues. The timing of a predictive prophecy's fulfillment is something that God seldom reveals. Bickle comments, "God never works as fast as people think He should."[535] He further states, "It seems as though God holds out to the last possible moment to reveal whether we will panic or trust Him in our times of uncertainty."[536]

The prophecy may require time for obedience, preparation, prayer and character development before it will be fulfilled. Conditions may need to be met before the full promise can be realized. Cindy Jacobs encourages, "Remember, it rarely hurts to wait."[537]

5. Distinguish between revelation and interpretation. In the hearing of a prophecy, be sure to separate the genuine revelation from whatever uninspired interpretation or application the prophetic minister may have conveyed.

Recently a close friend shared with me an incident in which a visiting prophet called him and his wife to the platform in front of the whole church. The prophet proceeded to deliver a powerful and very meaningful prophetic word that obviously came straight from the heart of God. They were deeply moved and encouraged. But then the prophet began to interpret his own message, saying, "Now, what this means for you is that...." The prophet then proceeded with a lengthy interpretation that brought great confusion to the couple. In fact, they returned to their seats feeling deflated.

When my friend shared this story with me, I was able to encourage him by telling him that the prophet's erroneous interpretation does not negate the legitimacy of the original prophetic word. After taking this perspective into consideration, my friend and his wife were then able to accept that God had

---

[535] Ibid., 176.

[536] Ibid., 109.

[537] Jacobs, 86.

truly spoken to them, and that prophetic message became the encouraging word that the Father wanted it to be. Separating revelation from interpretation is important.

Mike Bickle observes, "The problems in the church caused by prophetic ministry are *almost always* caused, not by incorrect prophecies, but by presumptuous interpretations and applications."[538]

6. Write down the prophecy for further reference and evaluation. Tape recording prophetic words is also a good idea.

7. Ask, "Are there conditions in the prophecy that need to be met?" If there are conditions to be met, then faithfully follow Jesus as He leads you into the meeting of those conditions.

8. Ask, "Is the word consistent with that which God has already been saying?"[539] Remember that you are in a relationship with your heavenly Father, and He is continually seeking to communicate with you. The message that you receive through a prophetic minister is probably not God's first attempt to get His message through. A prophetic word from God might be best understood as one statement in an ongoing conversation, and He does not contradict Himself.

---

[538] Bickle, 177.

[539] Ibid., 85.

CHAPTER 19

DEALING WITH HEAVY PROPHECY

While the normative mode for New Testament prophetic ministry aims toward "strengthening, encouragement and comfort,"[540] occasionally the church may have to deal with "heavy prophecy" and take special care to make sure that it is not abused. Here we will consider three types of heavy prophecy: *predictive* prophecy, *directive* prophecy and *corrective* prophecy."[541]

Predictive Prophecy

Why is it that some predictive prophecies do not come to pass? Here are a few possible reasons:

1. The original "prophetic word" was not truly a prophetic word from God.
2. The conditions for the prophecy's fulfillment were not met.
3. The person prophesying only had a partial understanding of what God was saying.
4. The person prophesying added too much of his or her own interpretation to the message, making the original revelation unclear.
5. The timing of the prophecy's fulfillment was misunderstood. More time needs to pass.

If it becomes clear that a given predictive prophecy was not a true word from God, the church may have to take responsibility to address the issue. Michael Sullivant instructs, "If such an errant utterance has been given

---

[540] 1 Corinthians 14:3.

[541] Sullivant, 137.

publicly, then some kind of public statement needs to be made to clear up the matter."[542]

Directive Prophecy

Directive or directional words are prophetic messages to individuals or groups requiring a specific action, correction or change of direction. Such words need time and a procedure for processing.[543]

There is a potential for negative impact with directive prophecy, especially when it is delivered publicly in the hearing of the entire congregation. When such prophecies are not truly inspired by the Spirit, church leaders are faced with the awkward responsibility to deal with the error publicly. It is difficult to confront erroneous prophecy publicly in an edifying manner.

Floyd McClung suggests the following procedure for facilitating directive or directional prophecy:

1. Prophetic individuals who believe they have received revelations regarding direction for the church are encouraged to submit their input to a prophetic team or to the elders.
2. The prophetic team discerns the viability and relevance of those revelations, and they work together with other church leaders to determine the needed response.
3. They may choose to act on the matter behind-the-scenes, or, on the basis of the input, they may choose to draft a prophetic statement to the entire congregation. In such a statement they may list promises contained in the prophecy together with their corresponding conditions.[544]

---

[542] Sullivant, 138.

[543] Floyd McClung, Jr., "The Prophetic Journey," a prophetic ministry conference, Westmore Church of God, Cleveland, Tennessee, 2005.

[544] Ibid.

Corrective Prophecy

What is to be done if a person receives a prophetic revelation regarding another person or group of people that is of a negative nature—something that may warrant corrective action? If a negative word is received about a person, Michael Sullivant suggests the following:

1. Discipline should not be administered on the basis of a subjective revelation. God expects us to take such heavy action on the basis of verified facts.
2. God may have revealed the problem for the purpose of inspiring intercession on behalf of that person.
3. It is advisable to wait for the right time to approach a person to ask about the specific issue. When you do approach, asking questions rather than leveling accusations is the appropriate way to respond. It may not even be necessary to speak of the revelation you have received.
4. If you are doubting whether to speak with someone along these lines, ask the Lord to set up a situation that will convince you that it is the appropriate time.[545]

Mike Bickle further instructs,

> The principles of Matthew 18 and Galatians 6 must be carefully followed when it comes to correcting someone who is in sin, even if his sin has been revealed through the operation of prophecy. These principles instruct us to go to a person privately about his sin before going to him publicly, and they tell us to go gently after examining ourselves in trial regard first.[546]

---

[545] Sullivant, 144-145.

[546] Bickle, 115.

CHAPTER 20

EVALUATING PROPHETS AND PROPHECIES

Some have the misconception that when a church opens itself to the operation of the manifestation gifts that they are making way for an "anything goes" mindset. If the appropriate function of the gifts is taught, and if church leaders fulfill their mandate to lead, guide and govern, the chaos is highly unlikely to occur. Having procedures in place to evaluate prophets and prophecies helps to keep everything functioning in order. The Bible says, "Do not put out the Spirit's fire; do not treat prophecies with contempt. Test everything. Hold on to the good."[547]

When a Prophetic Person "Misses It"

What is the responsibility of the church when a prophetic person "misses it"? Here are a few suggested guidelines:

1. Elders should correct false prophecies privately, if possible.[548] However, if it is a major error heard by the gathered body of believers, then open correction with kindness is in order.[549]

---

[547] 1 Thessalonians 5:19-20.

[548] Floyd McClung, Jr., "The Prophetic Journey," a prophetic ministry conference, Westmore Church of God, Cleveland, Tennessee, 2005.

[549] Ibid.

2. Floyd McClung teaches that the best way to deal with the concern about false prophecies is to "fellowship the problem."[550] Both Floyd McClung and Rickie Moore stated that church leaders will have trouble testing prophecy if relationship is not there.[551]

A Word of Caution to the Cautious

In our zeal to be discerning, we must be careful in several areas:

1. We must not put out the Spirit's fire.[552]
2. We must not treat prophecies with contempt.[553]
3. We must remember that the objective is not judgmentalism; rather, the objective is to "hold on to the good."[554]

Bruce Yocum observes and states, "As soon as we speak of prophets, people are immediately worried about false prophets.... The community can judge the worth of prophecy after it happens, but let it happen first."[555]

Although false prophecies and the people who speak them need to be held accountable, the church should be careful to not hastily label a person as a false prophet, especially if they are in the early stages of functioning in the prophetic gift. Even the Old Testament makes room for the *development* of the prophetic. Jonah and Jeremiah are examples. These prophets were corrected, yet they were not labeled as false prophets. [556]

---

[550] Ibid.

[551] Floyd McClung, Jr. and Rickie Moore, "The Prophetic Journey," a prophetic ministry conference, Westmore Church of God, Cleveland, Tennessee, 2005.

[552] 1 Thessalonians 5:19.

[553] 1 Thessalonians 5:20.

[554] 1 Thessalonians 5:21.

[555] Yocum, 25.

[556] Rickie Moore.

Three Types of Spurious Prophecies

Michael Sullivant describes three types of spurious prophecy[557] and suggests appropriate responses for each of them: unanointed, errors and prophecies inspired by demonic deception.

1. **Unanointed.** An unanointed word is one that is not necessarily wrong in its content, but it does not carry the sense of the Holy Spirit being upon it. Such words rise more out of the human mind than out of a regenerated spirit. Sullivant suggests that when it seems a person has a pattern of speaking unanointed messages, leadership should gently inform that person how he or she is coming across. Instruction and coaching should be offered. It is also important to not discourage the believer. Rather, affirm the person for taking the risk.[558]

2. **Errors.** A prophetic word spoken in error is one in which either the content is off track or its delivery is inappropriate. Content errors may be doctrinal in nature, or they may be informational inaccuracies. Content errors may also occur when a person adds too much of their own understanding or interpretation to a revelation. Delivery errors may involve issues of timing, attitude or motivation. Sullivant notes, "Sincere believers are quite capable of this kind of thing, and although they need to be corrected, they must not be labeled as 'false prophets.'" Severe offenses that negatively impact the congregation may need to be addressed publicly; however, if at all possible, most cases of error should be addressed privately and with gentleness.[559]

3. **Inspired by demonic deception.** In my experience, prophecies inspired by demons have been rare. In fact, to my knowledge, I have never witnessed such an occurrence. Sullivant says that if it does occur, "Firm and decisive action must be taken in these instances to bring immediate

---

557 Sullivant, 155ff.

558 Ibid., 156.

559 Ibid., 156-157.

correction."[560] Sometimes it is a demon that has caused the second type of spurious prophecy noted above: "Errors."[561]

Consideration of the First Century Context

Bruce Yocum notes that in first century Christian life, right judgments regarding prophecies rested on several important contextual elements: First, Christians lived a highly communal life and knew one another quite well.[562] Second, each community of faith was governed by an elder or a group of elders who protected them from false prophets and teachers.[563] Third, the greater concern in the New Testament was with discerning *prophets* rather than discerning *prophecies*.[564]

Why was the concern more with discerning *prophets* rather than *prophecies*? Several factors warrant consideration. First, due to the fact that most New Testament prophecies are inspirational in nature, they usually do not require a direct response.[565] Second, a community rarely has to depend solely upon one prophecy to perceive God's message.[566] Third, Christians can usually trust the word of a prophet when they know him to be a true prophet.[567]

How can the church recognize a true prophet? Yocum notes the following three keys as evidences of a true prophet:

---

560 Ibid., 157.

561 According to Roxanne Brant, a prophetic word can have three possible sources: (1) the Spirit of God (the Spirit of Truth), (2) the spirit of error (demonic spirits), or (3) the flesh. Roxanne Brant, *How to Test Prophecy, Preaching and Guidance* (O'Brien, Florida: Roxanne Brant Ministries, 1981), 26.

562 Yocum, 62.

563 Acts 20:28-31; Titus 1:10-16; 2 Timothy 4:1-5. Ibid., 63.

564 Ibid., 63.

565 Ibid.

566 Yocum, 64.

567 Ibid., 64.

a. The fruit of his life and service[568]

> Luke 6:43-44a
> "No good tree bears bad fruit, nor does a bad tree bear good fruit. Each tree is recognized by its own fruit."

b. His submission to and regard for human authority[569]

c. His submission to and regard for God's authority

Bruce Yocum states, "Any messenger must have two things before he can legitimately proclaim a message on behalf of another person: the message itself and the proper authorization to proclaim it."[570]

Weighing Prophetic Words

Typically, individual believers should have little difficulty in recognizing the Lord's voice. We know the Shepherd's voice.[571] However, a prophetic word should also be attested to by the community of faith.[572] Bruce Yocum states, "It is right for a prophet who has been tested and proved reliable to have confidence in exercising his gift. But he must remember that the basis of his own confidence is the confidence which the Christian community has placed in him."[573]

Once a prophetic word has been evaluated, it is either accepted or rejected. Harold R. Eberle states, "A preacher's words may be evaluated, but a prophet's words must be accepted or rejected, submitted to or resisted."[574]

---

568 Ibid., 65-66.

569 Ibid., 68.

570 Ibid., 75.

571 John 10:2-5.

572 Yocum, 107.

573 Yocum, 109.

574 Eberle, 22.

The Bible says, "Dear friends, do not believe every spirit, but test the spirits to see whether they are from God, because many false prophets have gone out into the world."[575] Here we will consider a list of tests for discerning prophecies:

1. **Does it align with Scripture?** [576] The Bible teaches, "All Scripture is God-breathed and is useful for teaching, rebuking, correcting and training in righteousness…."[577] John Bevere states, "The more skilled we become in the Scriptures, the more evident and clear the delineation becomes between true and false, right and wrong. The Word is our safeguard from deception."[578] Mike Bickle states, "The subjective side of our faith is always to be scrutinized in the light of the objective side, but both are essential."[579]

2. **If it is a predictive prophecy, does it come to pass?** [580] This test only works, if there is time to wait for the fulfillment. Pytches notes, "The problem here may sometimes be that if we wait to see, it may be too late."[581]

3. **What kind of fruit does the prophecy produce?** [582] Is the prophecy ultimately life-giving? Does it draw people to Jesus? Does it strengthen, encourage and edify those who hear?

---

[575] 1 John 4:1.

[576] Pytches, 162. All who write on this subject stress the importance of the Scriptures in the task of evaluating prophecies. The following sources are among those making the same point: Yocum, 112. Jacobs, 74.

[577] 2 Timothy 3:16.

[578] John Bevere, *Thus Saith the Lord?* (Lake Mary, Florida: Creation House, 1999), 20. This book is not a preferred resource for those who want to learn the positive aspects of prophetic ministry.

[579] Bickle, 74.

[580] Deuteronomy 18:21-22.

[581] Pytches, 163.

[582] Ibid.

4. Are there any confirmations regarding the prophecy? [583] Some say that if a prophecy is authentic, it will confirm that which God is already speaking to you. However, there are times when the prophetic message is the first time the hearer has been introduced to the revelation. In such cases, confirmation will typically come at some point after the prophecy. In short, sometimes the confirmation comes from something received prior to the prophecy, and at other times the confirmation comes after the prophecy. David Pytches suggests, "When all is said and done, it would be most unwise to act in more than a tentative way in response to any prophecy without confirmation from some completely independent source."[584]

5. Was the prophecy delivered in an attitude of submission to authority? [585] Disregard for authority is rebellion, and an attitude of rebellion toward God's appointed authorities can open the door for demonic activity. Pytches states,

> While Scripture shows that prophets who had words from the Lord for those in authority often delivered them boldly (cf. Nathan in Samuel 12:1-14 and Elijah in 1 Kings 21:17-34), nevertheless Scripture is quite specific that the prophetic ministry must be exercised in a fitting and orderly way (1 Corinthians 14:40). This means that it must be exercised among God's people in submission to those in authority (Heb. 13:7).[586]

6. Is the person delivering the word a person of integrity? Jesus said, "By their fruit you will recognize them."[587] Pytches observes,

> This is not an absolute test. God specifically pronounced Abraham a prophet (Gen. 20:7) even though he had just blatantly lied about his wife (Gen. 21:2). Balaam had a good prophecy (Num. 24), but he fell into bad ways (Jude 11). The old prophet in 1 Kings 13:14-26 also lied to the man of

---

583 Ibid., 164.

584 Ibid.

585 Ibid.

586 Ibid.

587 Matthew 7:16a.

God from Judah and then prophesied truly. Therefore, this test is not foolproof, and we shall need to use the other tests alongside it.[588]

7. Are there other influences tainting the prophecy? Three questions adapted from Cindy Jacobs' checkpoints can help us concerning this matter. First, is the speaker critical or judgmental?[589] Second, is there any evidence of a religious agenda or bias?[590] Third, is it possible that human love for the hearers may be tainting the word?[591]

8. Does the spiritual tone resonate with our own spirit?[592] There are times when the content of a prophecy can seem so true, yet something does not *feel* right about it. Some prophecies come from lying spirits.[593] Satan and demons have been known to speak things that are true for the sake of advancing their own agendas.[594] People prophesying from their own human spirit can also cause a sense of uneasiness. The gift of the discerning of spirits enables the church to rightly determine of what spirit a person speaks.[595]

9. Does the prophecy glorify the Lord Jesus and display His character? [596] Is it consistent with what Scripture reveals about Jesus? Does it draw you closer to the Lord or take you further from Him?[597]

---

588 Pytches, 164.

589 Jacobs, 78.

590 Ibid.

591 Ibid., 186.

592 Yocum, 115-116. Jacobs, 78.

593 1 Kings 22:22.

594 Matthew 4:6; Acts 16:17-18.

595 1 Corinthians 12:10.

596 Yocum, 117. Jacobs, 76.

597 Deuteronomy 13:1-3.

Reasons Why a Prophecy May Not Come to Pass

Do all prophecies come to pass? No. Why not? There are several reasons why some prophecies may not be fulfilled.

1. The first possibility is that the word was not truly a message from God. Sometimes people prophesy from the flesh more than from the spirit. At other times, they may receive a true revelation from God, but they may only have a partial understanding of what it means. When there is incomplete understanding, those who speak may be inclined to modify or add to the prophecy in an effort to force it to make sense to them. Such revision can so alter the message's original intent that it no longer represents God's heart on the matter. As a result, hearers are left looking for a fulfillment that God never intended.

2. The second possibility is that the circumstances for which the prophecy was intended have changed. This scenario can happen when a prophetic warning has been issued regarding a sin issue or some other matter in which change is required. If repentance takes place or the necessary change occurs, the negative consequences originally prophesied are cancelled out. The warning has been heeded. The story of Nineveh's repentance in response to Jonah's prophetic warning serves as a good example.

3. The third possibility is that prayer has changed the outcome. Occasionally prophets may predict natural disasters, political upheavals or other disastrous events. What happens when God's people pray against such things? Often in response to prayer, God will prevent the disaster, interrupt the predicted political shift or stop the destructive chain of events. A biblical example of prayer changing the outcome is found in the story of Hezekiah. Isaiah prophesied that Hezekiah would die. Isaiah left the room, and Hezekiah prayed. In his prayer, he reminded the Lord of his devotion. Immediately Isaiah returned and prophesied that Hezekiah's life would be extended.[598] When prayer has changed the outcome, it can appear to some that the prophecy was a false prophecy. On the contrary, such prophecies are of the most powerful kind, spurring believers into a ministry of intercession.

---

[598] 2 Kings 20:1-6.

4. The fourth possibility is that the conditions of a prophetic word have *not* been met. Often prophetic words have conditions. God may say, "If you will do *this,* then I will do *that.*" Prophetic words should not be viewed as unconditional promises. As Mike Bickle is careful to point out, "Many prophetic words are not guarantees but invitations to cooperate with God."[599] When a person receives a prophetic word that they discern to be a message from God, the first thing to do is to believe it. The second thing to do is to carefully steward opportunities that align with that word. Without the wise stewardship of opportunities and the fulfillment of conditions, the blessing that God had in mind can be missed. A biblical example of prophetic conditions not being met is found in the story of Saul. He was anointed as king, but he did not keep the commandments of God; consequently, the throne was promised to another.[600]

5. A fifth possibility is that the fulfillment of the prophecy is intended for another time. Timing is one factor in prophetic fulfillment that is seldom clear, because God rarely reveals the precise time when something is going to happen. God fills time, but He also exists beyond time; therefore, He has an entirely different perspective on time than we do. Some prophecies will not come to pass in the season in which we expect fulfillment. When that occurs, we may be inclined to label the prophecy as a false reading regarding the will of God in a matter. It may be best to shelve that word rather than flush it. Its fulfillment may be reserved for a time yet to come. In the Bible, many of the messianic prophecies of the Old Testament would fit this category. When some of those Old Testament prophecies were given, there were people who hoped for their complete fulfillment in their own time, but the eventual fulfillment was reserved for the dawn of the New Testament era.

---

[599] Bickle, 165.

[600] 1 Samuel 10:1; 13:13-14.

CHAPTER 21

A CHECKLIST FOR PROCESSING REVELATIONS

Over time, the processing of prophetic revelations can become intuitive. However, when believers are in training mode concerning the prophetic, a checklist may prove helpful. A checklist for processing revelations follows.

1. Is this impression originating from God, or is it the product of my own imagination? If there is doubt, asking the Holy Spirit for a confirming word may prove helpful.

2. Could anything be tainting my perception of what God is saying? For instance, if a person is personally invested into a situation or into the life of another person, it may be difficult to filter out personal biases **and** preferences in times or prophesying regarding that situation or person.

3. What is the purpose of this revelation? Is it just the result of my growing intimacy with Christ, and could it be that He has no other purpose in mind except to share with me His thoughts and His heart? If so, I should consider the possibility that the revelation I am receiving is only for me to ponder. I should remain silent.

Is it just for my training? If so, I should consider the possibility that I should remain silent. Is the Lord just teaching me how to recognize His voice? Am I being tested in my ability to keep His secrets?

Is it just for my own personal edification or guidance? If so, I should remain silent. Is it for the purpose of informing my prayers? Is it for the purpose of prompting my own personal obedience?

Is it to be spoken to others? Am I authorized by the Spirit to speak? It is important to receive the authorization of the Holy Spirit to speak. With the reception of every word of knowledge the prophetic minister should seek a word of wisdom so that he might know what to do with the revelation he has received. It is not difficult to perceive that strong sense of authorization. Ezekiel spoke of his sense of divine authorization in these words: "The spirit which had lifted me up seized me, and I went off spiritually stirred, while the hand of the Lord rested heavily upon me."[601]

Have I been released by church leaders to prophesy? If so, to whom am I to speak? When a revelation is received, it should be spoken to those for whom it is intended. For instance, if the prophecy is of a directional nature for the mission of the church, then that item would be for the elders to hear; they are the ones who would have the authority to act. In such cases, a public declaration of prophetic insight might be premature or even inappropriate.[602]

4. If it is to be spoken to others, how should this prophetic word be delivered? Should it be delivered privately to a particular individual? Should it be delivered publicly to the church?

5. Is now the time to deliver this revelation, or has it been given for a later time?[603] If in doubt, hold it. If it becomes like a fire within that cannot be held back, now may be the time to speak. If it remains in the realm of doubt or if its significance seems to fade for the moment, it is probably for another time.

6. Is it in the same flow as what God is doing with the service?[604] Michael Sullivant instructs,

---

601 Ezekiel 3:14.

602 Floyd McClung, Jr., "The Prophetic Journey," a prophetic ministry conference, Westmore Church of God, Cleveland, Tennessee, 2005.

603 Jacobs, 182-183.

604 Ibid., 182.

> Discern the purpose of any given meeting and the mood and timing within the particular meeting. Come spiritually prepared and 'prayed up' rather than relying on the music to help get you into spiritual sync.[605]

He continues,

> "Wait for the right timing to speak. Often there comes a sense of the manifest presence of God when it is time to prophesy. Seek to flow with the current of the Spirit's broader movement and mood in the gathering. Double-check before speaking forth something that will redirect the course of the meeting."[606]

7. Am I familiar with the local church's protocol?[607] If in doubt regarding the protocol, ask someone. Remember, that the culture of the house always prevails. Honor the house.

8. Is it a correctional word? Is it a directional word? If so, it should be submitted to the leadership for them to pray over and judge.[608]

9. Is it a predictive word? If so, be careful about naming dates and times. Be very careful in the areas of "romance, childbirths and money matters."[609] It is advisable for newcomers to the prophetic to refrain from prophesying specifics regarding dates, times, mates, child births and money.

---

[605] Sullivant, 191.

[606] Ibid., 192.

[607] Jacobs, 182.

[608] Ibid., 183.

[609] Sullivant, 143.

CHAPTER 22

MISCONCEPTIONS RELATED TO THE PROPHETIC

After repeated exposure to prophetic ministry, one cannot help but be awestruck with the fact that God has chosen to so work through us mortals. Through the agency of the Holy Spirit, he allows us to perceive His heart. He enables us to know and see hidden things—even the future. He empowers us to speak such revelations with such authority that our very words reshape reality. The discouraged become suddenly encouraged. The weak become strong. Broken things become mended. Lives are changed and are redirected toward a hopeful future. Prophetic ministry is without a doubt amazing and wonderful. However, fascination with the prophetic can lead to a number of misconceptions regarding prophetic gifts.

1. Misconception #1: prophetic people are spiritually superior. Mike Bickle, author of *Growing in the Prophetic,* comments,

> One of the most important things to do in a church that wants to nurture and administrate prophetic ministry is to dial down the mysticism and the carnal desire to look superspiritual. We need to keep our eyes off people and remain focused on Jesus and His purpose for us. This is not a spiritual beauty contest, but it can turn into one very quickly if people see gifts as merit badges rather than something to bless the church. It is not about the vessel. It's about loving the Lord and building up His church.[610]

2. Misconception #2: prophetic anointing is an indicator of spiritual maturity, godly character and divine approval. No *gift* of the Spirit is such an

---

[610] Bickle, 57.

indicator. The *fruit* of the Spirit[611] is the indicator. When character and anointing align, the manifestation of supernatural power may confirm that a person is on track with God's mission, as in the case of Jesus,[612] but not without character. The case of King Saul is a negative example of this point. He was anointed and was even known to be prophetic, but his character did not align with the anointing. As a result, Saul lost favor with God. The kingdom was taken from him and given to a man after God's own heart.[613]

Concerning the operation of spiritual gifts through carnal people, Mike Bickle comments,

> The message for prophets, leaders and church people is this: God's gifts are freely given as a sign of His mercy, not His approval. Don't disdain valid spiritual gifts manifested through spiritually immature people. But also, do not be fooled by God's grace and patience with prophetic vessels who remain anointed for a season as they continue in their carnality. Eventually He will call us all to account as stewards of the gifts He has entrusted to us.[614]

3. Misconception #3: prophets should lead the way. *Some* prophetic people are good leaders, but such is not always the case. According to Mike Bickle, it is not usually good for prophets to be the primary leader of the church. He says, "Remember, most prophetic people don't have the gift of leadership that is essential for a church to be healthy, balanced and safe. A church led only by prophets is not a safe environment for God's people."[615] Prophetic leaders usually have God's heart as to where the church should go and what it should become, but they often lack insight concerning the practical requirements for getting there. They are also known for missing the present needs of the people. In situations where the primary leader is highly

---

611 Galatians 5:22-23.

612 Matthew 11:4-5; Luke 7:22.

613 1 Samuel 13:13-14.

614 Bickle., 58.

615 Ibid., 57.

prophetic, that leader needs to work together with the other four of the five-fold leaders: apostles, pastors, teachers and evangelists.[616]

4. Misconception #4: prophetic anointing equals 100 percent doctrinal accuracy.[617] Although all church leaders should aim for doctrinal accuracy, the guardianship over doctrinal accuracy rests primarily upon the teaching gift. Prophets are prophets; they are not typically teachers. Mike Bickle rightly emphasizes, "It is so important that prophetic ministers are part of a local church team that includes gifted teachers. If they are not in a team, then they are often tempted to assume too much responsibility and thereby venture outside their calling."[618]

5. Misconception #5: prophetic churches are uniquely positioned to be the center of God's purpose and plan for their region. [619] If God has positioned a church to serve the churches of a region in a unique way, it probably has little to do with the church being prophetic. Mike Bickle warns prophetic churches not to have an over-realized sense of their importance. God is not too interested in raising up superstar churches that dominate the spiritual landscape of a region. As Mike Bickle says, "God is committed to using the whole church in unity in each area."[620]

---

[616] Ephesians 4:11-12.

[617] Bickel.

[618] Ibid., 64.

[619] Ibid., 47.

[620] Ibid., 48.

Chapter 23

Avoiding Pitfalls

Prophetic ministry conducted within biblical guidelines is a powerful and positive force in the earth. However, one should not rush into this realm without being aware of its potential pitfalls. I have discovered many of these pitfalls through the school of life experience, and others I have gleaned from practitioners like Mike Bickle, Harold Eberle, Jack Deere, Michael Sullivant, Cindy Jacobs, Floyd McClung and Kris Vallotton. This chapter provides a list of prophetic pitfalls to avoid.

1. Prophesying out of anger. There is an anger side of God, but His anger is motivated by love. He is angry against injustice and the things stand in the way of people experiencing His love. When it comes to heavy prophecies, think redemption. Think Fatherly warning and instruction. These are the motivations behind prophetic utterances that will correct injustices, redirect destructive patterns and remove hindrances. These are the motivations that will ultimately bring edification, comfort, strength and encouragement.[621] It is important for prophetic people to become aware of their own emotions and to not mistake their human emotions as a reliable representation of the heart of the Father—especially when those emotions are negative. As James says, "The anger of man does not work the righteousness of God."[622]

2. The desire to please people.[623] In the more advanced levels of prophetic ministry where warnings and corrections occur, a desire to please people can obviously pose a problem. If motivated by a desire to please, who

---

[621] 1 Corinthians 14:3.

[622] James 1:20.

[623] Deere, 206.

would even dare to speak a word that might upset someone? This desire often stems from inner struggles with identity and feelings of insignificance. Do you know who you are and whose you are? Do you know how valuable you are to Him? When that revelation breaks in upon a person, pleasing *Him* is all that matters!

3. The desire to be awesome.[624] Such motivation sets one up for a fall; it is a form of pride and selfish ambition.[625] There is nothing about signs, wonders and miracles that is about us being awesome. It is all about demonstrating that God is awesome.

4. Rationalizing mistakes.[626] If you make a mistake in the prophetic, humbly admit it and move on. Doing so increases your credibility. By trying to explain away your mistakes, you actually reduce your credibility in the eyes of others.

5. Using the gift for personal gain. Jack Deere refers to this pitfall as the "Gehazi" ministry.[627] Gehazi was the servant of the prophet Elisha. His name appears in the story of Elisha ministering healing to Naaman. After Naaman was healed, he offered money to Elisha, but Elisha refused to receive payment for a miracle. When Gehazi saw Elisha's refusal of the gift, he later went after Naaman and told him that his master, Elisha, had changed his mind. He lied and said that the money was now needed to take care of the needs of two young men. Naaman gave the money to Gehazi, but Gehazi kept the money hidden for himself. As a result of Gehazi's covetousness and deception, he became a leper.[628]

---

[624] Ibid., 207. Michael Sullivant also warns of the desire to impress others. Sullivant, 113.

[625] Proverbs 16:18; Philippians 2:3-4.

[626] Deere, 208.

[627] See 2 Kings 5. Deere, 209.

[628] 2 Kings 5.

6. Calling out sins publicly.[629] Prophetic anointing does not excuse believers from following biblical guidelines for confronting the sins of other believers. In Matthew 18, Jesus clearly outlines how erring believers should be approached. First, meet with them privately, one-on-one, to point out their fault. Second, if they refuse to heed your words, take one or two people with you, and confront them again. Third, if they still refuse to listen, take the matter to the church. Please note that taking the matter to the church may or may not require voicing the offense publicly. Before any sin is exposed publicly, congregational leaders must be involved in the process, and they should be the ones to discern whether or not the entire assembly of believers needs to be informed. Fourth, if they do not receive the warning of the church, then Jesus said they are to be treated as a tax collector or pagan. How were tax collectors and pagans treated in Jesus' day? They were sinners in need of a savior. The church does not give up on such people. The church keeps praying, keeps reaching and continues to love with the hope that the erring person comes to repentance.[630]

Some may object to my point by citing the Apostle Paul's words in 1 Corinthians 14:24-25:

> But if an unbeliever or an inquirer comes in while everyone is prophesying, they are convicted of sin and are brought under judgment by all, as the secrets of their hearts are laid bare. So they will fall down and worship God, exclaiming, "God is really among you!"

The words "convicted of sin" come from a word meaning to refute, rebuke or correct, and the word translated "brought under judgment" conveys the idea of examination, not condemnation. The passage relates to people being brought to a place of repentance, but let us not forget how people are brought to that point. Romans 2:4 teaches that God's kindness leads to repentance. People are seldom brought to repentance through public shame. The public prophetic declaration of God's heart for the sinner is what convicts of sin and draws that person into the realm of saving grace.

---

[629] Deere, 211.

[630] Matthew 18:15-17.

7. The "God-told-me" trap.[631] Prefacing prophetic words with "God told me" or "thus saith the Lord" is unnecessary. If a word is truly from God, the words will carry their own sense of divine authority without the speaker having to point it out. Besides, when a prophecy begins with "God told me," the hearer is left with an awkward sense of obligation to accept the message as fully reliable. There seems to be little room for weighing the message. After all, who would even dare to question God?

8. Believing that God is always talking. God *is* always available to commune with us. In our fellowship with Him, He *often* whispers to us. He allows us to sense His presence. Ongoing alignment with His heart *is* a worthy pursuit. His wisdom *is* always accessible, if we will ask for it,[632] and we *can* repeatedly replay the memory of those times when God has spoken to us. However, He is *not* constantly giving authoritative revelations for prophetic people to declare openly.

Although he may be overstating his point, I believe that Michael Sullivant raises a needed caution. In his opinion, God is *not* always talking. He states,

> Some sincere people have the conception that they are hearing almost constantly directly from God. Many have been taught that God is always 'talking,' but that most Christians just aren't good listeners. They really believe that if they become sensitive and mature enough they will be in a constant direct dialogue with God. In light of this, many purpose in their hearts to be different than those so dull of hearing. Their sincerity can be counterproductive. They try too hard to 'read God's mind,' and they begin to fantasize that they are hearing from God although He is not actually speaking to them. It's virtually impossible to lead a group of people into long-term healthy relationships and unity within the church who deeply believe that they're often and infallibly hearing the voice of God. I overheard a wise prophetic servant of God say, "God isn't talking half as much as some people think He is, and when He does speak, He means it twice as much as most people think He does!"[633]

---

[631] Deere, 213.

[632] James 1:5.

[633] Sullivant, 98.

My counter-emphasis is that I believe God *does* want to communicate with us much more than we are allowing. I *do* believe we need to become better listeners. Where I agree with Sullivant is in the point that some are so eager to hear God's voice on a continual basis that they cross the line into prophesying out of their human imaginations. I also agree that it is a problem when a prophetic person starts believing that they are constantly and infallibly receiving divine revelation. While Sullivant's point of caution is necessary, I am equally careful not to discourage people from a lifestyle of constant listening and constant expectation that they will in some way hear God's voice. Father is always near and always ready to commune with us at some level.

9. Overreliance on prophetic words for personal guidance. Sullivant rightly emphasizes that God wants us to prove His good, acceptable and perfect will more through the renewing of our minds than through receiving prophetic words.[634] He also states, "For some, the prophetic gift appears to be a shortcut to guidance in contrast to the longer route of praying, searching the Scriptures, receiving wise counsel, suffering, character building, learning from experience and so forth."[635]

10. Overreliance on the prophetic leader. Mike Bickle indicates that as a congregational leader he is careful to tone down any appearance of prophetic gifting.[636] If senior ministers are prophetically gifted, people can become wrongly attached to them. The focus needs to be on the Lord.[637]

11. Personal identity becoming wrapped around gifting.[638] Identity comes from the believer's relationship with God. We are His sons and daughters. We are saints. We are royalty.

---

[634] Ibid., 100. Romans 12:1-2.

[635] Sullivant, 103.

[636] Bickle, 135.

[637] Ibid., 136.

[638] Sullivant, 104.

12. Neglect of other vital things.[639] The prophetic aspect of the faith community's life is not just inwardly focused. The church exists in a world of all kinds of evil and injustices, and it exists as a prophetic community to speak into that world.[640]

13. Pride and the potential for arrogance.[641] Harold R. Eberle notes, "Knowledge of the spiritual realm or of the future tends to make one arrogant (1 Corinthians 8:1).... Be a servant. Cry. Pray. Weep even more."[642] Mike Bickle notes, "God often sends a thorn in the flesh to those to whom He gives abundant revelation, in order to protect their hearts from destructive pride."[643]

14. Deviations from sound doctrine. Taking a concept conveyed in a prophetic utterance and making an authoritative doctrine out of it would be an error. Doctrines should only rise out of a careful study of Scripture. Prophets need to have teachers in their lives to hold them accountable to sound biblical doctrine.

15. Taking offense. When prophetically gifted people present a revelation for consideration, if their message is not received or processed as they think it should be, they need to guard their hearts against offense. Likewise, if no one credits a particular prophet for being the recipient of the revelation, he should not take offense. If the prophet's sense of significance is properly established in his identity with Christ, it should make no difference whether or not he is given credit. Furthermore, it is important that offense is not taken when people do not respond.[644]

---

[639] Sullivant, 109.

[640] Floyd McClung, Jr., "The Prophetic Journey," a prophetic ministry conference, Westmore Church of God, Cleveland, Tennessee, 2005.

[641] Sullivant, 110.

[642] Eberle, 175.

[643] Bickle, 82.

[644] This caution is based on insights gleaned from Floyd McClung, Jr., "The Prophetic Journey," a prophetic ministry conference, Westmore Church of God, Cleveland, Tennessee, 2005.

16. Prophecy becoming an end in itself. Mike Bickle rightly states, "Prophecy is not something in which a church should major. It's one of the many tools used to build the house, but it's not the house...."[645] He further says, "Prophetic ministry cannot be an end in itself. Its purpose is always to strengthen and promote something greater and more valuable than itself."[646]

17. Inability to deal with the pain of the prophetic calling.[647] Mike Bickle offers several helpful insights regarding the personal pain that prophetically gifted people often suffer. Here we will note two of them. First, prophetic people often suffer persecution, rejection and demonic attack. Second, they can be prone to experience disappointment with God.

a. Persecution, rejection and demonic attack. In advanced levels of prophetic ministry, prophets sometimes have to deliver a hard word from God. Severe words often draw persecution from people who do not perceive that God is mercifully reaching out to them through such messages.[648] Demons are also troubled by the prophetic voice and will attempt to bring oppression into the prophet's life.

Mike Bickle instructs prophetic people to find their joy in loving God. They should not expect their charismatic gift to bring them personal fulfillment. Bickle observes,

> I have never met a prophetic person whose life was made significantly happy because of his or her gift. Typically they have experienced demonic attack, opposition from godly people and great perplexity in their own souls. They may see so much, but they often can't understand the full meaning of what they see.[649]

---

[645] Bickle, 24-25.

[646] Ibid., 73.

[647] Adapted from J. Randolph Turpin, Jr., "A Synthesis and Critique of 'The Prophetic Journey': The 2005 Prophetic Ministry Conference Conducted at Westmore Church of God" (an unpublished paper, Church of God Theological Seminary, 2005).

[648] Based on insights gained from Bickle, 114.

[649] Bickle, 130.

b. Disappointment with God. If prophetic people do not properly sustain their fixation on the goodness of God, they can easily become disappointed with Him. Why would that be the case? Mike Bickle explains,

> Prophetic ministers seem to have more disappointment with God than the average person. They often see clearly how things should be or how God plans for them to be. But they have to wait in faith for a longer time because they have seen farther ahead. They are much more prone to the Proverbs 13:12 difficulty: "Hope deferred makes the heart sick." Because their expectations are typically higher, they are more deeply disappointed.[650]

Another way of stating this insight is that prophetic people suffer by having to live with the disparity between what "is" and what "ought" to be.[651]

18. Not rightly esteeming the value of non-prophetic people. When prophetic people receive a word or insight from God, if they are not careful, they can have an attitude that says, "God has spoken. If you don't agree and run with the word God has spoken to me, then you are missing the will of God."

Prophetic people need to understand that they do not have the exclusive word of the Lord. Sometimes God will even speak through people who are not considered prophetic. Take for instance a case where God has prophetically shown a lead pastor that a new two-thousand seat auditorium needs to be constructed. Then church's business manager speaks up and says, "But pastor, we don't have the assets or cash flow to justify that level of indebtedness."

The lead pastor has a choice to make. He can either label the business manager as a person full of unbelief—a person resisting the will of God for the church, or he can discern the value of having such a pragmatic individual on his team. It is not a matter of one being right and the other being wrong. In this case, both are probably right. If the lead pastor will rightly esteem the value of this non-prophetic pragmatic person, the non-prophetic person can actually help the church reach its prophetic destination. Somebody needs to

---

[650] Bickle, 130-131.

[651] Ibid., 131.

be thinking budget. Somebody needs to be thinking cash flow. Somebody needs to have the freedom to say, "We have no money," without fear of being labeled a doubter. Somebody needs to be thinking about the steps needed for fulfilling the vision. Prophetic leaders often do not see the necessary steps toward the thing that has been foreseen. Consequently, they feel tempted to create their own route, taking action in areas where they have little or no giftedness. The result can be disastrous. Others gifts are needed in the process. A pragmatist can be a prophetic leader's best friend.

CHAPTER 24

PROBLEMATIC ISSUES WITH THE PROPHETIC

Prophetic ministry and leadership is normative for the New Testament church. However, that does not mean that it is immune from problems. When this mode of ministry administration is embraced, attention may need to be given to issues of theology, accountability and what some may call "balance."

Theological Weaknesses and Deviations

Prophetic leaders are not necessarily good theologians. The enabling gift of "prophet" and the enabling gift of "teacher" are two distinct anointings. Occasionally the two will occur together in one person, but that combination is probably the exception. For this reason, it is important for prophets and prophetic leaders to be relationally connected with Spirit-empowered teachers—individuals of theological soundness who are open to the legitimacy of the prophetic element in ministry.

The Question of Accountability

Because of the fact that prophets and prophetic leaders are people who claim to receive their guidance directly from God, they can easily fall into the trap that they need to be accountable only to God Himself. What is needed is an understanding that New Testament prophetic ministry can make no claim to absolute infallibility. The role of the community of faith is indispensable to an accountable paradigm for prophetic leadership.

The Possibility of Discouragement

Prophetic leaders should be the happiest people on earth, for their eyes have been opened to see things to come from heaven's perspective. If what they have embraced is truly a prophetic view of their life and ministry, then their hearts should be alive with hope—an expectation of a favorable and glorious outcome.

However, if a prophetic leader becomes fixated on where things are in the present and dwells too much on the fact that the congregation is nowhere close to its prophetic destiny, that leader can become discouraged. The disparity between what *is* and what *should be* becomes burdensome. In such times, the leader would do well to become immersed once again in God's presence. That leader should remind himself or herself of what God has said—God's promise. In the face of discouragement, declarations of God's revealed will are needed to lift the matter out of the realm of *striving* and elevate it to the place where it belongs—in the realm of *promise*. Perhaps even a faith-driven prophetic act is needed to reactivate the faith of the leader and the faith of those who follow.

The Question of "Balance"

The moment that I utter or write the word "balance," someone is likely shout, "Amen!" Let's not be too quick to get excited. Caution is needed. As a matter of fact, I have even considered writing an article entitled, "The Dangers of Balance."

Why do I say caution is needed? Isn't balance a good thing? Follow me closely, and perhaps you will understand why I am personally reluctant to approach life and ministry with a view toward what many call "balance."

Often when church leaders address issues related to spiritual gifts, they will call for balance. What is meant by "balance"? It seems probable that for many the intent is to promote a *holistic* approach to spiritual matters rather than to accomplish *balance* in the strictest philosophical sense of the word, and if such is the case, then perhaps there is little reason for concern. However, due to the fact many do pursue what they call "balance" to the detriment of charismatic ministry, a critique of the concept will now be offered.

Consider the origin of the concept. Balance is not a biblical concept; it is a Greek concept. Heraclitus taught that "opposites are necessary for life, but they are unified in a system of balanced exchanges.... To maintain the balance of the world, we must posit an equal and opposite reaction to every change."[652]

This distinctively Greek idea was foreign to the Hebraic worldview. As a matter of fact, to first century Jews, it was a repulsive idea, for it was part of the whole Greek-Roman invasion of Jewish culture.[653] With balance, a competing and even adversarial relationship between components is assumed, necessitating compromise on the part of those components for the sake of eliminating tension and producing a harmonious result.

It is potentially detrimental to apply this flawed concept to Christian life and ministry. To illustrate the point, the church sometimes erroneously speaks of the need for balancing the Spirit with the Word. With the understanding of balance as set forth here, the call to balance the Spirit with the Word would imply that the two are in a competing relationship with one another and that some give and take on the part of each would be necessary in order for the dynamic between them to work properly. In this light, a call for a balance between the Spirit and the Word would be absurd, for the two do not compete; both are in perfect accord.

If this thing called balance is inappropriate, then is there an alternative concept that we should consider? Rather than advance the idea of balance, it may be more fitting to promote a mode of *total obedience* or to call for *the pursuit of an integrated and holistic ministry*. When the church is totally obedient to the Spirit and totally obedient to the Word, ultimately the desired harmonious effect is achieved. The need is not for less of the Word and more of the Spirit, and the need is not for less of the Spirit and more of the Word. The need is for the church to be completely devoted to both.

---

[652] "Heraclitus," *The Internet Encyclopedia of Philosophy*, accessed February 5, 2005, available from http:// www.utm.edu/research/iep/h/heraclit.htm.

[653] Randall D. Smith, "The Life and Ministry of Jesus" (a lecture series delivered on a pastors' study tour sponsored by Christian Travel Study Programs, Jerusalem, Israel, December 1996).

When it comes to matters of the Scriptures or matters related to the *charismata,* it is not typically the case that *less* is needed. In those cases where the revelatory gifts have been abused, it does not mean that the church has plunged too deeply into matters of the Spirit. Rather, it signals that the church has not gone far enough in embracing that dynamic. Within the fullness of the Spirit is found the wholeness, harmony and safeguards that the church both needs and desires.

In some cases, imbalance is actually preferred and necessary. There are many occasions in the Bible when divinely ordered prophetic interventions had every appearance of being unbalanced. On the Day of Pentecost when believers ran into the streets speaking in tongues, was that a balanced occurrence? When Jesus overturned tables and drove out moneychangers in the temple, did that action have the appearance of balance? The very nature of prophetic ministry is to disrupt the status quo; it is for this reason that a preoccupation with balance could result in the unintended result of quenching the Spirit, missing the will of God and ultimately failing in our mission. Therein is the danger.

CHAPTER 25

PROMOTING THE PROPHETIC IN THE LOCAL CHURCH

Once congregational leaders catch the vision for how prophetic ministry can strengthen the church, they typically want to see their churches become more prophetic. Is there anything that can be done do to cultivate and promote the prophetic? Here we will consider practical suggestions for promoting and releasing the prophetic and other "gifts of the Spirit" into a ministry culture.

1. Teach on the gifts. As Jamie Buckingham says, "Gifts do not just happen; they are modeled and explained."[654] That which is taught in a church typically starts happening in that church.

2. Cultivate an atmosphere of expectant faith. Bruce Yocum observes, "Prophecy and other charismatic gifts flourish in an atmosphere of expectant faith."[655]

3. Wait before the Lord in services and even in administrative meetings.[656] If the Holy Spirit is allowed more time and space in which to work, He will do more. He will not typically force His way into a worship gathering or administrative meeting.

---

[654] Jamie Buckingham, afterword to, David Pytches, *Some Said It Thundered: a Personal Encounter with the Kansas City Prophets* (Nashville, Tennessee: Oliver-Nelson, 1991), 153.

[655] Yocum, 24.

[656] Jamie Buckingham, afterword to, David Pytches, 153.

4. Take time to explain the operation of gifts when they occur.[657] People become less fearful of and less resistant to the supernatural when they are given an opportunity to understand it.

5. Make room for the gifts to be manifested. Here is where local congregations need to think through issues of schedule, ministry setting and spiritual oversight. Will the people be encouraged to function in the gifts in the larger corporate gathering, small group gatherings or individually on their own? Is adequate time being allotted in service planning for the move of the Spirit? Is there adequate spiritual and pastoral oversight in place?

6. Provide safe opportunities for people to risk taking their first steps into the prophetic. Churches should encourage the practice of the gifts in small groups; a lot of processing can take place in small groups.[658]

7. Encourage people to take their first steps by speaking words of encouragement. Floyd McClung suggests that the place to start is to marry the prophetic to encouragement.[659] Yes, sometimes prophecy may speak of judgment, but even the prophetic impulse in the Old Testament is that in the midst of judgment there is always redemption. When it comes to prophecy, redemption is the objective. In the church, encouragement is the place to start. Once that aspect of prophesy has been faithfully embraced by a believer, the Lord can entrust him with other aspects of the prophetic. [660]

8. Lead the congregation in response to prophetic manifestations.[661] If a prophecy has been shared, the congregational leader should respond and

---

[657] Ibid., 153.

[658] Floyd McClung, Jr., "The Prophetic Journey," a prophetic ministry conference, Westmore Church of God, Cleveland, Tennessee, 2005.

[659] 1 Corinthians 14:3 says, "But everyone who prophesies speaks to men for their strengthening, encouragement and comfort."

[660] Floyd McClung, Jr., "The Prophetic Journey," a prophetic ministry conference, Westmore Church of God, Cleveland, Tennessee, 2005.

[661] Jamie Buckingham, afterword to, David Pytches, 153.

even lead the church in a responsive action or prayer. In so doing, he or she demonstrates that authentic prophetic words should be heeded.

9. Take whatever steps are necessary to fan the gifts into flame.[662] Michael Sullivant exhorts, "Study, pray, seek God's face, put it into practice, but by all means stoke the fire until that gift returns to its original intensity.'"[663]

---

662 2 Timothy 1:6.

663 Sullivant, 20.

Chapter 26

Shared Discernment[664]

Who or what sets the agenda for the work of the church? Some have said that ministry is all about finding a need and filling it. Do perceived needs determine the agenda? How would that look? If perceived needs set the agenda, then get ready to be overwhelmed! There are more needs surrounding us than we could ever address in a lifetime.

Does the will of the people set the agenda for ministry? "Let the people decide," some would say. Conduct a few surveys and polls. Take a vote. Compile and interpret the results. Wouldn't that show us what really needs to happen? The problem here is found in the limitation to a naturalistic perspective. Surveys, voting and majority rule may have some value, but when it comes to decisions where spiritual precision is necessary and when it comes to the executing of heaven's priorities in the earth, more is needed.

Who sets the agenda for ministry? *God* is the author of the agenda. Ministry is the extension of His wisdom and goodness. It is much more than a manifestation of human goodwill in response to apparent need.

To whom does God desire to minister at any given time? Who does He want to use in the work? What precisely does He want to do? When does He want to do it; what is His timing? Where and how is the work to be accomplished? How do we arrive at answers that represent God's point of view? The business of heaven calls for something beyond meetings at conference tables, diagrams on flip charts and figures on spread sheets.

---

[664] Based on J. Randolph Turpin, *Shared Discernment: A Workbook for Ministry Planning Teams* (Scarborough, Maine: DrawNear, 2011), 1-9. Large portions in this chapter have been included verbatim from the *Shared Discernment* text.

Someone needs to connect with heaven. We need God to reveal the answers, and some person or some group of people needs to receive the revelation. The call here is for the embracing of a *prophetic* mode of leadership—a leadership style that receives and acts upon whatever God reveals.

Leading by Reason and Revelation

The essence of leadership is to influence others to conduct themselves toward a desired destination or objective. In other words, a leader or leadership team leads people from where they are "already" to where they are "not yet."[665] In order to lead in such a manner, the discerning leader must have some level of knowledge of the place or objective to which he is taking people.

Knowledge of the desired destination or objective can be pursued in two ways: by reason or by revelation. By *reason* leaders can assess a situation and make a judgment call based on that assessment. However, while the engaging of reason is a vital aspect of a leader's thinking, it does have limitations:

1. Reason cannot access knowledge of the future.
2. Reason cannot access knowledge of the spiritual forces and realities at work.
3. Reason alone cannot always rightly discern the will of God.
4. Reason alone does not engage the leader in relational communion with God.

Western Christianity seems to have little difficulty in embracing reason as a way of knowing, but the possibility of contemporary revelation is often met with suspicion. Roger Stronstad comments, "In too many places the Church views itself as a didactic community rather than as a prophetic community,

---

[665] This description of the nature of leadership is an adaptation and application of the two-age motif underlying New Testament eschatology. George Eldon Ladd, *A Theology of the New Testament* (Grand Rapids, Michigan: William B. Eerdmans, 1993), 91. This application is especially appropriate for prophetic leadership, in view of its embracing of the dynamic of the Spirit—the Power of the age to come.

where sound doctrine is treasured above charismatic action."[666] The conveyance of knowledge through preaching or teaching is readily welcomed, but the prophetic is often categorically held at a distance.

There is a great need in the church for leadership by *revelation*. Revelation is needed because the agenda for ministry is not set by natural factors; as previously stated, only God determines that agenda. The ongoing and ultimate question for leadership in Christian ministry is this: "What is the will of God?"

The Prophetic Leader and the Prophetic Community

Prophetic leadership is both an individual and a corporate concern. There are individuals who are distinctly prophetic ministry leaders. They do not necessarily have to be prophets, but they do seek out prophetic guidance and order their actions accordingly. There are also entire churches and leadership teams that conduct themselves in a prophetic manner. They are devoted to a dynamic way of relating and communicating—interacting with God, the church body and one another. In this mode of ministry oversight, the prophetic anointing is regarded as both an individual and corporate anointing. Prophetic leaders are catalysts to the community to learn to hear God together. They serve within the church to help it fulfill its prophetic function. It has always been God's desire to speak to His people as a whole.[667]

Prophetic Leadership as Team Ministry

How do individual leaders function within the context of community-based leadership? In contemporary Western culture, the idea of "team work" is a metaphor that often helps to explain how a covenant community and its leaders share responsibility, authority and anointing. With Moses and Aaron we see an example of team ministry in prophetic leadership in particular. Both Moses and Aaron were enabled to speak prophetically for the sake of leading

---

[666] Roger Stronstad, *The Prophethood of All Believers: a Study in Luke's Charismatic Theology* (Sheffield: Sheffield Academic Press, 1999), 123.

[667] Numbers 11:29.

the people.[668] Moses was ordained to be like God before Pharaoh, and Aaron stood as Moses' prophet.[669]

In humility and a teachable spirit, prophetic leaders need to listen for God's guidance through means other than their own prophetic anointing. Once again, Moses serves as an example. Although he was the primary prophetic leader, Moses accepted instruction from a non-prophetic leader, Jethro, resulting in an effective strategy for delegating responsibilities.[670]

There may be times when one and only one person in a group may rightly discern the voice of God; however, the New Testament norm is that the discernment of heaven's purpose falls to God's people in community. The Scriptures provide ample examples of community-based discernment:

1. As a community of leaders, the first Apostles identified Judas Iscariot's replacement through a shared process of discerning God's will.[671]

2. When the Grecian Jews in Jerusalem felt that the needs of their widows were being neglected, the Apostles released them to discern God's will regarding the selection of seven men who would address the need.[672]

3. Although Peter was initially criticized by believers for entering the house of a Gentile, when he fully explained what God was doing among the Gentiles, they discerned the heart of God in the matter and concluded, "So then, God has granted even the Gentiles repentance unto life."[673]

4. When the Jerusalem council convened to address the non-compliance of Gentile believers to certain aspects of the Mosaic Law, many voices were heard, but the matter was concluded when James stated the consensus of the

---

668 Exodus 4:15-16.

669 Exodus 6:28-7:6.

670 Exodus 18:13-26.

671 Acts 1:15-17, 20-26.

672 Acts 6:1-7.

673 Acts 11:1-18.

Spirit that had manifested through the corporate process: "We should not make it difficult for the Gentiles who are turning to God."[674]

The very fact that God has ordained diversity in gifting among unified members of the body calls for team work. Prophetic leadership values the prophetic-cluster of manifestation gifts. There is a functional relationship between the prophetic cluster and other aspects of charismatic ministry.[675]

God has also placed five equipping gifts in the church for the sake of preparing His people for the work of the ministry.[676] These gifts are that of the apostle, prophet, evangelist, pastor and teacher. The *apostles* lead the church toward becoming apostolic. An apostolic church is aware of its authority, purpose and mission. The *prophets* lead the church toward becoming prophetic. A prophetic church is led of the Spirit, and its primary mode is to speak and act on the basis of revelation. The *evangelists* lead the church toward becoming evangelistic. An evangelistic church is outwardly focused and is concerned about communicating the essentials of the Gospel for the sake of the harvest. The *pastors* lead the church toward becoming pastoral or caring. The members of a caring church live in covenant with one another, and they are continually growing in the areas of care and compassion for people both inside and outside of the church. The *teachers* lead the church toward becoming a church devoted to the Scriptures. A church devoted to the Scriptures has an objective reference point and anchor for all of its subjective experiences.

---

[674] Acts 15:1-35.

[675] How do the gifts interrelate? (1) The revelatory gifts enable the prophetic minister to either act or speak on the basis of that which he has received by revelation. Once the revelation has been received, it is at that point that the prophetic vocal gifts can be engaged. (2) When the word from the Lord has been authoritatively verbalized, faith is generated in the hearts of those who hear; "faith comes by hearing, and hearing by the word of God."[675] (3) With the power gift of faith activated, two other power gifts can become operative: i.e., gifts of healing and the working of miracles.

[676] Ephesians 4:7-16.

The equipping gifts work together. Floyd McClung suggests that each of the five equipping gifts has a unique role of great significance, but they would be ineffective outside of relationship with one another. For instance, prophetic calling needs to be integrated with the other callings. Prophecy is given to help join people's lives together. Here is an example of the practical outworking of this truth:

1. A revelation comes to one person.
2. Others discern the accuracy of that revelation and introduce that person to another with a similar revelation.
3. Connections are made, and the church is built.

Prophetic leadership calls for relationships of mutual submission and deference. The natural inclination of any individual is for that person to think that he or she is always right; however, the corporate nature of charismatic gifts requires the preferring of one another.[677]

Providing the Opportunity for Shared Discernment

What has often been missing is the opportunity and process by which the people of God may discern the will of God together. Individual congregational leaders are often inclined to stand alone before a group of people and say in effect, "Okay people, here is what God has told me we are to do, so here goes. We're going to start moving in that direction. Who is with me?"

Where are the times, processes and opportunities for others to hear the sounds of heaven as well? The will of God *can* be rightly discerned through a shared process. I would go so far as to say that the will of God can be perceived more perfectly in a community of Spirit-empowered people than it can be perceived by one person praying and acting alone. While we must honor and respect congregational leaders (i.e., apostles, prophets, pastors, teachers and evangelists), they do not hold a monopoly on hearing the voice of God.

[677] Floyd McClung, Jr., "The Prophetic Journey," a prophetic ministry conference, Westmore Church of God, Cleveland, Tennessee, 2005.

The concept of shared discernment is based on the belief that God's will can be discerned and that the discernment of His will is best accomplished as believers seek Him through a shared process. This shared process requires an intentional engagement with the dynamic of the Holy Spirit. The encountering of God's presence and the hearing of His voice are anticipated as team members work through four movements of shared discernment. The four movements are (1) encountering God through *worship and prayer,* (2) *listening* for what the Spirit has to say about ministry action and development, (3) *sharing* with one another insights gained and (4) on the basis of the preceding three movements, *discerning* God's will as it pertains to ministry action and development in the group's shared context.

Overview of the Shared Discernment Model[678]

Jesus taught His followers to pray these words: "Our Father in heaven,... your kingdom come, *your will be done* on earth as it is in heaven."[679] Our concern as Christ's disciples is that the will of God might always be done. We are to pray for the Father's will to be done, but we must also know that we are agents of the fulfillment of His will in the earth. In other words, God's will is done when God's people do His will. Prayer for the Father's will leads to rightly perceiving or discerning His will in heaven, and the discernment of His will leads us into obedient acts of service to accomplish His purposes in the earth. In this way, the will of God is done on earth as it is in heaven.

Let us not be passive regarding the will of God. Some are of the opinion that no matter what man does, the will of God will be done. Not so. Every day that we live, God's will is not done someplace in the earth. Every day, someone is ignoring His Word, turning a deaf ear to His voice, neglecting the priorities of heaven and consequently not doing His will on earth. Today someplace on this planet some deed of kindness or some venture of faith that was supposed to take place did not take place. Why? Either His voice was *not*

---

678 J. Randolph Turpin, *Shared Discernment: A Workbook for Ministry Planning Teams* (Scarborough, Maine: DrawNear, 2011), 13-16.

679 Matthew 6:9-10, NIV.

discerned, or it *was* discerned but not heeded. Are we listening? Are we hearing? Are we responding? For heaven's purposes to be fulfilled in the earth, it is critical that we devote ourselves to the hearing and doing of God's revealed will. Whatever He says, we must do it.

God does not usually withhold His desires, plans and purposes from His people. He delights in revealing His will, yet His will needs to be discerned. How might we discern His will?

Discernment requires more than intellect; it requires prophetic guidance. A worshipful and prayerful heart and an ear attuned to the sound of God's voice are needed. Furthermore, because the present-day workings of the Holy Spirit occur in the context of the church as a body, discernment should be regarded as a *shared* experience.[680] Once we hear God's voice, share what we have heard, and consider what others believe they have heard, then we are better prepared to rightly discern His will.

It is with this understanding of divine guidance that the four-phase cyclical approach to shared discernment is suggested:

Worship and pray together,
Listen for God's voice,
Share with one another insights gained--what we believe He is saying, and
Discern God's will and its potential impact on our shared ministry.

This approach requires a set-apart time at a set-apart location (e.g., a retreat center) where a ministry planning team can draw aside to bring their decision-making into the presence of God. The team consists of its individual team members plus one person designated as the facilitator.

The shared discernment approach to ministry planning centers upon these movements working in a cycle. The discerning of God's will is an ongoing process. Once we have rightly discerned God's will, we continue to worship and pray. As we worship and pray, He continues to speak. We listen, we share, we discern, and the process goes on and on.

This approach keeps us positioned humbly before our God. Here we continually acknowledge before Him that our understandings of what He is

---

680 Review 1 Corinthians 12-14.

saying are subject to revision. Think of this matter in terms of our relationship to the Holy Scriptures. The Word—the Bible—is absolute, but our human understanding and application of the Word is not absolute. God's Word never changes, but the contexts and situations in which we seek to comprehend and apply that Word are continuously changing.

Prophetic guidance is similar. What God speaks to us is without error, but our perception, interpretation and application of His leadings may change and even be off track from time to time. There will always be a need to listen and discern again.

The shared discernment cycle also keeps us in an attitude of humility toward one another. None of us individually holds exclusive insight concerning the mind of God. New Testament discernment is not a solo act. We need one another. No matter how experienced we may think ourselves to be concerning spiritual matters, we need to be open to the possibility that God may want to speak to us through some other person.

Phase 1: Worship and Pray[681]

The first phase in the shared discernment process is to worship and pray. If our resolve is to pursue ministry planning according to the will of God and the perspective of heaven, then we must *know* His will and be engaged with His presence. To know His will, we need to *hear* His voice. Only *He* perfectly knows where we are in our journey, and only *He* perfectly knows where we ought to be heading. While our reasoned attempts to arrive at solutions and plans may be good, in the end, it is His voice that we must hear. Through worship and prayer, we prepare our hearts to hear the voice of the Lord.

The "Worship and Pray" phase emphasizes prayer, repentant worship, discernment of Christ's body, reflections on the objective Word of God and the intentional embracing of the dynamic of the Holy Spirit. Having engaged the heart of the Father through worship and prayer, it is then that we bring to Him specific petitions relevant to the needs of our ministry context.

---

[681] J. Randolph Turpin, *Shared Discernment: A Workbook for Ministry Planning Teams* (Scarborough, Maine: DrawNear, 2011), 17-23.

1. Opening Prayer. This process begins by petitioning God for His protection, guidance and presence.[682] Pray for His protection. Remember that this level of spiritual activity is an offensive act of spiritual warfare. Pray for His guidance. This process relies on much more than human reason; revelatory guidance is required. Pray for His presence. We need His presence, for ministry is a matter of partnership with God. We need more than a *visitation* of the Spirit. We need the *habitation* of the Spirit. We want Him to abide with us—to settle in and feel right at home among us. Fellowship and friendship with God is of far greater value in this process than emerging from our think tank with an impressive ministry plan.

In this opening prayer, the facilitator also leads the group in bringing the primary presenting issue before the Lord. In other words, the people say, "Lord, this is why we are here. This is the need before us. Here are the challenges we are facing. We come to you seeking your guidance."

While the primary objective of the team's planning retreat is to address matters related to ministry action and development, the group should also anticipate the Holy Spirit's dealings in areas of personal action and development. For this reason, this opening prayer time should include an invitation to the Holy Spirit to encounter each participant deeply on a personal level.

2. Repentant Worship. All true worship is repentant worship. The essence of *repentance* is to think and act differently after we have encountered truth. It is a turning away from former and lesser things and a turning toward the One who is far greater than all else. Likewise, when we *worship,* we are turning away from lesser things, and we are turning our faces toward the greater One—totally abandoning all else for the sake of Him whom our hearts desire. This turning unto God constitutes repentant worship.

Worship elevates our thoughts and affections unto God's throne—the seat of all government and control. It is in worship that we also touch the

---

[682] The author first observed this three-fold prayer in practice as Douglas and Barbara Small conducted the opening session of a Prayer Summit for the Church of God in Minnesota in 2003. Douglas Small is the founder of Alive Ministries (http://www.projectpray.org).

reality of *our* position in the heavenly realm. There we are seated with Christ at the Father's right hand—a position of authority and power.[683] There we encounter the glorious presence of God, gain heaven's perspective and behold the One who is highly exalted above all that might resist His purposes in the earth. The work of the church begins in this unearthly place. Here is where the discernment of God's will begins. The priority of worship cannot be overstated.

3. Discernment of the Body. While it is of great importance to discern what God wants us to *do,* it is of equal (if not greater) importance to rightly discern what He wants us to *be.* Perhaps it would be more appropriate to say that we must rightly discern *who we are.* Who are we? We *are* the body of Christ, and we are to *"be"* and function in a manner that is becoming of members of His body. Expressed plainly, we must rightly discern the worth of every member of the church, and we need to somehow grasp the mission and purpose that we are to fulfill together. As the church, we are not just a crowd of individuals. The Bible describes us as a body; we are interrelated, and we are to function in ways that are mutually beneficial.

Discerning the body in the context of ministry planning has to do with giving and receiving to and from one another those insights and gifts which may prove beneficial to the overall ministry development endeavor. On one hand, this process calls for individuals to have the *courage* to step out in faith, believing that God can in fact use each one—even though they may perceive themselves as insignificant. On the other hand, the process requires the group to be *humble*—to be willing to receive from one another, believing that God can use even the most unlikely people to deliver what is needed.[684]

Two biblical practices especially capture the essence of what it means to discern the body. First, the Apostle Paul associated the esteeming of the Lord's Body (i.e., the church) with the practice of communion—the Lord's Supper.[685] As members of the faith community partake of the bread and the

---

683 Ephesians 1:17-23; 2:6.

684 1 Corinthians 12:12-27 and Ephesians 4:16.

685 1 Corinthians 11:17-34.

wine together, they experience Christ's presence as one. In so doing, they encounter the reality of their common union in and with Christ.

Second, the Gospels present the practice of washing the believers' feet as a demonstration of what it means to be Christian together. In association with communion, Jesus washed the feet of His disciples and encouraged them to continue the practice in the days and years to come. The washing of feet was not only an act of mutual submission and service; it also expressed the mutual concern that members of the Body had for one another's cleansing and spiritual wellbeing.[686]

With these two practices integrated into the planning process, the idea of being the "Body of Christ" is elevated to something more than a metaphorical concept; it becomes a tangible reality central to our pursuit of Christian life and mission. We are reminded of our equal standing before the cross; we are equally in need of mercy and grace. We are reminded that none of us will accomplish God's purposes alone; we need one another. We are reminded that whatever we do in the name of ministry, it must be redemptive in nature and serve the good of the faith community as a whole. We are reminded that the *people* we serve are of far greater importance than our ministry *projects*. Integrating communion and the washing of feet into the opening portion of the planning retreat helps to establish the atmosphere of humility and mutual deference needed for a shared discernment process.

4. The Dynamic of the Holy Spirit. The central component of the shared discernment model is the dynamic of the Holy Spirit. On the day that Jesus ascended into heaven, He did not look at the remaining eleven disciples and say, "Just do the best that you can, boys." No, He left them with the promise that the Gift of the Spirit would be given to them.[687] With the coming of the Holy Spirit, they would be equipped with all that they would need to fulfill Christ's mission on the earth.

There are very specific ways in which the Holy Spirit equips, guides and enables the ministry of the church—namely through the *charismata*. Through

---

[686] John 13:1-17.

[687] Acts 1:8.

words of knowledge, words of wisdom and the discerning of spirits, God brings revelation to His people. Through prophecy, tongues and interpretation of tongues He speaks to His people. Through the gift of faith, gifts of healing and miracles, He supernaturally enables His people to demonstrate the power and authority of heaven.[688] These gifts of the Spirit are not optional blessings; according to the Apostle Paul, they are *necessary* for the strengthening of the church.[689] The shared discernment model calls for the cultivation of an environment where manifestations of the Spirit are welcome.

With this planning model, engagement with the Holy Spirit is intentional. When leaders come together to discern the heart of God and plan ministry endeavors accordingly, they *expect* the Spirit to show up. They learn to rely upon Him, and they refuse to take on any project or program that does not require His presence. Ministry becomes a matter of linking up with what the Holy Spirit has already purposed to do.

I am convinced that if the church would provide more time and space for the Holy Spirit to work, He would do much more. Are we in too much of a hurry? Let us make more *time* to be still before Him. Are our plans too full of *our* thoughts, ideas and plans? For a time, let us push the clutter of our own inventions aside to make *space* for the Holy Spirit to work.

God is always speaking, but is He always being heard? At this very moment hundreds of broadcast frequencies are moving through this room. However, I cannot hear them because my radio is not on—I am not tuned in to those frequencies. Even if my radio were on, at night I would be overwhelmed with that awful nighttime AM band noise—that racket caused by hundreds of signals competing for the same spot on the dial. I need a way to turn on my radio, filter out the interference and fine tune to a specific frequency. Otherwise, listening will be futile.

Worship and prayer help to filter out the multitude of voices that compete for our attention. Worship and prayer fine tune us to a point of receptivity to the voice of the Spirit—the "frequency" where God is speaking.

---

688 1 Corinthians 12:4-11.

689 1 Corinthians 14:26.

When the Spirit has our undivided attention, it is then that He will speak. And when He does speak, let us be careful to *listen*.

An Example. A number of years before I knew how to articulate this shared discernment concept, I had an experience in a local church council meeting that demonstrates the power of worship and prayer in the context of decision-making. Although everyone at the table was in relational harmony with each other, we seemed to be at odds with one another regarding a particular agenda item. The atmosphere was a bit tense, and I sensed that we were nowhere near making progress. We needed God to show up.

"Brothers, why don't we spend a few minutes in worship and prayer," I suggested. "I think that we all can sense that we need God's help on this matter."

We started praying, and then we started singing. God's Spirit settled upon us. Immediately the atmosphere cleared, and we gained heaven's perspective. When we came back to the table we had a unified sense of what needed to be done, and a unanimous decision was made in a spirit of joy. To God be the glory!

What made the difference? I think that Colossians 3:1-3 hints at why we experienced such a breakthrough on that day:

> Since, then, you have been raised with Christ, set your hearts on things above, where Christ is, seated at the right hand of God. Set your minds on things above, not on earthly things. For you died, and your life is now hidden with Christ in God.

The practice of worship and prayer sets our hearts and minds on things above. We are elevated to heaven's perspective as we are brought into God's presence.

The old idea that a person can be so heavenly minded that he or she is of no earthly good is faulty and misleading. Let us replace that idea with this one: in the context of ministry, it is not until a person *is* heavenly minded that he or she can be of any earthly good. To apply this thought to the decision-making context, it is not until a decision-making body comes into a heavenly mindset that they are able to faithfully execute the purposes of heaven in the earth. The practice of worship and prayer helps planning teams come to that point of consensus regarding God's will.

Phase 2: Listen[690]

A number of years ago my son and I had the opportunity to visit a sheep farm in Maine. One of the farm hands took us out into the pasture to show us how they would gather the sheep and lead them back to the barn. However, his demonstration backfired. As the farm hand approached the sheep, the sheep scattered. He made several attempts to approach them, but they ran away every time. He eventually gave up. As the three of us returned to the barn with no sheep following, he explained, "I have not spent much time with these sheep lately. They don't recognize my voice."

Jesus said, "My sheep listen to my voice; I know them, and they follow me."[691] The context for this passage shows us that the sheep follow Jesus because He has devoted Himself fully to establishing a *relationship of trust* with them—"I know them." They will not follow a stranger.[692]

From the Master's words we gain several helpful insights: (1) Jesus does in fact speak to His people. (2) If we are genuinely His people, we *will* listen to His voice. (3) His people can be confident that the voice they are hearing is truly His—not the voice of a stranger. (4) The hearing of His voice results in faithful response—we follow.

In Phase Two of the shared discernment cycle, we will learn to place our confidence in the relationship of trust that Christ established with us. Here we can rest assured that our Shepherd *wants* to speak to us and *will* speak to us. Whether our concern is for personal matters or ministry development matters, in either case, He will not leave us without guidance.

In the shared discernment cycle, we want to be very intentional about taking time and making space for the Holy Spirit to meet us. We enter that

---

690 J. Randolph Turpin, *Shared Discernment: A Workbook for Ministry Planning Teams* (Scarborough, Maine: DrawNear, 2011), 25-33.

691 John 10:27, NIV.

692 John 10:4-5.

place with expectation—expecting that the Shepherd will speak to His flock. We come anticipating that we will receive insight as we heed both the objective Word (i.e., the Scriptures) and the subjective Word (i.e., other ways in which God may speak that are subject to verification).

Reflections on the Objective Word of God. In our approach to ministry planning, opinion and personal preference are of little interest. We want to know *God's* will. What does *He* want us to do? Where does *He* want us to go? What kind of people does *He* want us to be?

Most of what we need to know in answer to these questions can be gained by studying and reflecting on the objective Word of God—the Bible. In fact, the Bible *is* our primary source for such wisdom. God has already spoken. He has made His will known. From the earliest days of the Old Testament Patriarchs until the final days of the New Testament Apostles, the Holy Spirit moved upon holy men, and they penned the very words of God.

I refer to the Holy Scriptures as the *objective* Word of God to distinguish them from the more subjective ways in which God speaks. In this context, the word "objective" means, "not influenced by personal feelings, interpretations, or prejudice; based on facts; unbiased." If we are to consider the possibility that God also speaks to us in subjective ways (e.g., dreams, visions, words of knowledge, words of wisdom, discernment of spirits, prophecy and interpretation of tongues), then we really need an objective standard by which such subjective means of guidance can be measured or judged. The Bible provides such an authoritative objective standard.

Objective points of reference are needed to help guide the planning process within the parameters of foundational principles. To demonstrate the role that the objective Word of God plays in this process, let us consider how the scriptures could be used in a case where the presenting issue might pertain to the need for a greater sense of love or friendship within a particular ministry context. In such a case, the group could consider this question: *Where are we in relation to the Great Commandment?* Jesus reminds us of the Great Commandment in Mark 12:28-31, stating,

> One of the teachers of the law came and heard them debating. Noticing that Jesus had given them a good answer, he asked him, "Of all the commandments, which is the most important?"

"The most important one," answered Jesus, "is this: 'Hear, O Israel, the Lord our God, the Lord is one. Love the Lord your God with all your heart and with all your soul and with all your mind and with all your strength.' The second is this: 'Love your neighbor as yourself.' There is no commandment greater than these."[693]

The relevance of this passage can be brought to light with an additional question: *How has God used this passage to speak into your life?*

Whatever scripture is selected for this reflection exercise, it should serve as an objective point of reference throughout the planning process. When ministry plans are drafted on the basis of God's authoritative Word, the church can then execute those plans with faith and confidence that God will enable and bless the resulting efforts.

The Voice of the Spirit. The Spirit does speak to the church through the objective Word of God—the Scriptures; however, He also speaks in other ways. He speaks to us personally through more subjective means such as dreams, visions, words of knowledge, words of wisdom, the discerning of spirits, quiet inaudible whispers in our mind or spirit and on rare occasions, with an audible voice or an angelic visitation. Most of these means of revelation come through the person, presence and power of the Holy Spirit. Decision-makers who utilize this shared discernment model aim to cultivate the presence of God in their lives, and their lifestyle is characterized by being continually filled with and immersed in the Spirit.

Reliance on Father's Voice. Jesus relied on subjective means of guidance. On one occasion He said, "I tell you the truth, the Son can do nothing by himself; he can do only what he sees his Father doing, because whatever the Father does the Son also does."[694]

---

[693] Mark 12:28-31, NIV.

[694] John 5:19, NIV.

Not even Jesus could work apart from revelation. He depended upon His Father revealing what must be done. On many occasions He would disengage from the multitude so that He might engage with His Father in solitude. His ministry followed a reoccurring pattern of engagement and disengagement. In those times of disengagement from ministry, He was being refreshed in the Father's presence, and He received guidance as to what He was to do next. If it was necessary for the Son of God to rely on the Father for such guidance, how much more so should we. Jesus' pattern of engagement and disengagement serves as an example to all who serve in ministry leadership. Discerning what Father is doing is all important.

Precision versus Imprecision. Listening for God's voice will make the difference between precision and imprecision in ministry. It is like the difference between shooting a shot gun and shooting a rifle equipped with a scope in target practice. With all of those pieces of lead bursting forth from the barrel of a shot gun, you will hit many random spots on the target, but you may or may not hit the bulls-eye. On the other hand, with a rifle and scope, your chances of hitting that bulls-eye with precision will greatly increase.

In ministry planning we can have a tendency to take the shot gun approach—to fire many different things at a ministry situation hoping that something works. Why not get a sharp focus on the exact thing that is needed from the very beginning? In the shared discernment cycle, that is what listening for the voice of God is all about—receiving the precise guidance needed for the matter at hand.

For a church, a track record of randomness in ministry planning can lead to disillusionment among members. Many things are tried, but nothing seems to work. On the other hand, a church that is intentional about listening for and discerning God's will, can cultivate an excitement for ministry with its members. Over time, a pattern of precision, effectiveness and faithfulness will become apparent to all. People will feel that ministry is worth their time and effort in that kind of environment.

Reflections on the Subjective Word of God. What is the Lord saying to you regarding the needs you are facing and His calling or will for your life, your ministry, and your congregation? Not sure? Could it be that the reason we do not know for sure what He is saying is that we have not yet taken the time to block out all other voices, draw aside in solitude and listen for His voice?

Bear in mind that while discerning God's will does relate to the needs with which we deal, it also goes beyond a concern for needs. God's will also has to do with passion and proactive visionary matters. Yes, His will can inform us in responding to needs, but His will should also be shaping our goals and plans even when no need is apparent.

Over the years, I have conducted numerous ministry planning retreats with leaders throughout America. One of the most important points in those retreats was when I would send them back to their rooms with these listening instructions:

Tomorrow we will be reflecting on areas of ***need***. We will also be reflecting on ***His calling*** and ***His will*** for our lives, our congregations, and our ministries. As we return to our rooms tonight, this is our assignment: Let us not be distracted. Let us set apart time and ask the Lord to tell us where we are in relation to His will. Ask Him to speak to you about areas of need—both personal needs and ministry needs. Ask Him to speak to you about His calling upon your life, your ministry, our congregation. Where are you in relation to His will concerning these things? What does He have to say about these matters? Listen for His voice. Write down what He whispers to you. We'll come back together in the morning and share what He has spoken.

At least an hour should be spent in solitary reflection and meditation. Actually, meditating into the evening, through the night and into the following morning is preferred. After all, God does still speak to people in dreams. Listen to what the Spirit is saying, and write down reflections. Listen for what God is saying regarding personal matters as well as whatever ministry related presenting issue is at hand.

In such times of solitary reflection, remember that God's subjective Word or guidance comes in various ways:

1. Flash images in the mind
2. The impression of a single word or phrase
3. A "gut level" feeling about a matter—a "hunch"
4. A sense of compassion regarding a situation.
5. An almost audible hearing of the Spirit's voice
6. On rare occasions, even an audible hearing of the Spirit's voice
7. A leading to read and meditate on a particular passage of Scripture
8. Words that may run through your mind as you pray in tongues
9. Words that you may spontaneously speak without forethought—in other words, prophecy
10. Dreams and visions
11. An awareness of God's presence

Interpreting What We Have Received. Do not jump too quickly into trying to interpret what you believe you have received. There is a worshipful and prayerful process going on here that will require more listening, and it will require the involvement of others. You may feel certain that you have heard from God, but at this point in the process, refrain from forming final conclusions. On the other hand, you may *think* that you are hearing from God, but you are not sure. What you are hearing does not make sense. Or you may come through this whole listening exercise feeling that you must conclude that God is *not* speaking to you. Do not settle on that conclusion just yet.

If you think that you are receiving something from God but it does not make sense, what does that mean? Yes, it is possible that it may just be your imagination. However, jumping to that conclusion would be premature at this point. Read on.

The Bible says that "we know in part and we prophesy in part."[695] Typically, each of us individually will receive only a "part" of the needed

[695] 1 Corinthians 13:9, NIV.

revelatory guidance. Think of this prophetic exercise in these terms: it is like putting together a picture puzzle. Each of us receives only a piece of the puzzle—a "part." No one receives the whole puzzle. It is not until we come together with others and place all of our individual puzzle pieces on the table that the total picture starts coming into view. What I receive may not make sense to me, but once I share it with others, it may make sense as it is considered together with the pieces others have received.

If you listen and yet hear nothing, what does it mean? There are several possibilities:

a. Perhaps God is speaking, but you are not recognizing His voice. In your time of meditation, are there unusual thoughts going through your mind that you assumed were part of your own wild imagination? Those thoughts may (or may not) be messages from the Lord.

b. Perhaps no additional guidance is needed. Could it be that you have already been given wisdom for the situation?

c. Perhaps you have forgotten or overlooked a piece of prophetic guidance previously given. If you are in the practice of journaling, you may discover a forgotten word of guidance by reviewing past journal entries.

d. Perhaps you have not yet fully responded to some previous word of guidance that God has given you. Fulfilling the previously revealed instruction may be necessary before the next step or instruction can be revealed. (It is helpful to cultivate the habit of being promptly and totally obedient to the voice of the Lord.)

e. Perhaps the guidance that you need will come through another person. The next phase of the shared discernment cycle is Share. In the sharing you may hear someone speak the very word that you need to hear.

f. Perhaps the silence is an indicator that you need to spend a little more time in the objective Word—the Bible. Read until the words jump off of the page and into your heart.

g. Finally, it could possibly be the case that some unresolved issue (e.g., unforgiveness or unconfessed sin) needs to be addressed.

How can we know for sure that we are receiving guidance from the Lord? In the New Testament, prophetic guidance typically takes place in the context of the faith community. As one person expresses what he or she believes God to be saying, other members of that community are involved in judging or discerning that which has been spoken.[696] God will use other Spirit-filled believers to help us in this discernment process. Thus the reason for the next phase in shared discernment: *Share.*

Phase 3: Share[697]

Emerging from their places of solitary reflection, team members reassemble to share. The revelation of heaven's purposes continues. Phase Three is really an extension of Phase Two. Here participants are still listening; they are listening for what God wants to say through one another.

As team members prepare to share, they ask,

> What might the Lord be speaking to us collectively through these reflections? What common themes are emerging among us? Could it be that each of us has brought a 'piece of the puzzle' to the table and that there is a larger corporate picture that He wants us to see?

God already sees the whole picture, but He apparently only allows decision-makers to see it a piece at a time with the various parts of the revelation being distributed among several or many in the body. The only way to get the big picture is to embrace the faith community, regard one another with honor and receive the gift that each person offers.

The Quality of Shared Prophetic Insights. In times of sharing, occasionally someone may bring a thought to the table that does not seem to fit. Remember that honoring one another in the time of sharing is extremely important. No matter how far-fetched an expressed insight may seem to be, it may still serve some purpose.

---

[696] 1 Corinthians 14:29.

[697] J. Randolph Turpin, *Shared Discernment: A Workbook for Ministry Planning Teams* (Scarborough, Maine: DrawNear, 2011), 35-36.

Although longsuffering should be exercised toward those whose contributions do not seem to fit, the quality of prophetic insights is an important consideration. In the New Testament, the receiving of revelatory guidance was of such a quality that the church made major decisions and acted on the basis of a prophetic word. In Acts 11:27-30, the faith community took prophetic action preparing for famine relief as a result of Agabus' prophecy. In Acts 13:1-4, Barnabas and Saul were commissioned by the faith community at Antioch on the basis of prophetic leading. In Acts 15:6-21, 28, James, an apostle, discerned God's will (i.e., the Holy Spirit's leading) on a very weighty matter after hearing the deliberations of other apostles and elders in the Jerusalem council. In light of these examples, the apparent need is for contemporary prophetic guidance to become of such a quality that it becomes a viable factor in decision-making and ministry planning processes.

The sharing that takes place in Phase Three helps to sharpen the focus. As one insight is heard after another, it improves the possibility that each prophetic item will be understood correctly. In the hearing of what is shared, a more holistic picture begins to take shape. The sharing contributes significantly to the sense that God is truly guiding the group.

Recording Shared Insights. The facilitator or an appointed scribe should record what participants say. Key words can be written on flipchart paper and taped to the wall for further reference as the ministry planning retreat progresses. With these recorded notes in view of all, the group can more easily participate in the next phase of this process—Discern.

Phase 4: Discern[698]

Once everyone on the planning team has had an opportunity to share their individual insights, the facilitator will help the group pull together the various pieces so that God's revealed will for the presenting issue might be discerned. If notes from the Phase Three discussion were written on flip chart paper for all to see, then here in Phase Four the facilitator should make reference to those notes.

---

698 J. Randolph Turpin, *Shared Discernment: A Workbook for Ministry Planning Teams* (Scarborough, Maine: DrawNear, 2011), 37-43.

There are similarities between this shared discernment process and the steps often taken in biblical interpretation. Exercises in the Share phase resemble the observation step in Bible study where the question is "What has God said?" This Discern phase resembles the interpretation step where the question is "What do these words mean?" So, what do all of these shared insights mean?

Identifying Significant Elements. At this point the task for the group is to identify elements of significance in the list or compilation of shared thoughts. What might the Lord be speaking to the group collectively through these reflections? What are the reoccurring themes? Does there seem to be a relationship between thoughts that were shared? Which of the noted items seem to be standing out above all of the rest? Do the pieces fit together like pieces of a puzzle? What does it all mean? Is there a single underlying thought that seems to be running through most of that which has been shared?

An Example. A few years ago, just a few days before completing the manuscript for my book, *Shared Discernment,* we witnessed shared discernment at its best in our Sunday night prayer meeting. I had already sensed that God wanted the church to devote the upcoming month to prayer and fasting with an emphasis on pressing into breakthrough and revival. I gave a few instructions to the group after a short exhortation from the scriptures:

For the next twenty minutes, let us individually wait before the Lord and ask Him to give us the blueprint for how he wants us to press in to prayer next month. I believe that God has shown me that we are to be pressing in for personal, corporate and regional revival. How does He want us to do that?

As you are waiting before the Lord, expect that He will speak to you. All you have to do is *listen.* He may impress images on your mind. He may lead you to a scripture. You may receive a word of knowledge. You may just get a gut-level feeling. Don't worry if it does not make sense. Just write it down. When we come back together we will *share* what we have received and *discern* what it all might mean.

We turned on the recorded worship music and let it play while congregants found places to sit or kneel alone in the sanctuary. After twenty minutes, we came back together. Then I gave this invitation:

If anyone feels they have received something that would be beneficial to our understanding of how we should proceed with our prayer emphasis next month, I invite you to come forward to the microphone.

There was no hesitation. They stepped forward one by one, and they started sharing. First, someone prophesied, "It is all going to transition next month." Another person echoed, "We will enter a new season." Then a number of very good items were mentioned such as prayer for personal cleansing, prayer for personal revival, prayer for Israel, prayer for America, prayer for our state, and so forth. Interspersed with these thoughts were statements about slowing down, being still and waiting upon the Lord.

While the people continued sharing I glanced down at the notes I had been taking, and on the paper I saw a pattern in what participants were saying:

Slow down.

Practice stillness.

Wait upon the Lord.

Be still and know that I am God.

Rest. Enter my rest.

"Listen to what we are saying!" I remarked. "Are you seeing a pattern?"

After a short time of Spirit-led discussion, we perceived that this season of pressing into breakthrough was not to be a time of striving. Rather, it was to be a time for trusting in the grace of God and entering into His rest—cultivating an atmosphere of His presence.

Having discerned what God was saying, the people entered into more prayer with emphasis on the theme of stillness and presence that had emerged. While many were still praying around the altar, I sat down, and my wife leaned to me and said, "Randy, we have just witnessed shared discernment."

Over the following days we worked on practical ways to act upon what was revealed. For instance, establishing times for meditative prayer at the church were scheduled to help cultivate a mindset of stillness and presence. Other items mentioned during the sharing time were integrated into the strategy as well, but the overriding emphasis related to the theme of stillness and presence. This incident was informal and somewhat spontaneous, yet it produced results that brought focus to the group. Imagine how this process might impact ministry planning situations in your context.

Evaluating and Responding to Shared Prophetic Insights. Not all things shared will have equal bearing on the ministry planning process. However, it is important to take heed to any points that the Holy Spirit may be trying to get across. How does a group sort out what is and what is not a true prophetic leading? The following are suggested guidelines for evaluating and responding to prophetic items in the context of a group's decision-making:

a. Receive each item as a *potential* word from God.
b. Use each prophetic item as a "springboard" into further prayer and the study of the Word.
c. In the hearing of each prophetic item, be sure to separate the genuine revelation from whatever uninspired interpretation or application the prophetic person may have conveyed.
d. Write down prophecies for further reference and evaluation.
e. Generally speaking, the group should seek and wait for confirmation. Is the word consistent with that which God has already been saying? Due to the possibility that the group's own desires could taint a prophetic word, at times a confirmation from an outside source may be needed.
f. Be aware of timing issues. In some instances, a shared insight may not make sense to the group simply because God did not intend it to be of immediate relevance. In such cases, the item may need to be placed aside for consideration at a later time. On the other hand, God may in fact intend the item to be considered immediately, but time may still be needed for obedience, preparation, prayer and character development before it can be fulfilled.

g. If the group bears witness that the prophetic word seems to be from God, they should ask, "Are there conditions in the prophecy that need to be met?"
h. If the prophecy requires action on the part of the team, how will that action affect current responsibilities? Are there financial ramifications? What stresses on the relational and ministry systems may this action add or relieve? Is the ministering body willing to sacrifice what will be required?[699]

Evaluation and response to shared prophetic insights must always be done in the light of the scriptures. How do the scriptures—the objective Word of God—shed further light on that which the group is discerning? Remember that this shared discernment process is like putting together a picture puzzle. Each team member individually has a piece of revelation or insight to bring to the table. The task of pulling all of the pieces together to form one unified picture may sometimes seem difficult; however, the good news is that the border for the puzzle has already been put together for the team! The border represents the scriptures—the objective Word of God. All of the prophetic pieces will be placed within the framework of the written Word. With this thought in mind, the team should consider the possibility that further study of the scriptures may be needed in order to rightly discern how the prophetic items fit together and what God might be saying.

Clarifying Needs and Callings. To bring closure to this Discern phase, the team should draft a clear statement of their shared perception of needs and the callings of God pertinent to those needs. Needs and callings in the following areas will likely emerge:

a. **Personal development.** What needs have surfaced related to personal development? What has been perceived as the calling of God relevant to personal development? Goals will be set on the basis of these needs and callings, and plans will be drafted on the basis of the goals. Whatever personal needs and callings are identified, these will become items that team members will address on an individual basis between team meetings. During regular

---

[699] This guideline is an adaptation of insights from Cindy Jacobs' writing concerning the processing of personal prophecies. Jacobs, 85.

team meetings, participants may report on their progress and receive support from the other team members.

b. **Personal action.** What actions need to be taken by team members on a personal level? Unto what action might God be calling each team member? Goals will be set toward the executing of these actions, and plans will be drafted on the basis of the goals. Whatever personal actions are identified, team members will address these items on an individual basis between team meetings. In their meetings, participants may report on these actions and receive support from the team.

c. **Ministry development.** What ministry development needs have surfaced relevant to the shared ministry context of the team? What has been perceived as the calling of God relevant to ministry development? Goals will be set on the basis of these needs and callings, and plans will be drafted on the basis of the goals. Whatever needs and callings are identified, these will become items that the team will address together in their regular meetings as well as through agreed-upon tasks and projects between meetings.

d. **Ministry action.** What ministry actions need to be taken by the team? Unto what actions might God be calling the team? Goals will be set toward the executing of these actions, and plans will be drafted on the basis of the goals. Whatever ministry actions are identified, the team will work together to execute these actions both within and outside the team meeting setting.

Beyond the Four Phases. After working through these phases, if the team's sense of direction still seems vague, it may be necessary to go through abbreviated versions of the four-phase cycle again until clarity has come. Once there is a sense of consensus that the Holy Spirit has spoken, the group can move on. The team can always revisit issues should they feel future adjustments are needed. Periodic meetings should be scheduled to assess progress on the project or primary issue at hand.

Chapter 27

Exercises for Training in the Prophetic[700]

Prophetic gifting cannot be generated in a person through teaching or training. The prophetic can only come from the Holy Spirit. However, believers can earnestly desire and pray for the prophetic, and they can be trained in how to be more receptive to the Spirit's ways regarding this area of gifting. With that understanding, the following reflective and experiential exercises for training in the prophetic are offered.

Exercise #1: Prayer for God's Presence, Guidance and Protection

Start the prophetic training session inviting participants to pray for the Lord to (1) manifest His presence, (2) guide everything that happens in the training session and (3) protect the students as well as their families that may be at home. Due to the potential for spiritual warfare, praying that our families be protected reduces the likelihood that they will suffer from spiritual backlash.

---

[700] Adapted from J. Randolph Turpin, Jr., "A Synthesis and Critique of 'The Prophetic Journey': The 2005 Prophetic Ministry Conference Conducted at Westmore Church of God" (an unpublished paper, Church of God Theological Seminary, 2005).

Exercise #2: Personal Cleansing

Conduct this exercise early in the training series to make sure potential hindrances to the prophetic are removed. Introduce this exercise by reading from a selected portion of Scripture addressing a set of God-given commandments or expectations. The Ten Commandments may be a good selection for this purpose. After reading each particular commandment or expectation, make a brief comment about each one. Then read Ephesians 1:7 and 1 John 1:9, passages that highlight mercy and forgiveness. Once an introduction to this exercise has been made, participants should be instructed to do the following:

1. Get alone with God.
2. Ask the Lord to reveal to you sins or hindrances in your life.
3. As the Lord reveals those things, confess them and repent of them. In repentance, renounce those things that are sin.
4. Receive the Lord's forgiveness, and ask Him to wash you clean.
5. Ask the Lord to fill you with His Spirit.
6. Thank Him for the work of His grace that you are receiving by faith.

Exercise #3: Praying in the Spirit

Experience has taught that one of the best ways for Spirit-filled believers to "warm up" for the potential manifestation of gifts is for them to pray in tongues frequently and for extended periods of time. For this exercise, participants can be encouraged to pray in tongues for ten to fifteen minutes.

Those who have not yet received tongues and those who do not feel comfortable with the idea of human-initiated tongues may engage in an alternate exercise. Alternate exercises may include the following:

1. Praying the Scriptures
2. Devoting this time to unceasing praise to the Lord.

Exercise #4:
Soaking Prayer

"Soaking" prayer is also known in some traditions as "tarrying." However, the idea of soaking prayer is that there be no striving associated with the experience.

This type of prayer is a time of quiet rest and meditation before the Lord. The pray-er is in a receiving mode more so than a giving or producing mode. Sometimes the playing of soft music can help to set the mood.

The facilitating of soaking prayer may vary according to the church culture with which participants are familiar. Some traditions would allow for individuals to take a restful posture such as lying on the floor. Others might think that practice to be too strange and would prefer to sit on the floor or in a chair. The idea is to minimize the potential for movement. Pacing tends to distract from this kind of praying.

The objective of soaking prayer is to meet heart-to-heart with the Lord. Sometimes it is helpful to come with this question in mind: "What do *you* want to say to me Lord?" At the conclusion of the soaking time, participants should write down any impressions or images that may have come to them. Typically these items are not to be shared; they are to be pondered in the heart.

Exercise #5:
Mutual Prayer for One Request

Near the beginning of the training series, involve participants in a reflective exercise that carries no expectation or pressure for anyone to do anything "prophetic." A low-risk "ice-breaker" is needed. This exercise would be of that nature, involving these actions:

1. Pair off with one other person of the same gender, preferably a person that you do not know.
2. Share with one another one prayer request based on either of these two questions:

   a. "What one thing do you want the Lord to do for, in or through you in this training series?"

   b. "Is there an area of need or concern weighing heavy on you right now? If so, what is it, and what would you desire of the Lord regarding the matter?"

3. Pray with one another about the expressed prayer requests.

Exercise #6:
Prayer for Spiritual Gifts

1 Corinthians 14:1 says, "Eagerly desire spiritual gifts, especially the gift of prophecy."

1. Form groups of three.
2. Each person in the group should express which spiritual gifts they would desire to receive.
3. Members of the group should pray over one another on the basis of the request.
4. If the Holy Spirit gives impressions for a specific way to pray, follow that leading.

Exercise #7:
Sharing a Scriptural Word of Encouragement

One of the best low-risk ways to introduce people to the nature of prophetic ministry is to urge them to ask of the Lord an encouraging word to share with another person. This exercise integrates the subjective and objective aspects of God's communication with man.

1. Form groups of three.
2. Remain silent; do not enter into conversation.
3. With a Bible in hand, quietly ask the Lord to impress on your heart a short encouraging passage of Scripture to share with your group.

4. Wait quietly before the Lord in an attitude of prayer for at least ten minutes.

5. Take note of the passages that the Lord impresses on your mind, but do not share them until everyone in the group has completed their time of meditative prayer.

6. Share with the group the passage that the Lord impressed on your mind. While sharing the passage, offer no interpretation or application. Speak only the biblical passage itself.

7. The other members of the group should respond as to how the passage might have related to them specifically.

8. Pray for one another on the basis of the Scriptures that you have shared with one another.

Exercise #8:
Prophetic Intercession

This exercise trains participants to wait for the Holy Sprit to reveal what the "prayer list" should be. In other words, through words of knowledge, words of wisdom and visions the intercessor will receive guidance for his or her praying.

1. Form groups of six to twelve people.

2. Take an extended period of time to wait before the Lord, asking Him to impress upon you what He would desire to be the focus of the group's prayers.

3. At the conclusion of the waiting time, those who have received impressions should share those revelations with the group.

4. If only a partial revelation has been received, then only that part should be shared, even if it does not make sense. Often we receive just one piece of the message and someone else may receive another piece that helps to make the message complete. 1 Corinthians 13:9 says, "We know in part and we prophesy in part."

5. The facilitator of the group should compile the various pieces of revelation and attempt to frame a prayer to the Lord based on that which has been received. Others may want to suggest ways for the petition to be shaped as well.

6. The group should then pray according to the guidance that they have received from the Holy Spirit.

Exercise #9:
Personal Prophecy

By the end of the training series, participants may be so tuned in to the flow of the Spirit that they are ready to deliver an anointed personal prophecy.

1. Pair off with one other person of the same gender.

2. Wait before the Lord asking Him to impress upon you anything that He might want to reveal for the benefit of your partner. Be prepared for the possibility of the following:

    a. A revelation of an affliction. This revelation may come in the form of a pain or a sensation in your own body, or it may come in some other manner.

    b. A revelation of some other need.

    c. A revelation of a needed word of encouragement.

3. If you receive no revelations, simply state that you have received nothing in particular.

4. If you have received a revelation, present it in the form of a question. For instance, if you think you have received a revelation of a back problem, ask, "Are you having problems with your back?"

5. If your partner confirms that you are on target with the revelation, then proceed to pray according to the revelation received.

6. If no revelation has been received, pray for your partner anyway. As you pray, it may be that the Lord may so guide your prayer that it will yet have a prophetic impact.

7. If you have "missed it," simply admit it, and do not try to reshape it to make it fit your partner's situation. Proceed with prayer for your partner; it may be that more accurate prophetic guidance will come as you are praying.

Chapter 28

Living a Prophetic Life

There is a kind of life available that brings into this world a constant manifestation of heaven. It is the prophetic life. I am talking about living on the basis of every word that comes from God's mouth.[701] It is a life lived according to what God is feeling, thinking, saying and doing. It is a life lived on the basis of where God is going. It is a life lived on the basis of what God is revealing.

Jesus lived the kind of life I am describing. He once said, "I tell you the truth, the Son can do nothing by himself; he can do only what he sees his Father doing, because whatever the Father does the Son also does."[702] Jesus' relationship with His Father was intimate. He constantly watched for what His Father was doing, and He listened for what His Father was saying. He felt His heartbeat. Whenever He discerned what His Father was doing, He aligned His actions accordingly. Whenever He heard what His Father was saying, He aligned His words accordingly.

A prophetic life is future oriented. It is living a life that is somewhat ahead of its time. It is living with expectation that the things promised will come to pass. It is living toward your destiny. It is living with the expectation that "He who began a good work in you will carry it on to completion until the day of Christ Jesus."[703]

---

[701] Matthew 4:4.

[702] John 5:19.

[703] Philippians 1:6.

A prophetic life is intentionally dependent on revelation. A person living this kind of life does not want to go where God is not going, does not want to do what God is not doing and does not want to say what God is not saying. Sensitivity to the leading of the Holy Spirit is a core value for the person desiring to live the prophetic life.

Over the years, God has been faithful to prepare me for a prophetic life. Here I will list a few of the things he has said to me in my journey—lessons that I believe to be instructive to any who are in pursuit of a prophetic life.

1. "Keep the canvas of your mind clean. I want to paint my pictures there." The screen of the human imagination is the same screen upon which the Holy Spirit will project visions and dreams.

2. "Keep your tongue sanctified." These things defile the tongue: gossip, lying, prideful boasting, complaining, arguing, speaking in anger and the use of inappropriate language. Can both polluted and pure water flow out of the same spring?

3. "Keep my secrets." Not everything that God reveals to the prophetic person needs to be spoken. He is looking for someone He can trust with secrets. In prophetic ministry, the hidden things of people's lives will be revealed to us. Typically such matters are revealed for the purpose of prayer or private ministry with the person; they are not to be shared with anyone. In prophetic ministry, heaven's strategies will be revealed to us. There is an appropriate timing and an appropriate way to unveil such things, and in some cases we are to never make them known. Wisdom from heaven is needed.

4. "Be loving and humble." God gives grace to the humble, and faith works by love. Fasting is a great way to gain a renewed heart of humility, and doing acts of self-less service is a great way to ignite love.

5. "Be promptly and thoroughly obedient." Do not delay, and do not modify what God has directed you to say or do.

6. "Be faithful over a little." This adage is sometimes called the "little-big principle." If we are faithful over a small amount of revelation, God will entrust to us more. The way that we handle little is the same way that we will handle much. In some cases, the Lord may require a person to be faithful over something that is not prophetic in nature at all as a prerequisite to being entrusted with prophetic anointing.

7. "Place a high value on what you hear." Jesus said, "Consider carefully what you hear. With the measure you use, it will be measured to you—and even more."[704] If we highly value what we hear, we will not want to ignore or forget it. We will not want to procrastinate regarding the things we have heard. We will write it down, and we will promptly act on it according to the wisdom the Spirit has given.

8. "I need you to be less concerned about being understood by others. I need you to be willing to be misunderstood." Prophetic living goes against the grain of the status quo. Prophetic people live like people who are out of synch with time; they are like time travelers from the future. When functioning in prophetic mode, future realities sometimes become so vivid that they appear to be in the present. Prophetic people see what others cannot see yet; therefore, the potential for being misunderstood by others is high. If we are too concerned about being understood, we may shrink back functioning prophetically. Keeping our prophetic edge requires a willingness to be misunderstood.

9. "The surest way to keep and increase whatever I give you is to give it away." Jesus said, "Freely you have received; freely give."[705] Not only are we to give our gift away by releasing prophecies to others, but we are to also impart the prophetic anointing to others, as the Spirit leads.

10. "Be passionate for my presence. I desire intimate fellowship with you." Converse with God. Listen more. Cultivate fellowship with the Holy Spirit.

11. "Honor and celebrate the prophetic gifting of others." Jesus said, "Anyone who receives a prophet because he is a prophet will receive a prophet's reward, and anyone who receives a righteous man because he is a

---

[704] Mark 4:24.

[705] Matthew 10:8.

righteous man will receive a righteous man's reward."[706] When we honor and celebrate the prophetic gifting of others, we increase the potential of the prophetic operating in our own lives.

[706] Matthew 10:41.

CHAPTER 29

SPIRIT-EMPOWERED PRAYER MINISTRY

I was awestruck with what I was seeing. It was the early 1990s, and someone had loaned our church John Wimber's video series on "Power Healing." "Holy Spirit come," Wimber would quietly pray, and then it would happen. There was no organ music, no hype, no shouting, no dramatic gestures and no superstars—just a simple little prayer, and then it happened. As Wimber and others gently touched seekers, the Spirit came upon them delivering healing.

Having almost forgotten about the Wimber video, in 1994 while attending renewal services in Toronto, I had a dramatic personal encounter with God's power that awakened me once again to my own relative ignorance regarding the things of the Spirit. In addition to the personal significance of this transforming experience, I observed once again this powerful yet gentle way of ministering to people that was a bit different from what I had known.[707] A quest for more began, and key people came across my path to assist in the exploration.

---

[707] This encounter occurred at the Toronto Airport Vineyard (Toronto, Ontario) in November of 1994. This incident together with subsequent events brought the author into relationship with several leaders who are a part of what C. Peter Wagner has called the Third Wave. In addition to this revival's personal impact on the author, it also modeled an approach to prayer ministry (altar ministry) that has informed this project: (1) Seekers and prayer ministers alike were encouraged to give the Holy Spirit time to work. (2) Seekers were directed in the simplicity of receiving from the Lord; the consistent emphasis was on receiving the Father's love. (3) Prayer was offered gently and quietly, and the supernatural was approached in ways that appeared quite natural. Ministry was administered in a systematic and orderly fashion while the Spirit was given freedom to move and work as He desired. (4) Whenever unusual

In 1999 while teaching in Central Africa, a meeting with an American minister, Kevin Porter, helped to bring greater definition to the things of the Spirit. As a fourth-generation Pentecostal, I was very familiar with the charismatic gifts, but Porter had unusual insight concerning how these gifts related to the normal functions of ministry. I was starting to see more clearly the essential role of the manifestation gifts in Christian practice. Values that had always been important to me as a Pentecostal were beginning to converge with values I had gleaned from Wimber and the Toronto revival. It was all coming together.

This chapter is about prayer ministry—individual believers and teams of praying believers ministering to people. It is also about the Holy Spirit being the essential agent of God in the work. What a powerful combination: God's people in unified teams combined with the power of the Spirit, simply allowing Him the time and space to "come" and do that which He delights in doing. He delights in manifesting God's kingdom through the manifestation of His amazing gifts of revelation, proclamation and power.

Why Pray?

Several years ago while preparing to conduct a prayer ministry seminar, I decided to poll my Facebook friends to learn what they thought to be important topics to cover in prayer ministry training. One of the most insightful responses I received came from my son-in-law, Jonathan Zajas, who said,

> We should not assume that people know *how* to pray. Neither should we assume that they know *why* they should pray. If believers do not grasp the *why* and the *how* of prayer, we should not be surprised when they do not consistently pray in a disciplined manner.

---

manifestations occurred, prayer workers were certain to evaluate the fruit of the experience. (5) There were no superstars; the people through whom most of the anointed prayer ministry was taking place were not vocational ministers.

If we do not grasp why we pray, we will not be very consistent or persistent with it. It is one of those activities that we will let slide. It will not be a priority. Why then do we pray? What difference does it make?

1. Prayer Glorifies God. Jesus promised, "I will do whatever you ask in my name, *so that the Son may bring glory to the Father*" [emphasis mine].[708]

2. Prayer is where we connect with God in holy friendship. We commune with God in prayer. We enjoy our time with Him. He listens to us, and we listen to Him. We give Him our hearts, and He gives us His.

3. Prayer accesses divine assistance. Jesus taught us to pray for our daily provision by praying, "Give us today our daily bread."[709]

4. Prayer is how God gets things done. Why bother praying if God is going to do whatever God wants anyway? If we do not pray, will God just do what He wants to do anyway? No, I do not believe that God will just do what He wants to do anyway. There may be some exceptions, but that is not typically how it works.

Jesus taught us to pray, "Your kingdom come, your will be done, on earth as it is in heaven."[710] How does God's will get done? God's will is done when God's people do His will and when God's people pray His will.

"Okay Dr. Turpin," someone may say, "Are you suggesting that God is sitting in heaven waiting for us to pray before He performs His acts in the earth?"

Yes, that is basically what I am saying. It might be slightly overstated, but generally speaking, yes—especially as it relates to His redemptive works in the earth. As Dutch Sheets has said, "God chose, from the beginning of Creation, to work on the earth through humans, not independent of them."[711]

---

[708] John 14:13.

[709] Matthew 6:11.

[710] Matthew 6:10.

[711] Dutch Sheets, *Intercessory Prayer* (Ventura, California: Regal Books, 1998), 29.

Think about it. Throughout Scripture, isn't it true? Consider the time the Hebrews worshipped a golden calf. God decreed judgment. Moses prayed. God withheld judgment.[712] Consider the time when Hezekiah was dying. Isaiah confirmed, "The Lord says you are going to die; you will not recover." Hezekiah prayed. The Lord healed him.[713] Obviously, human beings can make a difference regarding what God will do in the earth, simply through their praying.

Why do the prayers of mere mortals mean so much to God? From the beginning, God authorized the human race to rule in the affairs of earth. In Genesis 1:26-28, God said,

> "Let us make man in our image, in our likeness, and let them rule over the fish of the sea and the birds of the air, over the livestock, over all the earth, and over all the creatures that move along the ground. Be fruitful and increase in number; fill the earth and subdue it. Rule over the fish of the sea and the birds of the air and over every living creature that moves on the ground."

In Psalm 8:3-8, the psalmist said,

> "What is man that you are mindful of him, the son of man that you care for him? You made him a little lower than the heavenly beings and crowned him with glory and honor. You made him ruler over the works of your hands; you put everything under his feet...."

As Dutch Sheets said, "God chose, from the beginning of Creation, to work on the earth through humans, not independent of them." So, how is God's will done in the earth? God's will is done when God's people do His will and when they pray His will.

We cannot afford to be passive in this matter of the will of God. God's will is not just automatically done. Let us think this through. Somewhere today someone went into eternity without Christ. Was that God's will? Was God's will done in that situation? Of course, it was not. Scripture clearly

---

[712] Exodus 32.

[713] 2 Kings 20; Isaiah 38.

teaches that it is not His will that any perish.[714] God has many things that He wants to accomplish in the earth. He wants to manifest mercy instead of judgment, but He is waiting, even longing, for someone to act or pray on the basis of His will.

Sometimes people will pray a prayer, and the prayer is not answered. Some are too quick to make this assumption: "It must not have been God's will." Others conclude that God's will cannot be known. Let us gain clarity on this matter. God's will is something that He delights in revealing to His people, and when He reveals it, we are to act upon it, pray it and settle for nothing less than His will being done.

The line in the prayer Jesus taught us, "Your will be done,"[715] is not just some blanket statement that we thoughtlessly throw on top of our prayers. No, we are to find out what pleases the Lord, and then we are to pray that thing or do that thing.

Are there instances of God acting redemptively without someone praying? That is not likely to happen. Prayer is almost always required. There may be instances when it may not appear anyone is praying for certain redemptive things to occur, but in actuality, He has called upon someone to pray, and we just do not know about it.

Allow me to demonstrate how this works with a hypothetical example. A single mother in North Carolina has a young child with a fever. She is not a woman of prayer, and she does not have anyone in her life who knows how to pray. God in His compassion wants to heal the child, so He causes His Holy Spirit to move upon an available intercessor on the other side of the planet in Mongolia. The intercessor prays in the Spirit for twenty minutes or more, not knowing for whom he is praying. Suddenly, the child's fever breaks. Only heaven knows how this breakthrough has been arranged, but it involved the critical role of an available and willing intercessor in the earth. I would like to think that there are entire congregations that have made themselves available to pray in such a way.

---

[714] 2 Peter 3:9.

[715] Matthew 6:10.

So, why is prayer is critical? It is critical to the way God gets things done in the earth. Without prayer, most of what God wants to do would never be accomplished in the earth.

Let us consider another example. In Luke 10:2, Jesus said to his disciples, "The harvest is plentiful, but the workers are few. Ask the Lord of the harvest, therefore, to send out workers into His harvest field."

For the longest time, I thought this passage to be very strange. If Jesus is the Lord of the harvest and He wants workers sent out into His harvest field, why doesn't He just send them? Why does he have to involve His disciples in the asking, if He already wants it accomplished? He involves them because that is the way God works. God works in the earth through the agency of man. Generally speaking, if we do not pray it, it will not happen.

Prayer that Tarries

In my childhood years it was not uncommon to hear people talk about tarrying before God in prayer. In the context of tarrying (i.e., extended times of unhurried waiting), believers would pray until they "prayed through." In other words, they stayed in God's presence until something happened. To concede to nothing happening was not an option.

There are two modes of tarrying in the context of prayer. The first is meditative or soaking prayer, and the second is persistent intercessory prayer. During meditative prayer, pray-ers do not have to do or say much. They are primarily in receiving mode. Thoughts are directed to God and His Word. While engaged in meditative prayer, pray-ers should write down anything the Lord may reveal to them. If the praying is taking place in a group setting, when the time for meditation is closing, the leader may call the group back together. The group can then spend a few moments sharing whatever the Lord has revealed.

Persistent intercessory prayer, as understood in this context, is typically vocal and fervent. Believers pay aloud and with authority, allowing the Holy Spirit to be totally in control. If you praying in this mode with a group of people, stay engaged with the Spirit in prayer until such time that the breakthrough comes or until everyone has a sense that the Lord has released them. It usually takes at least an hour to reach this level of praying.

We do not always tarry because we *have* to. Sometimes we tarry because we *want* to. We are lovers of His presence. We want to hear His voice. We want to feel His touch. We want to catch a glimpse of heaven. We want to press in with an "is there anything more you want to say to us Lord" attitude. If we give the Holy Spirit more time and space in our lives and in our church services, He will do more.

Revelation, Vocal Authority and Power

Prayer is about the most awesome privilege and opportunity granted to man. When the righteous pray, there is movement in the heavenlies. The righteous pray, and the course of nations changes. The righteous pray, and sinners are saved. The righteous pray, and the afflicted are healed. The righteous pray, and the oppressed are set free. The righteous pray, and the dead are raised. The Bible says that "the prayer of a righteous man is powerful and effective."[716] With prayer being such a powerful matter, may we not water it down by offering half-hearted doubt-filled prayers. Let us pray by revelation, and with authority and power.

Spirit-empowered prayer ministers and teams value the integration of the manifestation gifts in the exercise of their ministry. They rely upon revelation through words of knowledge, words of wisdom, the discerning of spirits, dreams and visions to inform and guide their praying. They pray with vocal authority through the gifts of prophecy and tongues. They pray expecting powerful breakthroughs as they exercise the gift of faith, gifts of healing and the working of miracles.

What is meant by the term "vocal authority"? Vocal authority refers to the ability God has graciously given to His people to vocalize their prayers with authority. In other words, it is a matter of literally speaking out prayers and proclamations that flow forth directly from the Spirit of God Himself.

---

[716] James 5:16.

There are two primary ways that the believer can pray with vocal authority. One way to engage in such prayer is to pray directly from the passages of the already-written Word of God. Praying the Scriptures should be integrated into the prayer life of ever believer. Another way to pray with vocal authority is to engage two of the vocal gifts of the Spirit in the ministry of prayer: tongues and prophecy.

Prophetic Intercession

Prayer that is initiated by revelation and spoken with vocal authority will result in manifestations of power. This kind of praying on behalf of others is often called "prophetic intercession." Prophetic intercession takes places with the pray-er interceding from the vantage point of the future breakthrough even before it manifests. In a sense, the intercessor is praying from the future and into the present. Another way of saying it is that the intercessor is praying from heaven to earth—from the bliss heaven to the troubles of earth.

Spirit-Empowered Prayer Ministry Teams

Spirit-empowered prayer ministry teams can be commissioned to fulfill various types of assignments. They can be sent as evangelistic teams into the streets, led by the Spirit to pray with and prophecy to people. They can be intercessory support teams at the church, appointed to pray for the leaders, the congregation and the services. They can pray with people at the altar, ministering healing and breakthrough at their point of need. They can be assigned to the church's healing ministry, serving in hospital visitation or in healing rooms. Whatever the application of the team concept might be, many of the dynamics that drive prayer ministry teams are the same. The following chapter will give particular focus to engaging prayer ministry teams in the ministry of healing.

CHAPTER 30

THE MINISTRY OF HEALING

Although application of biblical truth has been made throughout this text, it is now time to pull it all together to form a comprehensive paradigm for Spirit-empowered ministry. Of particular concern is applying what we have learned to the ministry of healing. We will aim to create such a paradigm by applying the biblical models and patterns that we have observed.

To illustrate how we might apply biblical models and patterns to the way that we go about the ministry of healing, initially a narrative approach will be taken. While this prayer ministry model can be applied to other settings, here we will demonstrate its relevance by portraying a hypothetical prayer encounter in the context of local church altar ministry. We will refer to this church as Elk Ridge Worship Center under the leadership of Pastor Jacob Randall. Here the reader should be able to pick up on the various models and patterns that we have already noted from the Scriptures.

Altar Ministry at Elk Ridge Worship Center

Pastor Jacob Randall has concluded his sermon and is calling for people to come forward to the altar area to receive prayer. Knowing that there are a number of people in this service who have never been to church before, he perceives a need to guide them carefully through this first-time experience.[717] He says,

[717] It is important to note that while seeker sensitivity is certainly in order, here we are not promoting seeker sensitivity at the expense of compromising Holy Spirit sensitivity. Some see the seeker-sensitive approach and the Spirit-sensitive approach

> We are giving you an opportunity right now to come forward to receive prayer. This is a time in our service when Jesus does amazing things in people's lives. This is a time to receive prayer for healing, financial breakthrough or the meeting of other needs you may be facing. Maybe you need encouragement, or this could be the day that you invite Jesus to come into your life. We invite you to come.
>
> When you come forward, just stand across the front here in a line facing me, and our prayer ministry team will meet you and pray with you. When you get up here, you do not have to do anything except *receive* prayer. We will do the work. All you need to do is receive. You may come at this time.

At this point the Pastor Randall steps down into the altar ministry area and a few prayer team members step into the area as well. Additional prayer ministers will step forward as the need for them becomes apparent. Prayer teams consist of two to three people at a time. While a trainee may be standing behind the seeker in supportive prayer, one or two others should be standing in front of the seeker prepared to minister face-to-face.

As the seeker meets the prayer team, they are greeted with smiles and introductions: "Hi, my name is Tom, and this is my wife, Sally. What is your name?"

"My name is John," the middle-aged seeker answers.

Seeing that the seeker is a male, it is Tom who continues to take the lead in the prayer ministry encounter. Generally speaking, females minister to females, and males minister to males. In those times when ministry takes place across gender lines, the Elk Ridge team makes sure that someone of the seeker's gender is there with them for accountability purposes.

Tom asks, "John, what would you like for the Lord Jesus to do for you today?"

---

to ministry as being mutually exclusive; however, such does not necessarily have to be the case. Nevertheless, if ever faced with a choice whether one should be seeker-sensitive or Spirit-sensitive, the Spirit-sensitive route should always be the preference. The church must honor the Holy Spirit.

While John responds, both Tom and Sally are listening. They are listening both horizontally and vertically at the same time. In other words, they are listening to John, but they are also listening for the voice of the Spirit. While John may be expressing a real need, there may be something more or something different that the Lord would desire to do.

John responds, "I am having severe pain in my foot."

"Which foot is it?"

"It's my right foot," answers John.

"Is it hurting right now?" Tom asks.

John moves his foot a bit to see if the pain is still there. "Yes, it is very painful right now."

At this point some compassion and common sense are in order. Notice what Tom says next.

"Would you like to sit down while we pray with you?" Tom offers.

John pauses to think and then says, "No, that's okay. I'm placing most of my weight on my other foot, so I'm okay right now."

The next thing that Tom does is ask permission to place his hand on John. In an environment in which a church is hoping to draw totally unchurched people, we should not assume that seekers understand all of the procedures and movements involved in a time of prayer ministry. For some people, even an act as simple as placing a hand on them might seem strange; therefore, the Elk Ridge team has learned that it is a good idea to ask.

Tom asks, "May I place my hand on your shoulder here as we pray?"

"Sure," John responds.

When placing hands on a person, Tom is discreet as to where he places his hand, and he is also careful to not apply unnecessary pressure. In some ministry contexts, people do not feel that real ministry is taking place unless seekers fall in the floor under the power of the Spirit. At times the Spirit does overwhelm seekers in the altar resulting in them falling before the Lord. However, in no way does this team want to suggest to seekers that they *have to* fall. If a prayer minister applies pressure with his or her hand, the seeker may interpret that gesture as a suggestion for them to fall down. The key is to be gentle and natural with the touch.

Tom and Sally are ready to pray now, and Tom takes the lead. The trainee is standing behind John offering supportive prayer, but he may serve another role as well. Here at Elk Ridge, people frequently fall under the Spirit's power, and the church has found it necessary for trainees to be initially trained as "catchers."

Tom waits a few moments before the Lord for the Holy Spirit's leading. He starts to pray,

> Father, in the name of Jesus we bring John before you, and we thank you for your healing power. John, may the healing power of God move into your right foot right now. I declare healing and total relief from this pain.

While Tom is praying, Sally has been praying quietly in tongues and listening for the voice of the Spirit at the same time. As she has been praying in the Spirit, the words "his prodigal daughter" have appeared in front of her spiritual eyes. She cannot shake it. She knows that it is a word of knowledge from the Lord.

Sally leans toward her husband Tom and whispers, "I think that the Lord is showing me something."

Tom is still in the lead in this ministry situation, but here is where team work comes in. Tom says, "Go ahead, Sally, and share what the Lord is showing you."

Sally asks, "John, do the words 'his prodigal daughter' mean anything to you?"

Tears start to roll down his face. He is overcome with emotion, and for a few moments he cannot speak. At first, all he can do is shake his head to affirm that those words meant something to him, but then he manages to force out the words, "I haven't heard from my daughter in five years!"

As is usually the case, at this point the receiving of a word from the Lord generates a strong sense of faith with those who are praying. They proceed to pray with a great sense of authority and confidence. As they are praying, the

Lord guides Tom with a word of wisdom as to how to pray for this situation with precision. Tom prays, "Lord, I ask that before this week is over that John's daughter will contact him."

After the emotions have subsided a bit, Tom asks, "How does your foot feel now?"

John moves his right foot again. "It feels better."

Note that sometimes people will say that they feel better just because they don't want the prayer encounter to look like a failed attempt. For this reason, even if there is just a small hint of lingering pain, it is best to go into prayer once again over the affliction.

"On a scale of one to ten, how would you rate your pain?"

"About at three or four," John responds.

"On a scale of one to ten, where was it when you came up here a few minutes ago?'

"It was about an eight," John answered.

"Well, let's pray again," Tom says. "Are you still okay? Do you need to sit down?"

"No, I'm fine," John chuckles. His spirit is much lighter now.

They continue praying for the healing of his foot. Usually the healing will be completed in this second wave of prayer, but if for some reason it does not, the prayer team should either continue in prayer as long as the seeker will allow them to do so, or the seeker should be offered some encouraging scriptures regarding healing.

Sequence of Actions for Healing Ministry Teams

The following sequence of actions for healing ministry teams can be applied to any type of prayer ministry team. The prescribed steps have been drafted with altar ministry in mind, but these actions are not limited to altar ministry inside the walls of a church. These are helpful guidelines for ministering outside the walls of the church as well.

1. Invitation, Introduction and Interview. In a church service context, the *invitation* is given for seekers to step forward. Members of the prayer ministry team *introduce* themselves to the seeker, and the seeker is given the opportunity to introduce himself or herself as well. Then the prayer ministry team conducts a simple *interview*, asking the seeker what he or she needs from the Lord.

2. Wait. Following the interview, the team waits upon the Lord. They listen for His voice. They watch for what He wants to do. They wait for a sense of the manifest presence of God, for it is His presence that will make the difference in the situation at hand.

3. Pray. Having gained a sense of what God wants to do, the team then prays accordingly. One person on the team should pray so that the seeker can hear him or her, while the others pray supportive prayers, preferably in tongues. Pray the breakthrough, not the problem. Pray with confidence that *it is God's will* to grant what is being requested. This is not the place to be praying "if it be thy will" kinds of prayers.

4. Touch. A member of the team asks the seeker for permission to touch him or her. "May I take your hand?" or "May I place my hand on your shoulder?" the prayer minister may ask. Typically the laying on of hands upon the head of a person should be reserved for those authorized to do so by senior church leaders, for the placing of a hand upon the head of another person signifies a role of authority over that person.

5. Speak. Speak to the problem. Make a prophetic declaration of truth. Declare the breakthrough, healing or solution needed in the person's situation. Remember, Jesus did not tell His disciples to *pray* for the healing of the sick. He told them to actually *heal* them. They were *authorized by Jesus* to heal them. With that authorization in mind, believers are to authoritatively declare the needed breakthrough or healing.

6. Wait and Test. After speaking to the problem or situation, wait for a manifestation of the Holy Spirit's power. Watch for evidence indicating that something is happening. If the seeker has come forward for healing from pain, ask them to test the area where they were previously experiencing pain. If they had come needing healing from a hearing loss, have them test their hearing. If they were having an eyesight problem, ask them to test their eyesight. If they were walking with a limp, ask them to walk a few yards. If they were not able to lift their arm or bend their leg, ask them to slowly attempt to do so now. Often healings do not manifest until the moment that the person puts the healing to the test. Rejoice over every incremental improvement in the situation.

7. "Soak them" in prayer. Even if it seems that the breakthrough has come, keeping "soaking" the seeker in prayer. There is always more that the Lord wants to do. If the seeker falls under the Spirit's power, urge them to stay on the floor to continue receiving from the Lord in that position of rest.

8. Interview. Ask the person to describe what is happening to them. If it seems that they have not yet received their complete breakthrough, ask them if you might continue to pray with them a little longer. If so, go back to step one of the previous steps, and work through the sequence once again. If the interview reveals that they have had a significant breakthrough, make note of their testimony, and find a way to allow their testimony to be heard. Their story of God encounter may be the very word that someone else needs to hear to encourage them in their faith.

How Long Should We Pray?

How long should we pray with people? Ideally we should pray until something happens. I knew of one church in Florida where the prayer teams were instructed to pray with the afflicted for two hours or until they were healed—whichever came first. That particular church had a high success rate in seeing miraculous healings. The point is that we need to give the Holy Spirit time and space to work in the lives of people.

Healing Rooms

There are a number of models and methods that a congregation can use to facilitate a ministry of healing, but one approach that I have particularly found effective is the healing room model. For several months, I served in the healing room ministry at Bethel Church in Redding, California. With over one thousand volunteers serving on a rotating basis and between two hundred and five hundred people showing up for healing every Saturday, it is the largest healing room ministry in the world. John G. Lake has been credited with creating the basic idea for healing rooms that Bethel Church follows.

What do people experience when they show up for healing at the Bethel Church healing rooms? First, they enter a waiting room where they are given a group number and are asked to fill out paperwork identifying their affliction.

Second, they are taken into a classroom where someone explains what is going to happen in this process. They are also given simple nuggets of biblical truth related to healing to encourage their faith. While all of this is going on, designated workers are quietly praying over the people in the room.

Third, they are taken into the sanctuary where they sit quietly to soak in God's presence. Worship leaders and musicians fill the atmosphere with worship. Pray-ers walk around the room releasing God's presence to people as they wait.

Third, a group number is called, and individuals with that number are escorted from the sanctuary and into the prayer room. The prayer room is a large area with seating to one side and a lot of open space in the middle of the floor. Everyone remains seated until someone calls for them. Then each individual is taken to a spot on the floor where a three-member prayer team is prepared to minister healing. One experienced team member leads in face to face conversation and prayer with the person, a second team member assists, and typically the third team member is an observer being initiated to the ministry. Eyes are kept open during prayer, and prayers are conversational in tone and concise. Most of the prayers for healing are more like declarations than prayers. After a few moments in prayer, the person is asked to test the afflicted part of their body to see if they have experienced healing. If the individual has not experienced healing yet, the team prays a little longer. If healing has occurred, they praise God together and make record of the testimony. The entire prayer session in the prayer room takes only ten minutes or less.

Fourth, following the ministry time in the prayer room, the people are invited to sit in on a short optional class dealing with "Keeping Your

Healing." Every week our teams followed these procedures and witnessed amazing miracles.

What to Do and Not Do

1. Do release the presence of the Lord Jesus into the situation.
2. Do pray in faith, assuming that it is God's will to heal.
3. Do minister healing in an attitude hope, love and joy.
4. Do give glory to God for the breakthrough.
5. Don't fixate on the affliction. Stay focused on the breakthrough.
6. Don't place condemnation on people for their inability to get healed. Do not blame it on their lack of faith.
7. Don't tell people that they are totally healed. They are the ones who must verify their own healing.
8. Don't tell people to stop taking their medication or to cancel a medical procedure.

Suggested Assignments

Get together with others who are reading this text and discuss the hypothetical Elk Ridge prayer encounter case given in this chapter. What might they have done differently? What guidelines for prayer ministry might be gleaned from the example of Jesus and the first century church? What should prayer ministry look like in your ministry context?

If this text is being studied in the context of a course dealing with Spirit-empowered ministry, with the instructor's guidance, identify students in the class who are suffering afflictions in their bodies. If so, pray for them according to the model that has been set forth. After the prayer ministry time, be sure to spend some time together reflecting on the experience.

CHAPTER 31

DELIVERANCE

When Jesus first commissioned His twelve Apostles, He instructed them, saying, "As you go, preach, saying, 'The kingdom of heaven is at hand.' Heal the sick, cleanse the lepers, raise the dead, and cast out demons.'" The restoration of the afflicted is a common occurrence among Pentecostals, Charismatics and Neocharismatics, but raising the dead and casting out demons is not typically an everyday practice. Jesus' command to raise the dead will be addressed later, but here we will consider His command to cast out demons.

What Is a Demon?

What is demon? In the Bible, demons are referred to as unclean or evil spirits[718] and even lying spirits.[719] Many believe them to be fallen angels, but according to first century Jewish tradition, they were understood to be spirit-beings that entered the world through Nephilim activity in the years leading up to the Flood of Noah's day.[720] Whatever their origin might have been, Jesus mandated that their oppressive activity among humans cease. Jesus cast them out, and He wants His disciples to cast them out as well.

Levels of Demonic Activity

There are levels of demonic activity. *Temptation* is the most basic and common activity of demonic forces. Often people feel tormented with

---

718 Matthew 10:1

719 1 Kings 22:23.

720 Genesis 6.

tempting thoughts that are not of their own making—fiery darts from the evil one. The believer has been equipped with an effective shield of faith for deflecting such temptations. The sword of the Spirit—the word of God—is also indispensable in this warfare.[721]

The next level of demonic activity is what is often referred to as *oppression*. Oppression can manifest itself in depression, affliction, addictions and life-patterns that seem unbreakable. The oppressive works of darkness are subject to the authority of Jesus.

The most severe level of demonic activity is *possession*. When people are possessed, they are under what appears to be the complete control of a demon. A believer can silence a demon and stop its violent activities, in Jesus' name, but the total deliverance of a demon-possessed person requires a desire on that person's part to be delivered. Anyone who wants to be set free can be set free through the power and authority of Jesus. If a person lacks the soundness of mind to express a desire for freedom, intercession on their behalf by others is in order.

Authority over Demons

Demons are subject to the authority of Jesus. At the close of Matthew's Gospel, immediately before Jesus commanded His disciples to make disciples of all nations, He said, "All authority in heaven and on earth has been given to me."[722] In Luke 10:19, Jesus told His disciples that He was giving them authority over all the power of the enemy.

Paul told the Ephesians that the Father seated Jesus "at his right hand in the heavenly realms, far above all rule and authority, power and dominion, and every name that is invoked.... And God placed all things under his feet."[723] Then Paul said, "God raised us up with Christ and seated us with him in the heavenly realms in Christ Jesus."[724] Where is Jesus seated? Jesus is

---

[721] Ephesians 6:16-17.

[722] Matthew 28:18.

[723] Ephesians 1:20-22.

[724] Ephesians 2:6.

seated at the Father's right hand with all the powers of darkness beneath His feet. Where are believers seated? Believers are seated with Jesus in the same place. If all the powers of darkness are beneath the feet of Jesus, that means that all the powers of darkness are beneath the feet of those who believe as well.

On one occasion, Jesus sent out seventy of His disciples giving them authority over demons. When they returned, they rejoiced over the fact that demons were subject to them in Jesus' name. Jesus affirmed their confidence regarding evil spirits being subject to them in His name, saying, "I saw Satan fall like lightning from heaven. I have given you authority to trample on snakes and scorpions and to overcome all the power of the enemy; nothing will harm you." However, He continued, saying, "Do not rejoice that the spirits submit to you, but rejoice that your names are written in heaven."[725] He wanted His disciples to live in the humble recognition of the mercies of God at work in their own lives. Jesus' emphasis is a safeguard against spiritual pride.

Practical Guidelines

Theologically and biblically it is clear that believers have been authorized and commissioned to cast out evil spirits. By reviewing the chapter entitled, "A Biblical Introduction to the Manifestation Gifts," that theology becomes evident. How should it practically play out in actual confrontations with the forces of darkness? Here a few guidelines are offered.

1. Live *your* life in submission to the authority of Jesus. If you are not personally submitted to Jesus in humble obedience, you are not likely to have much effect in your attempt to take authority over evil spirits. A lifestyle of fasting and prayer is a good way to sustain a spirit of humble readiness to function in deliverance ministry.

2. Ask God for the gift of the discerning of spirits. The real issue might be a matter of the human spirit of the person and not a demon spirit. The Holy Spirit will help the believer make the distinction. There is no need to

---

[725] Luke 10:18-20.

take authority over demons that may not even be present when the real issue is the healing of a human spirit.

3. Follow the leading of the Holy Spirit. Trust God for words of knowledge, words of wisdom and the discerning of spirits to guide you in the ministry encounter. Wait for the Holy Spirit's signal as to when you are to issue the authoritative command for the demon to leave. He may prompt you to do so without delay, or He may lead you to wait.

4. Do not attempt deliverance ministry alone. At least two people are needed for a number of reasons:

a. The presence of two ministering believers provides a way to verify what transpires in the ministry session, just in case the oppressed individual leaves the session undelivered and making false accusations.

b. Agreement between two believers will reinforce the spiritual authority driving the ministry encounter.

c. When two are present, one person may pick up on a key that the other might miss.

d. If odd manifestations occur, the second person can summon additional assistance. If the manifestations become violent, a second person and possibly even a third person may be needed to bring the situation under control.

e. When two are present, one can confront the demon while the other can minister to the human person. Further explanation follows.

5. Remember that you are dealing with two entities: the person and the demon. While taking authority over the evil spirit, be sure to minister love and peace to the person.

6. Do not hold conversations with demons. Study the way Jesus dealt with them. He usually commanded them to be quiet while He confronted them.

7. Do not let the demon control the situation. Note that demons love to draw attention to themselves, and they love to make everybody think that they are in charge. Keep yourself in a spiritual posture of realizing the Jesus is in charge, and conduct yourself in the ministry encounter accordingly.

8. If possible, remove the oppressed person from public view while the ministry encounter is taking place. Taking the person to a side room removes the potential distraction that demonic manifestations might cause, and it also helps to preserve the person's dignity.

9. Do not allow the demon to violently thrash the person. You may have to command the evil spirit, saying, "In Jesus' name, I command you to not thrash this person. You will leave quietly."

10. Issue an authoritative command. Your command may sound something like this: "In Jesus' name, leave this person now, and go the place Jesus assigns you." This command should be spoken firmly, but it does not necessarily have to be loud.

After the Deliverance

After people have been set free, they need to be guided through a prayer of repentance. If they have not yet been born again, explain the way of salvation to them, and pray with them. Pray for the Holy Spirit to occupy the regions of the heart and life that have just been vacated by the evil spirit. It is also a good idea to talk with such people about living a deliverance lifestyle—not allowing themselves to return to patterns that lead to bondage. Encourage them to get involved in Christian community where they can gain the strength that they need.

Following the deliverance session, it also important for those who have ministered to give attention to themselves. First, receive prayer from others for a personal refreshing and for protection from any backlash from the enemy. Then check the heart to safeguard against pride; give God all of the glory. Be careful about how you speak of the deliverance that has taken place. If you do talk about it, report that you were a *witness* to what *Jesus* did. You also want to protect the dignity and confidentiality of the person who has been delivered.

CHAPTER 32

RAISING THE DEAD

Raising the dead is part of the Gospel commission. The words of Jesus in Matthew 10:7-8 suggest that raising the dead is one of the manifested evidences of the immediacy of the kingdom of heaven. Jesus came to give life. He said, "The thief comes only to steal and kill and destroy; I have come that they may have life, and have it to the full."[726] On one occasion, He even said, "I am the resurrection and the life."[727]

Biblical Examples

In addition to Jesus' own physical resurrection,[728] Scripture contains at least nine other examples of the dead being raised. Elijah raised the son of a widow from the dead,[729] and his disciple, Elisha, raised the son of a Shunammite woman.[730] Then years later, a dead man came back to life when his body touched Elisha's bones.[731] Jesus raised the son of the widow of Nain,[732] the daughter of Jairus[733] and finally his friend, Lazarus,[734] from the

---

726 John 10:10.

727 John 11:25.

728 Matthew 28:5-8; Mark 16:6; Luke 24:5, 6.

729 1 Kings 17:17-22.

730 2 Kings 4:32-35.

731 2 Kings 13:20, 21.

732 Luke 7:11-15.

733 Luke 8:41, 42, 49-55.

734 John 11:1-44.

dead. At the time of Jesus' resurrection, the Bible says that many dead saints arose from their graves.[735] Beyond the pages of the Gospels, we read that Peter raised Dorcas,[736] and Paul raised Eutychus.[737]

Observations and Patterns

The Widow of Nain's Son.[738] One of the premises of Spirit-empowered ministry is that Jesus is our example in all things. His compassion is one of the most consistent reoccurring features of His ministry. When Jesus saw the mother at Nain whose only son had died, He had compassion on her and comforted her saying, "Don't cry."[739] Jesus then touched the bier and said, "Young man, I say to you, get up!" The young man sat up alive. The working of this miracle followed sequence noted earlier in the chapter entitled, "A Biblical Introduction to the Manifestation Gifts":

1. Jesus saw the need.
2. He was moved with compassion.
3. He ministered comfort.
4. He touched.
5. He spoke an authoritative word that raised the dead.

Jairus' Daughter.[740] Jairus asked Jesus to come to his home to heal his dying twelve-year-old daughter. While Jesus was still on His way, the little girl died. When Jesus arrived, the mourners were already grieving the child's death. The biblical account suggests that Jesus made the mourners and doubters leave the room. Only Peter, John, James and the girl's parents remained. Jesus then took the child by the hand and called to her, saying,

---

[735] Matthew 27:50-53.

[736] Acts 9:36-41.

[737] Acts 20:9, 10.

[738] Luke 7:11-15.

[739] Luke 7:13.

[740] Luke 8:41, 42, 49-55.

"Little girl, arise."[741] Her spirit immediately returned to her body. This dead-raising incident presents this pattern:

1. Jesus responded to intercession.
2. He removed potential spiritual distractions, particularly parties who had already conceded to the child's death.
3. He touched.
4. He spoke an authoritative word that raised the dead.

Lazarus.[742] Several aspects of Spirit-empowered ministry are represented in the dramatic story of Jesus raising Lazarus from the dead. This account has already been reviewed in the chapter entitled, "A Biblical Introduction to the Manifestations Gifts."

In John 11:1-45, Mary and Martha sent a message to Jesus informing Him that Lazarus was sick. The Lord delayed two days before departing for Lazarus' home. When Jesus finally started toward Lazarus' home, by revelation[743] He already knew that Lazarus had died. By the time Jesus came near to the scene, Lazarus had already been in the grave four days. The atmosphere was filled with grief and disillusionment. Jesus empathized with the family's sorrow and wept.

The Lord Jesus approached the grave, instructed that the stone be removed from its opening and began to pray. It was not a long prayer. His prayer would have taken no more than thirty seconds. It is interesting that in the prayer, Jesus did not ask the Father to bring Lazarus back to life. In essence, the heart of His prayer was a prayer of thanksgiving; He said, "Father, I thank you that you have heard me." As He concluded His prayer, He cried with a loud voice, "Lazarus, come out!"[744] Lazarus came forth alive, and many believed on Jesus because of this miracle.

---

[741] Luke 8:54.

[742] John 11:1-44.

[743] The revelatory power in which Jesus is functioning appears to be the equivalent of the gift of the "word of knowledge."

[744] John 11:43.

This dramatic story demonstrates the following:

1. A delayed response to need might be divinely ordered.
2. Revelatory guidance enables confident and effective ministry, especially when natural circumstances appear contrary to such guidance.
3. When grief and disillusionment surround adverse situations, the focus needs to be brought back to faith in Jesus.
4. Empathy accompanies faithful and effective ministry.
5. A prayer of praise or thanksgiving may precede great miracles.
6. A vocal command may affect miraculous results.[745]

Dorcas.[746] In Joppa, a disciple named Dorcas (also known as Tabitha) had died. A woman named Lydda sent two men to Peter asking him to come quickly. When he arrived, he was taken into an upper room where the body of Dorcas had been placed. Peter put all of the mourners outside. Then Peter knelt down and prayed. We are not told what he prayed. After praying, Jesus turned to the body and said, "Tabitha, arise." She opened her eyes and sat up.[747]

This account includes the following elements:

1. Peter came in response to a request.
2. He removed potential spiritual distractions, particularly parties who had already conceded to the child's death.
3. He prayed.
4. He spoke an authoritative word that raised the dead.

Eutychus.[748] While Paul was visiting Troas, a young man named Eutychus fell out of a third story window and died. The miracle of him being

---

[745] These observations only should not be interpreted as a formula for producing miracles. Everything noted here is the result of clear divine guidance.

[746] Acts 9:36-41

[747] Acts 9:36-41.

[748] Acts 20:9, 10.

brought back to life is described in one single verse: "Paul went down, threw himself on the young man and put his arms around him. 'Don't be alarmed,' he said. 'He's alive!'"[749] The Apostle's physical contact with Eutychus appears to be the only action taken in this case.

Summary

It is important to not reduce the raising of the dead to a method or formula. In some cases, prayer was involved, but not in all cases. In some cases, physical contact was involved, but not in all. In most cases, an authoritative command was issued, but not in all. However, in *all* of the given cases, there was a response of *compassion*. What is essential for the dead to be raised? Essential to the raising of the dead is the belief that Jesus came to give life and the availability of a believer to act in Jesus' name to release that life to those who need it.

---

[749] Acts 20:10.

Chapter 33

Spirit-Empowered Evangelism

Signs, wonders and miracles accompanied the ministry of Jesus and His disciples as they proclaimed the Gospel of the kingdom of heaven. Often it was the manifestation of miracles that caused people to place their faith in Christ. The same is happening today. All around the world, Spirit-empowered ministry is resulting in a wave of people being drawn into the family of God.

Spirit-empowered evangelism relies upon prophetic guidance. One training model for this mode of evangelism has been developed by Kevin Dedmon, author of *The Ultimate Treasure Hunt: A Guide to Supernatural Evangelism Through Supernatural Encounters*.[750] This evangelist model is known as the "treasure hunt."

The treasure hunt begins with the evangelism team waiting upon God for words of knowledge. These revelations serve to lead them to where they should go and to guide them in how they should minister once they arrive at their destination. Team members are given the opportunity to share with one another what they believe God is impressing upon them. These insights and foresights are written down on a sheet of paper. When these clues are compiled, they comprise a "treasure map" that will guide the team to their divine appointment.

When I served as lead pastor in Maine, we conducted treasure hunts on several occasions. One Saturday morning our team gathered and found that we had received the following clues: a curb, a traffic light, a pizza restaurant,

---

[750] Kevin Dedmon, *The Ultimate Treasure Hunt: A Guide to Supernatural Evangelism Through Supernatural Encounters* (Shippensburg, Pennsylvania: Destiny Image, 2007).

a man wearing a baseball cap and pain in the neck and shoulder area. We quickly figured out that we were supposed to go to a pizza restaurant about two miles down the road. It was located at a major intersection with a traffic light, and, of course, there was a curb there as well.

So, we drove to the restaurant, got out of our vehicle, and within moments our team leader saw a young man walking across the parking lot wearing a baseball cap. He approached the young man, introduced himself and explained what we were doing. He said, "We are on a treasure hunt, and we believe that you are the treasure." Then he showed him his treasure map and said, "Some of our clues appear to be leading to you. By the way, are you experiencing pain in your neck and shoulder area?"

"Yes! How did you know?" he replied.

"Well, God is thinking about you, and He loves you so much that He let us know. He wants to show you how much He loves you. Do you mind if I pray for you?"

"Go ahead," the young man said.

All our leader did was barely touch him and speak a one sentence prayer, and the young man jumped back exclaiming, "Wow! How did you do that? What was that?" He had experienced a strong sensation of God's power.

"That's the power of God," our leader explained. "How does your neck feel now? Test it out."

"How did you do that? The pain is all gone!" the young man said as he moved his neck in every direction to try to find the pain.

This healing encounter opened the door for our team to pray with him further. He did not make a profession of faith in Christ on this day, but he certainly was brought nearer to the kingdom through the encounter that he experienced.

The treasure hunt approach is just a training tool. Kevin Dedmon explains that after awhile, team members no longer need the treasure map. The Holy Spirit will highlight to them people to approach, and He will spontaneously manifest words of knowledge and words of wisdom to guide the evangelistic encounter.

CHAPTER 34

PASTORING REVIVAL

When revival breaks out in a local church, a new vitality comes to God's people, but corporate renewal can also bring major shifts and changes. Revival can be unsettling. Revival upsets the status quo. In such times, it is especially important for congregational leaders to provide oversight and guidance. As Pastor Rod Parsley emphasizes, both glory and government are needed in a culture of revival.

Five-fold Oversight

Part of the needed government or oversight is found in the function of the five-fold equipping gifts: apostles, prophets, pastors, teachers and evangelists.[751] Apostles provide general leadership in cultivating kingdom culture. They keep everyone looking at the big picture. Prophets help the church to hear and speak what God is saying. Pastors maintain the unity and health of the local body in the midst of the revival movement. Teachers help everyone to understand what is going on from a biblical point of view. Evangelists prevent the revival from becoming introverted by keeping the focus on the world harvest of souls.

Not all lead pastors are actually functioning in a pastoral gifting, as far as a five-fold understanding of leadership is concerned. Many lead pastors are actually apostles. Some are prophets, some are teachers, and some are evangelists. If the primary congregational leader is an *apostle*, that leader should be surrounded by prophetic, pastoral, didactic and evangelistic leaders. If the primary leader is a *prophet*, that leader should include pastors, teachers, evangelists and an apostle on the team. If the primary leader *is* a

---

[751] Ephesians 4:11-14.

pastor, that leader's team should include prophets, teachers, evangelists and an apostle. If the primary leader is a *teacher*, that leader's team should include pastors, prophets, evangelists and an apostle. If the primary leader is an *evangelist*, that leader should include pastors, teachers, prophets and an apostle.

Empowerment of Others

Revival is not about the senior leaders becoming the anointed men and women of God to whom everyone else comes flocking. Anointed leaders are essential to revival, but becoming the anointed leader of a congregation or of a movement is not the objective. The reason that leaders need the anointing is that they may empower others to function. Apostles empower the church to be apostolic. Prophets empower the church to be prophetic. Pastors empower believers to be pastoral. Teachers empower them to be proficient with Scripture. Evangelists empower the church to be evangelistic. Revival is about the empowerment of God's people to bring the kingdom of heaven to the world.

In my years of ministry as a lead pastor, there were many worship services where I was not the person God used to manifest a healing or a breakthrough. My purpose was to empower and deploy others to do the work of the ministry. I trained qualified congregants to minister in prayer, healing and the prophetic. Then when it came to altar ministry time, I released them to do what they had been gifted and trained to do.

Maintaining Normal Church Life

When revival starts happening in your church, do not wear out your staff or your congregation with revival. They may love it, but they still have jobs to work, schools to attend and families to attend to. Revival is so supernaturally life-giving that it may seem for awhile that tending to the normal things of life may not be all that important. Here is where we need a little bit of realism. Find ways to facilitate and sustain revival that does not wear your people out.

In the late 1990's my wife, Kerry, attended a conference at the Toronto Airport Christian Fellowship (TACF)—the site of the Toronto Blessing. She decided to stay beyond the conference just to see what a normal Sunday morning was like for the local TACF congregation. Everything about the morning service was great, but prior to the service, Kerry had a conversation with a woman sitting behind her. Kerry said to her, "It must be exciting to be part of a church that is hosting a revival that is drawing the nations." The woman's blank stare and simple response was revealing. "I suppose," she said. "It's all good, but it's hard on those of us who live here and have made this our church home."

Over the years I have found the same challenge to be true of my own congregation in times of revival. I have heard my own members say, "It's all good, pastor, but with all of these new things happening and all of these new people arriving, it's hard to figure out where I belong anymore. It's feeling like a different place. Sometimes I feel like saying, 'What has happened to my church?'"

None of this is to say that these people are right or wrong in feeling the way they do. The point is that we need to be aware of the fact that not everyone is going to be excited about all of the changes that revival brings, and even those who are excited may begin to feel lost in the midst of all of the newness.

Cultivating Community

I once heard Bill Johnson say that there were two things that were of equal importance to him as far as the life of the local church is concerned: revival and community. Revival is all about love, and love is all about relationships. Yes, it is about the vertical relationship that we have with God: the receiving of the Father's extravagant love and the quickening of a vibrant passion for Jesus. However, it is also about the nurturing of the horizontal relationships that we have with one another. May the amazing *passion* for Jesus that is so characteristic of revival always manifest itself through *compassion* for others—a love for the body of Christ and a love for the world beyond the church.

Promoting a Multi-Generational Mindset

Even outside of revival culture, a multi-generational mindset is important to the sustained health of the church. Those who are young should honor the older generation, and the older generation should bless those who are young. This mindset is especially critical in the advancement of revival culture.

I like to view this dynamic through the metaphor of a relay race. It is all about passing and receiving the baton. In a relay race, one runner runs with the baton in hand, anticipating passing it off to the next runner. For a few moments, the first runner and the second runner run together as the baton is passed from one to the other. For a split second, both of their hands are on the baton at the same time. Then when the first runner is assured that the second runner has the baton securely in hand, the first runner releases it. The baton is released with the expectation that the second runner will carry the baton much further than the first runner was going to go.

So it is in revival culture. One generation runs carrying a spiritual legacy, anticipating passing it on to the next generation. For a season, both the old and the young run together—spiritual fathers and mothers running with their spiritual sons and daughters. The former generation has a sense of responsibility to make sure that their legacy is securely placed in the hands of the rising generation. As the legacy is passed on, older believers are full of hope knowing that the younger ones will carry the fire of revival much further. The old bless the young, and the young honor those who are older. At the finish, all generations will rejoice together.

Identifying Core Values

In the midst of revival, a local congregation would do well to identify its core values and work to sustain them. Of course, the in-breaking of God's kingdom may require some revision, but that process needs to be carefully guided by the leaders of the church. Wisdom from God is needed to make sure that things truly sacred are not compromised. Wisdom is also needed to make sure that "sacred cows"—antiquated traditions—are not retained. Some of the old things may need to stay, and other old things will have to go. Without a doubt, there will be new things to embrace. Revival typically brings with it what some call "aspirational values"—new values that should be introduced into the church's culture.

Stewarding Testimonies

Elsewhere in this text, attention has been given to the power of testimony. Part of pastoring revival involves stewarding the testimonies of what God is doing in the midst of the revival. Appoint someone as the chronicler, historian or scribe. When significant supernatural things have happened, make record of those occurrences. Give opportunity for some of these stories to be publicly shared. In doing so, Jesus will be glorified, and others will be encouraged to trust God for similar happenings in their own lives.

Coordinating Logistics

Revival typically attracts more people and new people. Revival requires more space and even new spaces. Revival involves shifting schedules and the addition of new times to gather. Revival requires training of workers, discipleship of converts, and the assimilation of new members. Coordinating the logistics associated with all of these changing dynamics is part of pastoring revival.

Dealing with Disorder and Unusual Manifestations

It may be unfair to place "disorder" and "unusual manifestations" in the same section, because many unusual manifestations are not necessarily out of order. The point here is that people in the congregation may need help processing unusual manifestations when they occur. For instance, how do church members deal with seeing a seeker at the altar break out into laughter? A church leader may need to point out that the Holy Spirit has just manifested supernatural joy in that person's life. How are observers to deal with seeing someone vibrating on the floor? Someone may need to point out that God's power is upon that person. Just a simple explanation will often put people at ease. A list and description of unusual manifestations will be presented later.

Sometimes unusual things happen that can only be classified as disorder. Simply stated, it should not be allowed to continue. Here is where designated personnel (e.g., ushers, deacons, elders) will have to inconspicuously and kindly step in to correct the situation. Confrontations should be conducted redemptively and without humiliating the individual.

Responding to the Critics

Even a casual reading of the Gospels will quickly reveal that whenever Jesus shows up, critics will show up as well. How are we to respond? If the church took time to respond to every criticism that comes along, they would never get anything else accomplished for the sake of the kingdom. Nehemiah's response to his opponents provides a good example to follow:

> When word came to Sanballat, Tobiah, Geshem the Arab and the rest of our enemies that I had rebuilt the wall and not a gap was left in it—though up to that time I had not set the doors in the gates—Sanballat and Geshem sent me this message: "Come, let us meet together in one of the villages on the plain of Ono."
>
> But they were scheming to harm me; so I sent messengers to them with this reply: "I am carrying on a great project and cannot go down. Why should the work stop while I leave it and go down to you?" Four times they sent me the same message, and each time I gave them the same answer.[752]

Care needs to be taken to distinguish between those who are committed to oppose the revival and those who are merely questioning. People who question what is going on are not necessarily enemies. Many of them are truly in pursuit of truth, and their pursuit will likely lead them into the middle of the revival that is taking place.

Sustaining Revival

How can a genuine revival be sustained? Often God will go as far as we want Him to go in a revival movement. If we hunger and thirst for Him, He will fill us. If we schedule more time and provide more space for Him to work, He will fill that time and space. If we obey every instruction He gives, He will give us even greater instructions. If we are faithful over a little, He will entrust us with much more.

When revival is met with criticism, persecution and other forms of spiritual backlash, church leaders can feel tempted to tone down the revival and even change directions. It can also be the case that prolonged revivals can bring on this thought: "Maybe we have done this long enough. Perhaps we

[752] Nehemiah 6:1-4.

should move on to some other emphasis." I like what Bill Johnson has said on multiple occasions regarding sustaining revival: "Do not change the subject." Stay with the spiritual momentum. Go with what God is doing, and do not stop until He stops.

CONCLUSION

Greater things now await you. That is what Jesus promised when He said, "I tell you the truth, anyone who has faith in me will do what I have been doing. He will do even greater things than these...."[753] It is His will and purpose for you to continue with the work that He started as He walked the earth. He even desires for you to take it further.

Jesus fully authorized and empowered us to heal the sick, raise the dead, cleanse the lepers and drive out demons.[754] He sent the Holy Spirit who has distributed to the church gifts of grace to enable what He has authorized. Today, by the agency of the Holy Spirit, Jesus still works signs and wonders in, among and through those who believe.

It is my belief and hope that those who have worked through this volume will discover that biblically-informed Spirit-empowered ministry models will produce more authentic and more effective outcomes than programs and plans devised without regard for the Spirit. The Spirit will always deliver the kingdom of heaven in a way that rightly represents the Father's heart—a heart of love and power.

Live a Jesus-centered life. Be continually filled with the Holy Spirit. Earnestly desire His gifts, and faithfully steward what He has given. Cultivate sensitivity to His voice. Follow His leading. Proclaim the Gospel. Prophetically declare a hopeful future. Rescue the perishing, and edify the church. Honor those who have been placed in your life to guide and assist you. With a love coupled with boldness, fulfill the call of Christ that is upon you. Heal the sick and the brokenhearted. Drive out demons. Deliver the

---

[753] John 14:12.

[754] Matthew 10:7-8.

oppressed. Raise the dead. May all of this be accomplished so that the Lamb that was slain may receive the full reward of His suffering.[755] To God be the glory!

[755] This statement is based on the call to Moravian missions: "May the Lamb that was slain receive the reward of His suffering."

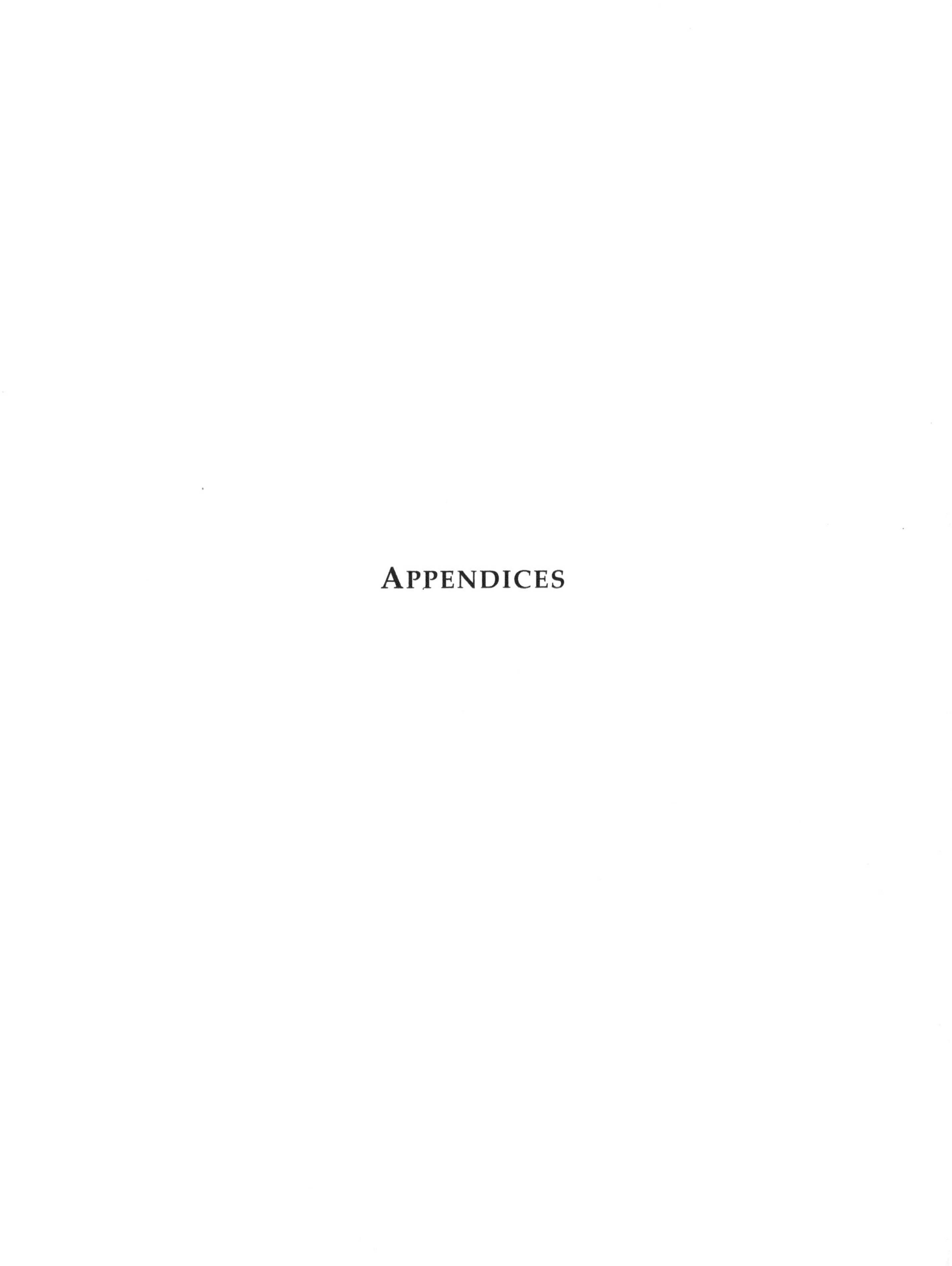

Appendices

APPENDIX A

THE CORINTHIAN PROBLEM

The church at Corinth had its share of difficulties, and some erroneously think that spiritual gifts were the source of their trouble. The problem at Corinth was not the spiritual gifts. The problems at Corinth were rooted in a number of other dysfunctions that compromised the operation of spiritual gifts in the church. Paul's corrective words in 1 Corinthians helped to preserve the integrity of spiritual gifts in the church.

Relational Issues

Relationships in the Corinthian church were out of order. For a church to become an environment in which the spiritual gifts function properly, its members need to be functioning properly in relationship with one another.

Paul's first letter to the Corinthians was addressed to "the church of God in Corinth."[756] "Church of God" and "Corinth" were almost contradictory terms. Apart from the grace of God, to speak of the "church of God" *in* "Corinth" would have been unthinkable. Corinth was an "every man for himself" self-serving society, and traces of that culture had made its way into the church.

Yes, the Corinthian church had its problems, yet Paul affirmed who they were in Christ. He continues in verse two, writing, "To the church of God in Corinth, to those *sanctified* in Christ Jesus and *called to be holy*." He further blessed them and affirmed their giftedness, saying,

> Grace and peace to you from God our Father and the Lord Jesus Christ. I always thank God for you because of his grace given you in Christ Jesus.

---

[756] 1 Corinthians 1:2.

> For in him you have been enriched in every way—in all your speaking and in all your knowledge.[757]

The "grace given" to them was that which enriched the Corinthian believers in their speaking and in their knowledge.

Paul's first reference to spiritual gifts in his first letter to the Corinthians is found in 1:7 where he said, "You do not lack any spiritual gift as you eagerly wait for our Lord Jesus Christ to be revealed." The Apostle acknowledges the sufficiency of the spiritual gifts in the Corinthian church, but then to this very spiritual church, he offers correction.

Not all was well at Corinth. There were divisions in the church. In 1:10, Paul wrote, "I appeal to you, brothers, in the name of our Lord Jesus Christ, that all of you agree with one another so that there may be no divisions among you and that you may be perfectly united in mind and thought."

Paul's call for agreement was not just a general preventative measure. It was a remedial measure, for a very real and specific division had taken place. In 1:11-12, he said, "Some from Chloe's household have informed me that there are quarrels among you. What I mean is this: One of you says, 'I follow Paul'; another, 'I follow Apollos'; another, 'I follow Cephas'; still another, 'I follow Christ.'" They took pride in their identification with certain teachers or leaders.

The Apostle then confronted their divisive attitude, saying in 1:13, "Is Christ divided? Was Paul crucified for you? Were you baptized into the name of Paul?" The obvious answer is "no." Scholars have referred to this thing that was going on in Corinth as a "party spirit."

Then to this spiritually gifted church, Paul brought another word of correction. In 3:3, he said, "You are still worldly. For since there is jealousy and quarreling among you, are you not worldly? Are you not acting like mere men?"

Paul said, "Are you not acting like *mere men*?" In other words, he is saying, "Are you not acting like you are *just human*?" Our initial response as

---

[757] 1 Corinthians 1:3-5.

readers might be, "Well, of course they are *just human*!" After all, is it not true that the one acceptable and justifiable excuse for weakness that we all can use is the claim that we are "just human"? Not so. From Paul's point of view, believers are *not* just human. We are supposed to live like we are truly the righteous sons and daughters of God. Jealousy and quarreling should have no place among us.

Pride

Not only did the Corinthian believers take pride in their identification with certain teachers or leaders, but they also took pride in their intellectual abilities and their knowledge of philosophy. In 1:25-31, Paul confronted this intellectual pride, stating,

> The foolishness of God is wiser than man's wisdom, and the weakness of God is stronger than man's strength. Brothers, think of what you were when you were called. Not many of you were wise by human standards; not many were influential; not many were of noble birth. But God chose the foolish things of the world to shame the wise; God chose the weak things of the world to shame the strong. He chose the lowly things of this world and the despised things—and the things that are not—to nullify the things that are, so that no one may boast before him. It is because of him that you are in Christ Jesus, who has become for us wisdom from God--that is, our righteousness, holiness and redemption. Therefore, as it is written: "Let him who boasts boast in the Lord."

In 2:1-5, he continued,

> When I came to you, brothers, I did not come with eloquence or superior wisdom as I proclaimed to you the testimony about God. For I resolved to know nothing while I was with you except Jesus Christ and him crucified. I came to you in weakness and fear, and with much trembling. My message and my preaching were not with wise and persuasive words, but with a demonstration of the Spirit's power, so that your faith might not rest on men's wisdom, but on God's power.

Paul's ministry among the Corinthians was totally unimpressive by Greek standards. However, a demonstration of the Holy Spirit's power accompanied his preaching. The result was that the people were focused more on "God's power" than they were on "men's wisdom."

Pagan Influence

Starting with 1 Corinthians 12:1, Paul speaks of things that do not initially make sense to us twenty-first century readers, but they made perfect sense to the original recipients of the letter who lived in the context of a pagan society:

> Now about spiritual gifts [spiritual matters or things], brothers, I do not want you to be ignorant. You know that when you were pagans, somehow or other you were influenced and led astray to mute idols. Therefore I tell you that no one who is speaking by the Spirit of God says, "Jesus be cursed," and no one can say, "Jesus is Lord," except by the Holy Spirit.[758]

Paul is speaking into a specific set of circumstances which we know little about, but it appears that some may have resisted or objected to supernatural manifestations. They were concerned about deception. In their former years of idolatry, they had become familiar with supernatural things driven by demonic forces. How could they be sure that these manifestations were truly God at work and not something else?

There are two important points for us to make here. First, spirits which are not of God will not exalt Jesus as Lord, and the Spirit which is of God will always exalt Jesus as Lord. Second, when a person is being moved by the Holy Spirit to speak prophetically, in tongues or in interpretation, he need not fear that he might say something that does not honor Christ. He will not say "Jesus is cursed," or anything like that, and the Holy Spirit speaking through him will always exalt Christ.

When we ask the Father to fill us with the Holy Spirit or to impart to us some gift of the Spirit, we are not to fear that we might get something that is not of God. Here we are reminded of Jesus' words in Luke 11:9-13:

> "So I say to you: Ask and it will be given to you; seek and you will find; knock and the door will be opened to you. For everyone who asks receives; he who seeks finds; and to him who knocks, the door will be opened. Which of you fathers, if your son asks for a fish, will give him a snake instead? Or if he asks for an egg, will give him a scorpion? If you then, though you are evil, know how to give good gifts to your children, how much more will your Father in heaven give the Holy Spirit to those who ask him!"

---

[758] 1 Corinthians 12:1-3.

In 1 Corinthians 12:4-6, Paul goes a little further in his attempt to preclude error and to relieve concerns and fears rooted in past pagan experiences: "There are different kinds of gifts, but the same Spirit. There are different kinds of service, but the same Lord. There are different kinds of working, but the same God works all of them in all men." Of course, we take it for granted that there is only One Spirit behind these gifts, ministries, workings and manifestations, but to these Corinthians who had come out of a pagan environment motivated by a multitude of evil spirits, the emphasis on one Spirit was necessary.

APPENDIX B

A BIBLICAL HISTORY OF THE PROPHETIC

An Old Testament View of Prophetic Ministry and Leadership

Turn through the pages of the Old Testament, and it appears that direct encounters with God were reserved for a select few. However, is that the way God wanted it to be? Wasn't it His desire from the beginning to walk with man? Of course, sin altered the relationship, but was it God who held Himself aloof, or was the distance perpetuated more by the doings of man?

In Exodus 20:18-19, the Bible says,

> When the people saw the thunder and lightning and heard the trumpet and saw the mountain in smoke, they trembled with fear. They stayed at a distance and said to Moses, "Speak to us yourself and we will listen. But do not have God speak to us or we will die."

Could it be that God actually would have preferred to speak to everyone and not just to one or to a few? The Hebrews preferred "distance" from God, and from that point forward, God used prophets and priests as mediators.

The following is an annotated list of examples where prophetic encounters occurred with the people of the Old Testament:

1. God communicating with Adam and Eve.[759] Here we see the first known series of prophetic messages, impacting the direction of the entire human race.

---

[759] Genesis 2:17; 3:14-19.

2. God communicating with Cain.[760] The Lord engaged in direct conversations with Cain as He attempted to lead Cain into a right response to His revealed will.

3. Enoch's walk with God.[761] Enoch, who may have been regarded as a patriarch in his time, is described in a relationship with God that was typical of prophets.

4. God communicating with Noah.[762] Prophetic revelations were given to Noah regarding the flood and the ark. Communications also took place between God and Noah following the flood, establishing a new order for the human race.[763]

5. God communicating with Abram.[764] In Abram's first recorded prophetic encounter with God, he was called out of his father's land. Abram's second and third recorded prophetic encounters with God brought forth promises related to the land.[765] God's covenant with Abram and his descendants was revealed through a prophetic encounter.[766] When the Lord thought to bring judgment upon Sodom and Gomorrah, He took the initiative to reveal to Abraham His plans regarding those cities for the sake of intercession.[767]

6. God communicating with and through Joseph.[768] Joseph's prophetic dreams revealed God's purposes for the children of Israel. After going into captivity, Joseph interpreted the dreams of the cupbearer and baker while in

---

[760] Genesis 4:6-15.

[761] Genesis 5:21-24.

[762] Genesis 6:1-7:4.

[763] Genesis 8:15-9:17.

[764] Genesis 12:1-3.

[765] Genesis 12:7; 13:14-17.

[766] Genesis 15:1-21.

[767] Genesis 18:17.

[768] Genesis 37:1-11.

prison.[769] He also interpreted Pharaoh's dreams and his own subsequent promotion.[770]

7. God communicating with and through Jacob/Israel. God spoke to Israel in a night vision, encouraging him to move to Egypt.[771] Then as he approached the end of his days, Israel prophetically pronounced blessings over his sons and their descendants.[772]

8. God communicating with and through Moses and Aaron. With Moses and Aaron we see an example of team ministry in the prophetic; both were enabled to speak prophetically for the sake of leading the people.[773] Moses' burning bush prophetic encounter, initiated his role as a prophetic leader.[774] Moses was ordained to be like God before Pharaoh, and Aaron was appointed to be as Moses' prophet.[775]

In humility and a teachable spirit, prophetic leaders need to listen for God's guidance through means other than their own prophetic anointing. Moses, the prophetic leader, accepted instruction from a non-prophetic leader, Jethro, resulting in an effective strategy for delegating responsibilities.[776]

The Scriptures seem to imply that limiting the prophetic to one or to a few may not have been God's first choice. It was the people that expressed *their* preference that God speak through one man, Moses, and not to them

---

[769] Genesis 40:1-23.

[770] Genesis 41:1-57.

[771] Genesis 46:1-4.

[772] Genesis 48:1-49:28.

[773] Exodus 4:15-16.

[774] Exodus 3:1-4:14.

[775] Exodus 6:28 – 7:6.

[776] Exodus 18:13-26.

directly.[777] Moses yearned for all of God's people to be prophetic and anointed of the Holy Spirit.[778]

9. God communicating with and through Joshua. Prophetic encouragement came to Joshua to be strong and courageous in taking the promised land.[779] Prophetic leadership was exemplified through him as he led the Hebrews in crossing the Jordan River.[780] The march around Jericho was a powerful act of prophetic leadership.[781]

10. God communicating with and through Deborah. Deborah was a prophetess and a prophetic leader.[782]

11. God communicating with and through Gideon. The story of Gideon is an exciting prophetic leadership adventure.[783]

12. God communicating with and through Samuel. In a time when the prophetic was rare, Samuel was available and responsive to the voice of God,[784] He became established as a prophet in Israel.[785] As a prophet, Samuel rebuked King Saul, noting that the Lord is in search of emerging leaders who are in pursuit of His heart.[786]

13. God communicating with and through Nathan. Through the prophet, Nathan, the Lord spoke to David regarding David's offspring and

---

[777] Exodus 20:18-19.

[778] Numbers 11:29.

[779] Joshua 1:7-8.

[780] Joshua 3:1-17.

[781] Joshua 6:1-27.

[782] Judges 4:1-5:31.

[783] Judges 6:1-8:35.

[784] 1 Samuel 3:1, 10.

[785] 1 Samuel 3:19-21.

[786] 1 Samuel 13:1-15.

the building of the temple.[787] As a prophet, Nathan also rebuked King David.[788]

14. God working through David in a prophetic manner. Although David is not usually regarded as a prophet, the manner in which he relied upon the prophetic sets him apart as a prophetic leader.

15. Communicating with and through Solomon. The Lord appeared to Solomon at Gibeon.[789] Solomon prayed for discernment so that he might be enabled to govern the people.[790] The Lord appeared to Solomon a second time, delivering a promise to establish Solomon's throne.[791]

16. God communicating with and through Elijah. With prophetic authority, Elijah confronted the prophets of Baal at Mount Carmel.[792] He boldly delivered God's message to Ahab, king of Israel.[793]

17. God communicating with and through Elisha. Elisha was called of God,[794] and the mantle of Elijah fell upon him.[795] He issued the prophetic order that Jehu be anointed as king of Israel.[796]

18. God communicating with and through Jehoshaphat. Jehoshaphat is an example of one who was a prophetic leader in the sense that he heeded prophetic influence outside of his own anointing and aligned his words and

---

[787] 2 Samuel 7:1-17.

[788] 2 Samuel 12:1-23.

[789] 1 Kings 3:5.

[790] 1 Kings 3:9.

[791] 1 Kings 9:1-7.

[792] 1 Kings 18:16-46.

[793] 1 Kings 21:17-34.

[794] 1 Kings 19:19-21.

[795] 2 Kings 2:1-18.

[796] 2 Kings 9:1-13.

actions accordingly. In a time of war, King Jehoshaphat led his people with the exhortation that faith in the Lord's prophets would result in success.[797]

19. God communicating with and through Hezekiah. Hezekiah is another example of one who was a prophetic leader in the sense that he heeded prophetic influence outside of his own anointing and aligned his words and actions accordingly. When threatened by enemies, the people gained confidence from the words of their prophetically guided king, Hezekiah.[798]

20. God accomplishing prophetic purposes through Nehemiah. Nehemiah was a prophetic leader who was not guided as much by revelation as he was the heart of God—a quality resulting in fervent and effectual prayers.[799]

21. God communicating with and through Isaiah. Isaiah's prophetic encounter with God's glory was a preparation for his prophetic mission and calling.[800]

22. God communicating with and through Jeremiah. The Lord spoke to Jeremiah, appointing him as a prophetic leader.[801] God placed His words in Jeremiah's mouth.[802] The record of his ministry portrays him as a *watchman* [803] and a *servant* of the Lord.[804] However, his critics regarded him as a man of

---

[797] 2 Chronicles 20:20.

[798] 2 Chronicles 32:7-8.

[799] Nehemiah 1:4.

[800] Isaiah 6:1-13.

[801] Jeremiah 1:5.

[802] Jeremiah 1:9.

[803] Jeremiah 6:17.

[804] Jeremiah 7:25; 24:24.

strife and contention.[805] Jeremiah's story leaves the impression that prophets are also intercessors.[806]

23. God communicating with and through Ezekiel. Ezekiel was called to prophesy,[807] and he carried a sense of strong prophetic authorization.[808] He is portrayed in the Scriptures as a watchman.[809]

24. God communicating with and through Daniel. The prophet Daniel interpreted king Nebuchadnezzar's dreams[810] and they mysterious handwriting on the wall.[811]

25. God communicated with and through Hosea. Hosea was made ready to prophesy with the heart of God through a series of prophetic actions involving his wife and children.[812]

26. God communicating with and through Jonah. Jonah's story includes his call to prophesy, his resistance of that call, and the consequences that he suffered.[813]

God has always desired to speak to His people as a whole. In Numbers 11:29, Moses said, "I wish that all the Lord's people were prophets and that the Lord would put his Spirit on them!"

Eventually Moses' desire would be fulfilled. That fulfillment would come after the cross, after the resurrection, after the ascension and on that day of the

---

[805] Jeremiah 15:10.

[806] Jeremiah 27:18.

[807] Ezekiel 1:1-3:15.

[808] Ezekiel 3:14.

[809] Ezekiel 3:17.

[810] Daniel 2:24; 4:19-27.

[811] Daniel 5:13-31.

[812] Hosea 1:2-2:1.

[813] Jonah 1:1-17.

great outpouring of the Spirit on Pentecost. The prophet Joel foresaw that day of fulfillment:

> And afterward, I will pour out my Spirit on all people. Your sons and daughters will prophesy, your old men will dream dreams, your young men will see visions. Even on my servants, both men and women, I will pour out my Spirit in those days.[814]

A New Testament History of Prophetic Ministry and Leadership

Joel prophesied it, and one hundred twenty disciples experienced in the same moment on the Day of Pentecost. The Holy Spirit came upon them all. This anointing is for "all flesh"—for people of every description.[815] From that day forward, the prophetic became normative for the church.[816]

Here we will consider a few examples of the prophetic in the New Testament:

1. God communicating with and through John the Baptist. Matthew 3:1-6 describes his ministry,

> In those days John the Baptist came, preaching in the Desert of Judea and saying, "Repent, for the kingdom of heaven is near." This is he who was spoken of through the prophet Isaiah:
>
> "A voice of one calling in the desert,
> 'Prepare the way for the Lord,
> make straight paths for him.'"
>
> John's clothes were made of camel's hair, and he had a leather belt around his waist. His food was locusts and wild honey. People went out to him from Jerusalem and all Judea and the whole region of the Jordan. Confessing their sins, they were baptized by him in the Jordan River.

---

[814] Joel 2:28-29.

[815] Acts 2:17-18.

[816] A biblical basis for New Testament prophets may be established through the multiple examples that follow and through a review of 1 Corinthians 12:28-29; Ephesians 2:20; and Ephesians 4:11-12.

Through John's ministry of prophetic preaching, he announced the coming of the kingdom of heaven and called the people to repentance. He had a forerunner anointing and functioned in the spirit and power of Elijah to turn the hearts of the fathers and the children toward one another.[817] A great following resulted from his faithfulness to this calling.

2. God communicating with and through Jesus. On at least three occasions, those who were in the company of Jesus heard God's voice as He spoke audibly with His Son.[818] Jesus relied upon every word that came from His Father's mouth; in fact, He declared that it was more important to hear and heed the voice of God that in was to eat physical bread. The sound of the Father's voice is life-giving.[819]

The doing of God's will on earth is dependent on revelation of His will from heaven.[820] The pattern of Jesus' life exemplifies this dependency. His engagements with people were followed by disengagement for the sake of engagement with the Father.[821] Someone has stated it in these words: "Jesus ministered between places of prayer."

Jesus ministered with a sense of divine focus and timing.[822] He was guided by His perception of His Father's words and actions.[823] In John 5:19-20, Jesus said,

> "I tell you the truth, the Son can do nothing by himself; he can do only what he sees his Father doing, because whatever the Father does the Son also does. For the Father loves the Son and shows him all he does."

---

[817] Mark 1:2-3 and Luke 1:17.

[818] Matthew 3:17; 17:5 and John12:27-33.

[819] Matthew 4:4.

[820] Matthew 6:10.

[821] Mark 1:35-38; 6:30-32.

[822] John 2:3-4; 7:6: 11:1-7; 12:23, 27; 13:1.

[823] John 5:17, 19, 30; 8:28; 12:49-50; 14:10, 24, 31.

The prayer that Jesus prayed in John 17 illustrates the powerful impact of His sense of timing. With supernatural insight into the timing of God's purposes, He entered into prophetic intercession.

3. God communicating with and through Peter. Peter's dependence on the Word of Christ enabled him to walk on water.[824] His prophetic sermon in Acts 2 announced that the Spirit had been poured out on all flesh, enabling all believers to minister prophetically.[825] Later he was supernaturally enabled to speak before religious rulers in defense of the Spirit's work.[826] He received a revelation of Ananias and Sapphira's sin, and the result was a manifestation of judgment, holy fear and the further demonstration of the Lord's power.[827] A divine appointment between Peter and Cornelius was arranged prophetically by visions, angels and the voice of the Spirit.[828] In the writing of 2 Peter, he noted that His message, as well as the message of the other Apostles, was received through a direct personal encounter with Jesus and His glory.[829]

4. God communicating with and through Philip. In Acts 8, Philip's actions were directed by an angel and the Holy Spirit.[830]

5. God communicating with and through Saul/Paul. The supernatural commissioning of Saul (later named Paul) by Jesus on the road to Damascus launched him into his prophetic destiny.[831] Throughout his ministry, Paul lived, ministered and led prophetically. He accurately predicted judgment against the sorcerer Elymas.[832] He prophetically pronounced a healing at

---

[824] Matthew 14:22-33.

[825] Acts 2:14-21.

[826] Acts 4:8.

[827] Acts 5:1-16.

[828] Acts 10:1-23; 11:1-8.

[829] 2 Peter 1:16-19.

[830] Acts 8:26-35.

[831] Acts 9:1-9; 22:6-16; 26:9-16.

[832] Acts 13:9-12.

Lystra.[833] Guided by a revelatory vision, Paul's own preconceived plans were prevented, yet the result was his call into Europe—the Macedonian call.[834]

In Acts 19, the Lord spoke to Paul in a vision, encouraging him regarding the work in Corinth.[835] As his ministry progressed, he was compelled by the Spirit to go to Jerusalem although he had also been prophetically warned that he would suffer.[836] By revelation he was informed that he would testify about Jesus in Rome.[837] En route to Rome, he accurately predicted that the ship carrying him to Rome would suffer shipwreck, and later an angel revealed that none would perish.[838] His prophetic experiences were so frequent that the Lord had to allow his "thorn in the flesh" just to keep him humble![839]

6. God communicating with and through the Apostle John. The book of Revelation is the only New Testament book that is entirely prophetic from beginning to end. Its twenty-two chapters attest to the fact that the Apostle John was a man who functioned powerfully under a prophetic anointing. It seems significant to me that John is also the apostle who lived his life under such a remarkable revelation regarding love. I wonder if there is a connection between the intensity of the prophetic in his life and the degree to which he comprehended the love of God.

7. God communicating with and through the faith community. The church of the New Testament was a prophetic community. Roger Stronstad expresses,

> "In too many places the Church views itself as a didactic community rather than as a prophetic community, where sound doctrine is treasured above charismatic action. Indeed, the preaching and teaching of the word

---

[833] Acts 14:9-10.

[834] Acts 16:6-10.

[835] Acts 18:9-11.

[836] Acts 20:22-23.

[837] Acts 23:11.

[838] Acts 27:10, 21-26.

[839] 2 Corinthians 12:1-10.

> displaces Spirit-filled, Spirit-led and Spirit-empowered ministry. The Spirit of prophecy has been quenched and the gifts of the Spirit have been sanitized and institutionalized...."[840]

Prophecy was taken seriously in the New Testament church. For instance, the faith community took prophetic action and prepared for famine relief when they heard the prophecy of a man named Agabus.[841] On another occasion, the church at Antioch commissioned two of their most valuable leaders—Barnabas and Saul—to take the Gospel into the Gentile world on the basis of prophetic leading.[842] The incident of James, an apostle, discerning God's will after hearing the deliberations of other apostles and elders in the Jerusalem council provides yet another example.[843]

These examples combined with numerous other New Testament teachings contribute toward the conclusion that the prophetic in ministry and leadership was normal for the New Testament church. If the church of the twenty-first century is to genuinely emulate a New Testament paradigm, the call to embrace prophetic ministry and leadership is unavoidable.

---

[840] Roger Stronstad, *The Prophethood of All Believers: a Study in Luke's Charismatic Theology* (Sheffield: Sheffield Academic Press, 1999), 123.

[841] Acts 11:27-30.

[842] Acts 13:1-4.

[843] Acts 15:6-21, 28.

APPENDIX C

A HISTORY OF SPIRIT-EMPOWERED MINISTRY IN THE PENTECOSTAL MOVEMENT

Current understandings of prophetic ministry and leadership have not been formed in a vacuum. They are the product of various biblical, theological and historical cultural influences that have converged upon ministry thought and practice. Here we will consider a chronology of voices and influences that have helped to shape the prophetic ministry paradigm.

The Holiness Revival

A revival of holiness was a necessary prelude to a revival of power. Character precedes gifting. The nineteenth century holiness revival emerged as Methodists were reminded of John Wesley's teachings on "entire sanctification" and "perfect love"--the complete orientation of the heart *toward* God and *away from* sin.[844]

In 1887, a Presbyterian minister named A. B. Simpson was preaching "Christ our Savior, Sanctifier, Healer and Coming King" at a former temperance campground in Old Orchard, Maine.[845] When Simpson linked up

---

[844] Chris Armstrong, "Phoebe Palmer: Did You Know? Interesting facts about the American Holiness revival," Christian History, accessed June 26, 2012, available from http:// www.christianitytoday.com/ ch/ 2004/ issue82/ 1.02.html.

[845] Ibid.

with Charles Cullis, a healing revival began on those grounds, and a contagious hunger for the baptism of the Holy Spirit began to spread.

Out of this movement rose Frank Sandford who founded Shiloh—a ministry training center in Durham, Maine. Shiloh drew in hundreds of emerging leaders yearning for revival—people like A. J. Tomlinson and Charles F. Parham, who would later become significant players in the Pentecostal movement.

The Welsh Revival[846]

In the nation of Wales, a spiritual awakening began, due largely to the prayers and ministry of a man named Evan Roberts. One account of the revival reports,

> People were changed in so many ways. The crime rate dropped, drunkards were reformed, pubs reported losses in trade. Bad language disappeared and never returned to the lips of many.... It was reported that the pit ponies failed to understand their born again colliers who seemed to speak the new language of Zion—without curse and blasphemy.... Even football and rugby became uninteresting in the light of new joy and direction received by the Converts.[847]

When news of the revival crossed the Atlantic, many Christians felt compelled to pray and ask God for a similar work of the Holy Spirit in America. Some even traveled to Wales to witness first-hand the miraculous transformation of lives that was taking place.

By 1905, a number of believers in Los Angeles, California had become convinced that the developments in Wales were part of a move of God toward the fulfilling of Joel 2:23-29—a prophecy that states,

---

[846] This account has been adapted from the author's previous work entitled, *A Man Called King: The Life and Legacy of King Turpin, Jr.* (Scarborough, Maine: DrawNear, 2010), 10-12.

[847] "The Welsh Revival: A History of 1904 and News of Today," accessed November 11, 2010, available from http://www.welshrevival.com.

> Be glad, O people of Zion, rejoice in the LORD your God, for he has given you the autumn rains in righteousness. He sends you abundant showers, both autumn and spring rains, as before.
>
> The threshing floors will be filled with grain; the vats will overflow with new wine and oil.
>
> I will repay you for the years the locusts have eaten....
>
> You will have plenty to eat, until you are full, and you will praise the name of the LORD your God, who has worked wonders for you; never again will my people be shamed.
>
> Then you will know that I am in Israel, that I am the LORD your God, and that there is no other; never again will my people be shamed.
>
> And afterward, I will pour out my Spirit on all people. Your sons and daughters will prophesy, your old men will dream dreams, your young men will see visions. Even on my servants, both men and women, I will pour out my Spirit in those days.

The Holiness and Welsh revival streams were about to converge.

The Azusa Street Revival[848]

Expectant Christians in Los Angeles began to pray for a visitation of the Holy Spirit; they yearned to have an encounter with God just as believers in Wales had experienced.

Los Angeles had been made ready for revival. In February of 1906, a black minister named William J. Seymour had been invited to preach. He preached about a manifestation of the Holy Spirit known as "speaking in tongues."[849] Seymour had not personally experienced this work of the Spirit, but based on teaching he had received under Charles F. Parham in Houston, Texas, he believed that speaking in tongues was the initial evidence of the baptism in the Holy Spirit.

---

848 Adapted from J. Randolph Turpin, *A Man Called King: The Life and Legacy of King Turpin, Jr.* (Scarborough, Maine: DrawNear, 2010), 12-13.

849 See Acts 2 and 1 Corinthians 12-14.

On April 9, 1906, Seymour was preaching at 214 North Bonnie Brae Street in Los Angeles, and the power of the Holy Spirit fell upon the gathering. On that day it is reported that one man received the baptism in the Holy Spirit and began to speak in tongues. On the days that followed, others started receiving the same experience. This move of the Spirit escalated, and the meetings had to be moved to Azusa Street. Thus this awakening became known as the Azusa Street Revival—the beginning of the modern-day Pentecostal movement.[850]

The Post World War II Healing Revival

The year 1946 marked the beginning of the post World War II healing revival. With that revival came the rise of an evangelist thought by many to be a prophet, William Branham.[851] Branham represents an era in the Pentecostal movement when charismatic personalities were widely accepted as mediators between God and the afflicted.

Some have suggested that Branham's influence on his contemporaries may have initiated a movement that eventually led to the general fascination with the prophetic that became so prevalent among Pentecostals and Charismatics in the latter half of the twentieth century.[852]

The Latter Rain Movement

In the 1950s a group of Christians in Saskatchewan, Canada became concerned that Pentecostals were not functioning as strongly in the charismatic gifts as they were in the beginning of the movement. Their hunger

---

[850] A similar outpouring of the Holy Spirit had taken place ten years earlier in 1896 at Camp Creek, North Carolina, among members of the Holiness Church—the group that later became known as the Church of God (Cleveland, Tennessee).

[851] Stanley M. Burgess, ed. *The New International Dictionary of Pentecostal and Charismatic Movements* (Grand Rapids, Michigan: Zondervan Publishing House, 2002), 440.

[852] C. Douglas Weaver, *The Healer-Prophet, William Marrion Branham: A Study of the Prophetic in American Pentecostalism* (Macon, Georgia: Mercer University Press, 1987), x.

resulted in a revival of the *charismata*, and a short yet significant movement began that later influenced both Pentecostals and Charismatics. The embracing of the five-fold enabling gifts and a rise in the practice of personal prophecy were notable features. The movement became known as the "Latter Rain Movement."

Although some measure of good was produced out of the Latter Rain, there were differences and emphases that caused mainstream Pentecostals to distance themselves from the movement. It is not our purpose here to argue the pros and cons of the views of either Pentecostals or Latter Rain adherents. Our purpose is to simply show that notable emphasis was given to the prophetic and that this emphasis carried over into the Charismatic movement that emerged a few years later.

The Charismatic and Neo-charismatic Renewal Movements

The emergence of the Charismatic renewal in the 1960s and the Neo-charismatic renewal of the 1980s helped to strengthen and perpetuate the prophetic fervor.

In 1981 John Wimber delivered a lecture at Fuller Theological Seminary entitled, "Signs, Wonders and Church Growth." That lecture preceded the course, "The Miraculous and Church Growth," which Wimber taught at Fuller from 1982 to 1985.[853] His contributions set into motion a new "Signs and Wonders" movement that gave particular attention to the revelatory gifts and gifts of healing.

The Prophetic Movement and the "Kansas City Prophets"

While the Signs and Wonders movement was emerging in the 1980s, the prophetic movement, rooted in earlier moves of the Spirit, regained momentum. This renewed emphasis on the prophetic was represented by the

---

[853] Burgess, 1200.

attention given to the "Kansas City Prophets" in 1986.[854] Among those prophets emerged a pastor, Mike Bickle. Bickle's church, Metro Christian Fellowship, became known worldwide for its prophetic orientation. In this same period, Bill Hamon emerged as a prominent authority regarding the revelatory gifts.[855]

The Toronto Revival

The Toronto Revival of 1994 added fuel to the flame of revived prophetic interest.[856] With the sudden influx of people claiming prophetic giftings, the need for a sound theology quickly became evident. While scholars such as Guy Chevreau[857] and Michael L. Brown[858] worked to address concerns related to unusual physical manifestations, Jack Deere filled the theological void related to prophetic issues. In 1996 Deere, who is a former Dallas Theological Seminary professor, wrote two books relevant to the need: *Surprised by the Power of the Spirit: Discovering How God Speaks and Heals Today* and *Surprised by the Voice of God: How God Speaks Today through Prophecies, Dreams, and Visions.* In addition to these works, in 2001 Jack Deere released a helpful guide entitled, *The Beginner's Guide to the Gift of Prophecy.*[859]

---

[854] Burgess, 816. David Pytches released a book in 1991 telling the story of the "Kansas City Prophets." David Pytches, Some *Said It Thundered: a Personal Encounter with the Kansas City Prophets* (Nashville, Tennessee: Oliver-Nelson, 1991).

[855] Bill Hamon, *Prophets and the Prophetic Movement: God's Prophetic Move Today* (Shippensburg, Pennsylvania: Destiny Image, 1990).

[856] In reference to the Toronto Revival, the British press coined the term, "Toronto Blessing." The leaders of the revival preferred to call it the "Father's Blessing."

[857] Guy Chevreau, Catch *the Fire: The Toronto Blessing: An Experience of Renewal and Revival* (London, Marshall Pickering, 1994).

[858] Michael L. Brown, *From Holy Laughter to Holy Fire: America on the Edge of Revival* (Shippensburg, Pennsylvania: Destiny Image Publishers, 1997).

[859] Jack Deere, *The Beginner's Guide to the Gift of Prophecy* (Ann Arbor, Michigan: Vine Books, 2001).

Bethel Church

During the Toronto Revival, a pastor from Northern California experienced such a significant encounter with God's presence that he purposed to devote the rest of his life to stewarding His presence. This pastor's name was Bill Johnson.

Shortly after Bill Johnson was impacted in Toronto, he moved to Redding, California to serve Bethel Church—a church where his father had once served as lead pastor. Empowering all believers to minister supernaturally continues to be a core value at Bethel. Everyone is encouraged to prophesy. This emphasis is held as consistent with 1 Corinthians 14, where Paul teaches:

1. The gift of prophecy is to be eagerly desired.[860]
2. A church where everyone speaks in tongues and prophesies would be ideal. However, prophesying is to be preferred above speaking in tongues, because prophecy has the potential to bring immediate edification to the church.[861]
3. A church where everyone is empowered to prophesy creates an environment where the awareness of God's presence and power increases.[862]
4. Biblical guidelines and accountability in prophetic ministry contribute to a culture in which everyone feels that they can contribute prophetically to the instruction and encouragement of the church.[863]

---

[860] 1 Corinthians 14:1.

[861] 1 Corinthians 14:5.

[862] 1 Corinthians 14:24-25.

[863] 1 Corinthians 14:31-32.

Appendix D

Supernatural Manifestations

When the Spirit of God moves upon gatherings of people or even upon individuals, unusual things can occur. When God—the consuming fire (Deuteronomy 4:24; Hebrews 12:29) enters the room, it is impossible for nothing to happen; evidence of his presence and power will certainly manifest. We are talking about heaven invading earth—the celestial penetrating the terrestrial. We are talking about the Almighty encountering weak mortal flesh. The possibility of manifestations of God's presence should come as no surprise.

Supernatural encounters are not limited to the Holy Spirit showing up. Angels can also enter the environment. Some may even suggest adding demons to the list of potential supernatural visitors, but in this context, if demons manifest, it is usually as they are departing.

Manifestations may occur in the physical surroundings or they may occur in or through individuals. Examples of manifestations in the physical surroundings include the following:

1. Luminous manifestations resembling fire[864]
2. The sound of wind[865]
3. Vocal musical sounds
4. The shaking of physical surroundings[866]

---

[864] Acts 2:3.

[865] Acts 2:2.

[866] Acts 4:31; 16:26a

5. Clouds, mists or a haze
6. Visible manifestation resembling a dove[867]

Most of the examples covered in this chapter will not be of manifestations in the physical surroundings. We will be given primary attention to manifestations occurring in or through individuals.

In a context of supernatural encounters, three categories of manifestations often occur: biblical, unbiblical and extra-biblical.

Biblical Manifestations

A biblical manifestation would be one that can be found in Scripture. Here we will review a list of biblical manifestations along with a few details related to each one.

1. Manifestation Gifts

The primary manifestation gifts are listed in 1 Corinthians 12:8-10: word of wisdom, word of knowledge, faith, gifts of healing, the working of miracles, prophecy, discerning of spirits, various kinds of tongues and the interpretation of tongues. Although not included in the 1 Corinthians list, dreams and visions fall in this same category.[868] Pastoral guidance for facilitating these manifestations is contained in 1 Corinthians 12-14 and is suggested elsewhere in this text as well.

2. Falling Before the Lord

When humans come into contact with the presence of God or angels, the impact of that encounter can cause a physical reaction. Being overwhelmed by the presence often results in a person falling to the ground. This manifestation is sometimes called being "slain in the Spirit" or "resting in the Lord." Similar reactions are found in Scripture. In the list below, some of the noted incidents involved a voluntary act of dropping to the ground rather than the person

---

[867] John 1:32.

[868] Acts 2:17.

involuntarily falling. However, it appears that several of these accounts clearly suggest an involuntary reaction.

a. Falling before the Lord to worship or pray.

Genesis 17:3
Abram fell facedown, and God said to him…

Joshua 5:14
"…but as commander of the army of the Lord I have now come." Then Joshua fell facedown to the ground in reverence, and asked him, "What message does my Lord have for his servant?"

b. Falling as a result of being overwhelmed by the Lord's presence.

Numbers 22:31
Then the Lord opened Balaam's eyes, and he saw the angel of the Lord standing in the road with his sword drawn. So he bowed low and fell facedown.

Judges 13:20
As the flame blazed up from the altar toward heaven, the angel of the Lord ascended in the flame. Seeing this, Manoah and his wife [Samson's parents] fell with their faces to the ground.

Ezekiel 1:28
Like the appearance of a rainbow in the clouds on a rainy day, so was the radiance around him. This was the appearance of the likeness of the glory of the Lord. When I saw it, I fell facedown, and I heard the voice of one speaking.

Ezekiel 3:23b
And the glory of the Lord was standing there, like the glory I had seen by the Kebar River, and I fell facedown.

Ezekiel 43:3
The vision I saw was like the vision I had seen when he came to destroy the city and like the visions I had seen by the Kebar River, and I fell facedown.

Ezekiel 44:4b
I looked and saw the glory of the Lord filling the temple of the Lord, and I fell facedown.

Daniel 8:17a
As he came near the place where I was standing, I was terrified and fell prostrate.

Daniel 8:27
I, Daniel, was worn out. I lay exhausted for several days. Then I got up and went about the king's business.

Daniel 10:8-11
So I was left alone, gazing at this great vision; I had no strength left, my face turned deathly pale and I was helpless. Then I heard him speaking, and as I listened to him, I fell into a deep sleep, my face to the ground. A hand touched me and set me trembling on my hands and knees. He said, "Daniel, you who are highly esteemed, consider carefully the words I am about to speak to you, and stand up, for I have now been sent to you." And when he said this to me, I stood up trembling.

Matthew 17:5-6
While he was still speaking, a bright cloud covered them, and a voice from the cloud said, "This is my Son, whom I love; with him I am well pleased. Listen to him!" When the disciples heard this, they fell facedown to the ground, terrified.

John 18:5b-6

"I am he," Jesus said. (And Judas the traitor was standing there with them.) When Jesus said, "I am he," they drew back and fell to the ground.

Acts 9:3-4 (26:14)

As he neared Damascus on his journey, suddenly a light from heaven flashed around him. He fell to the ground and heard a voice say to him, "Saul, Saul, why do you persecute me?"

Revelation 1:17

When I saw him, I fell at his feet as though dead.

c. Falling into a trance. Most often the expression "fell into a trance" simply means that the person shifted out of an awareness of their surroundings and into an awareness of God, heaven or something else that was revelatory. In at least one of the following accounts, the trance did also involve physical falling.

Numbers 24:4

The prophecy of one who hears the words of God, who sees a vision from the Almighty, who falls prostrate, and whose eyes are opened.

Acts 10:9-10

About noon the following day as they were on their journey and approaching the city, Peter went up on the roof to pray. He became hungry and wanted something to eat, and while the meal was being prepared, he fell into a trance.

Acts 22:17

"When I returned to Jerusalem and was praying at the temple, I fell into a trance."

d. Falling as the result of a "power encounter."

Mark 3:11
Whenever the impure spirits saw him, they fell down before him and cried out, "You are the Son of God."

Mark 9:20
So they brought him. When the spirit saw Jesus, it immediately threw the boy into a convulsion. He fell to the ground and rolled around, foaming at the mouth.

Luke 8:28
When he saw Jesus, he cried out and fell at his feet, shouting at the top of his voice, "What do you want with me, Jesus, Son of the Most High God? I beg you, don't torture me!"

3. "Drunkenness"

Acts 2:13-15
Some, however, made fun of them and said, "They have had too much wine." Then Peter stood up with the Eleven, raised his voice and addressed the crowd: "Fellow Jews and all of you who live in Jerusalem, let me explain this to you; listen carefully to what I say. These people are not drunk, as you suppose. It's only nine in the morning!

4. Loss of physical strength

Daniel 10:8
So I was left alone, gazing at this great vision; I had no strength left, my face turned deathly pale and I was helpless.

5. Trembling

Daniel 10:10-11
A hand touched me and set me trembling on my hands and knees. 11 He said, "Daniel, you who are highly esteemed,

consider carefully the words I am about to speak to you, and stand up, for I have now been sent to you." And when he said this to me, I stood up trembling.

6. Boldness

Acts 4:31b
And they were all filled with the Holy Spirit and spoke the word of God boldly.

7. Joy and Laughter

Genesis 21:6
Sarah said, "God has brought me laughter, and everyone who hears about this will laugh with me."

Psalm 126
When the Lord restored the fortunes of Zion,
we were like those who dreamed.
Our mouths were filled with laughter,
our tongues with songs of joy.
Then it was said among the nations,
"The Lord has done great things for them."
The Lord has done great things for us,
and we are filled with joy.
Restore our fortunes, Lord,
like streams in the Negev.
Those who sow with tears
will reap with songs of joy.
Those who go out weeping,
carrying seed to sow,
will return with songs of joy,
carrying sheaves with them.

Ecclesiastes 3:1, 4a
There is a time for everything,
and a season for every activity under the heavens:...
a time to weep and a time to laugh,...

Luke 6:21b
Blessed are you who weep now,
for you will laugh.

1 Chronicles 16:27
Splendor and majesty are before him;
strength and joy are in his dwelling place.

Nehemiah 8:10c
The joy of the Lord is your strength.

Nehemiah 12:43
And on that day they offered great sacrifices, rejoicing because God had given them great joy. The women and children also rejoiced. The sound of rejoicing in Jerusalem could be heard far away.

Psalm 16:11
You make known to me the path of life;
you will fill me with joy in your presence,
with eternal pleasures at your right hand.[869]

Psalm 30:11
You turned my wailing into dancing;
you removed my sackcloth and clothed me with joy.

Psalm 45:7
You love righteousness and hate wickedness;
therefore God, your God, has set you above your companions
by anointing you with the oil of joy.

---

[869] This passage is also quoted in Acts 2:28.

Psalm 126:2

Our mouths were filled with laughter,
our tongues with songs of joy.
Then it was said among the nations,
"The Lord has done great things for them."

Isaiah 56:7a

These I will bring to my holy mountain
and give them joy in my house of prayer.

Romans 14:17

For the kingdom of God is not a matter of eating and drinking, but of righteousness, peace and joy in the Holy Spirit.

Galatians 5:22-23

But the fruit of the Spirit is love, joy, peace, forbearance, kindness, goodness, faithfulness, gentleness and self-control.

1 Thessalonians 1:6

You became imitators of us and of the Lord, for you welcomed the message in the midst of severe suffering with the joy given by the Holy Spirit.

8. Weeping

Ecclesiastes 3:4

There is a time for everything,
and a season for every activity under the heavens:...
a time to weep and a time to laugh,
a time to mourn and a time to dance,...

9. Inability to speak

Daniel 10:15

While he was saying this to me, I bowed with my face toward the ground and was speechless.

Luke 1:19-20
The angel said to him, "I am Gabriel. I stand in the presence of God, and I have been sent to speak to you and to tell you this good news. And now you will be silent and not able to speak until the day this happens, because you did not believe my words, which will come true at their appointed time."

10. Leaping and dancing

Exodus 15:20
Then Miriam the prophet, Aaron's sister, took a timbrel in her hand, and all the women followed her, with timbrels and dancing.

2 Samuel 6:14-16
Wearing a linen ephod, David was dancing before the Lord with all his might, while he and all Israel were bringing up the ark of the Lord with shouts and the sound of trumpets. As the ark of the Lord was entering the City of David, Michal daughter of Saul watched from a window. And when she saw King David leaping and dancing before the Lord, she despised him in her heart.[870]

Psalm 30:11
You turned my wailing into dancing;
you removed my sackcloth and clothed me with joy.

Psalm 149:3
Let them praise his name with dancing
and make music to him with timbrel and harp.

Psalm 150:4
Praise him with timbrel and dancing.

[870] 1 Chronicles 15:29.

Ecclesiastes 3:4

There is a time for everything,
and a season for every activity under the heavens:...
a time to mourn and a time to dance,...

Luke 1:41-44

When Elizabeth heard Mary's greeting, the baby leaped in her womb, and Elizabeth was filled with the Holy Spirit. In a loud voice she exclaimed: "Blessed are you among women, and blessed is the child you will bear! But why am I so favored, that the mother of my Lord should come to me? As soon as the sound of your greeting reached my ears, the baby in my womb leaped for joy.

Luke 6:22-23

"Blessed are you when people hate you, when they exclude you and insult you and reject your name as evil, because of the Son of Man. Rejoice in that day and leap for joy, because great is your reward in heaven."

Acts 3:6-8

Then Peter said, "Silver or gold I do not have, but what I do have I give you. In the name of Jesus Christ of Nazareth, walk." Taking him by the right hand, he helped him up, and instantly the man's feet and ankles became strong. He jumped to his feet and began to walk. Then he went with them into the temple courts, walking and jumping, and praising God.

11. Running

1 Kings 18:46

The power of the Lord came on Elijah and, tucking his cloak into his belt, he ran ahead of Ahab all the way to Jezreel.

Unbiblical Manifestations

An unbiblical manifestation would be one that is condemned by Scripture. Communication with the spirits of deceased persons would be an example of an unbiblical manifestation, for necromancy is clearly forbidden in Scripture.

Extra-biblical Manifestations

An extra-biblical manifestation would be one that is not necessarily condemned by Scripture, yet it cannot be found in Scripture. Levitation would be an example of an extra-biblical manifestation. I have heard of more than one instance of individuals levitating a few inches off of the ground as they stood in the glory of the Lord during a prayer or worship time. It reportedly happened to my grandfather on one occasion. Levitating in the glory is not condemned by Scripture, yet it cannot be found in Scripture; therefore, it must be classified as extra-biblical.

Other examples of extra-biblical manifestations would include the following:

1. Indoor rain. Some have reported a gentle downpour of rain in the context of worship. Afterwards the ceiling and areas above the ceiling have been checked to rule out the possibility of water leaks.

2. Feathers. Many have witnessed the sudden appearing of feathers. In one worship service in Maine, several people witnessed a sudden explosion of a small quantity of feathers in mid-air in the area above the altar. After the service, maintenance personnel examined the ceiling and ventilation system. They ruled out the possibility of feathers appearing by any natural means.

3. Gold dust. Incidents of glittering dust appearing in Bibles, on hands, on other objects and floating in the air have been reported. Scientific analysis has revealed that in some cases the material is not actually gold, yet it is gold-like in appearance.

4. Gold-filled teeth. In some revival contexts, teeth have been supernaturally filled with gold. The Bible does not condemn this manifestation, yet neither does it speak of it; therefore, it is classified as extra-biblical.

Discernment of Unusual Manifestations

Whenever manifestations of any kind take place, church leaders are responsible to see that everything is done in an orderly fashion. It is especially important to protect the church from unbiblical manifestations and possibly from some that are extra-biblical. Although extra-biblical manifestations are not categorically condemned, the question must be asked, "Is this an authentic manifestation originating from the Holy Spirit's activity?" We should also assess the need for guidance as it relates to the manifestation.

"Is This God?" How can God's people know for sure? How does one discern the validity of a particular manifestation? Here are a couple of questions to ask. (1) What fruit is being produced? (2) Is the manifestation in harmony with Scripture? (3) Is the manifestation in harmony with what God is doing in this moment?

Let us take the manifestation of laughter as an example. When a person experiences what some call "holy laughter," what fruit is being produced? Perhaps that person is receiving much-needed joy. Is laughter in harmony with the Scripture? Yes. Is joy in harmony with Scripture? Yes, it is God's will for His people to be joyful. Anything that is revealed in Scripture as the will of God can be initiated by the Spirit of God. Is this instance of laughter in harmony with what God is doing in this moment for the church body? If not, it needs to be guided pastorally. For instance, if the individual is being blessed by laughter but the manifestation is out of synch with what God is doing with the rest of the church, that person may need to be kindly escorted to another room. By doing so, the individual continues to receive their blessing, and the congregation is no longer distracted.

BIBLIOGRAPHY

Algera, J. A. *Signs and Wonders of God's Kingdom*. Philadelphia, Pennsylvania: Westminster Theological Seminary, 1993.

Armstrong, Chris. "Phoebe Palmer: Did You Know? Interesting facts about the American Holiness revival." *Christian History*. Available from http://www.christianitytoday.com.

Arndt, W. *A Greek-English Lexicon of the New Testament and Other Early Christian Literature*. Chicago, Illinois: Chicago Press, 1979.

Arnott, Carol. Interview by the author. Toronto, Ontario, November 1994.

Arnott, John. *Experience the Blessing*. Ventura, California: Regal Books, 2000.

__________. *The Father's Blessing*. Orlando, Florida: Creation House, 1995.

__________. *Keep the Fire: Allowing the Spirit to Transform Your Life*. London: Marshall Pickering, 1996.

Arrington, French L. and Bill George. *Divine Order in the Church.* Cleveland, Tennessee: Pathway Press, 1978.

Assemblies of God. "Apostles and Prophets." A position paper. Springfield, Missouri: General Council of the Assemblies of God, 2001.

Assemblies of God Theological Seminary. *Signs and Wonders Conference.* Springfield, Missouri: Michael Cardone Media Center, 1995. Audiocassettes.

Backlund, Steve. "Renewing the Mind." Igniting Hope Ministries. Available from http:// ignitinghope.com/ renewing-the-mind.

Barratt, T. B. *The Gift of Prophecy*. Bedford: Cecil Polhill, 1909.

Basham, Don. *Can A Christian Have a Demon?* Monroeville, Pennsylvania: Whitaker Books, 1971.

__________. *Deliver Us From Evil*. London: Hodder & Stoughton, 1973.

__________. *Face Up with a Miracle*. Springdale, Pennsylvania: Whitaker House, 1967.

Bender, Harold S. *Divine Healing: A Symposium*. Scottdale, Pennsylvania: Herald Press, 1950.

Bernard, J. H. *A Critical and Exegetical Commentary on the Gospel According to St. John*, vol. 2. Edinburgh: T. & T. Clark, 1972.

Bevere, John. *Thus Saith the Lord?* Lake Mary, Florida: Creation House, 1999.

Bickle, Mike. *Growing in the Prophetic*. Lake Mary, Florida: Creation House, 1996.

__________. *Passion for Jesus*. Lake Mary, Florida: Creation House, 1993.

Blomgren, David. *Prophetic Gatherings in the Church*. Portland, Oregon: Bible Temple Publishing, 1979.

Boardman, W. E. *The Lord That Healeth Thee*. London: Morgan and Scott, 1881.

Bockmeuhl, Klaus. *Listening to the God Who Speaks*. Colorado Springs: Helmers and Howard, 1990.

Bond, K. M. *Signs and Wonders: Perspectives on John Wimber's Vineyard*. Langley, British Columbia: Northwest Baptist Theological Seminary, 1990.

Boschman, LaMar. *The Prophetic Song*. Shippensburg, Pennsylvania: Revival Press, 1986.

Bosworth, F. F. *Christ the Healer.* Grand Rapids, Michigan: Fleming H. Revell Company, 2001.

Bradshaw, F. E. *The Holy Spirit through the Ages, with Emphasis on the Charismata.* California Graduate School of Theology, 1976.

Brant, Roxanne. *How to Test Prophecy, Preaching and Guidance.* O'Brien, Florida: Roxanne Brant Ministries, 1981.

Bridges, James K., Christopher Gornold-Smith, Joseph Castleberry, M. Paul Brooks, H. Maurice Lednicky, M. Wayne Benson, and Opal L. Reddin. *Pentecostal Gifts and Ministries in a Postmodern Era.* Springfield, Missouri: Gospel Publishing House, 2004.

Brown, Michael L. *From Holy Laughter to Holy Fire: America on the Edge of Revival.* Shippensburg, Pennsylvania: Destiny Image Publishers, 1997.

__________. *Israel's Divine Healer.* Grand Rapids, Michigan: Zondervan Publishing Company, 1995.

Brueggemann, Walter. *The Prophetic Imagination*. Minneapolis: Fortress Press, 2001.

Bryant, C. V. *Rediscovering Our Spiritual Gifts: Building up the Body of Christ through the Gifts of the Spirit*. Nashville, Tennessee: Upper Room Books, 1991.

Bubeck, Mark I. *The Adversary.* Chicago, Illinois: Moody Press, 1975.

Buber, Martin. *The Prophetic Faith*. New York: Collier Books, 1985.

Burgess, Stanley M., ed. *The New International Dictionary of Pentecostal and Charismatic Movements.*Gra nd Rapids, Michigan: Zondervan Publishing House, 2002.

Canty, George. *The Practice of Pentecost: A Handbook on Discerning and Developing the Gifts of the Spirit.* Basingstoke: Marshall, Morgan & Scott, 1987.

Carson, Donald A. *Showing the Spirit: A Theological Exposition of 1 Corinthians 12-14.* Grand Rapids, Michigan: Baker Book House, 1987.

Chevreau, Guy. *Catch the Fire: The Toronto Blessing: An Experience of Renewal and Revival.* London, Marshall Pickering, 1994.

__________. *Pray with Fire: Interceding in the Spirit.* London, Marshall Pickering, 1995.

__________. *Share the Fire: The Toronto Blessing and Grace-based Evangelism.* Shippensburg, Pennsylvania: Revival Press, 1997.

Cooke, Graham. *Developing your Prophetic Gifting.* Grand Rapids, Michigan: Chosen Books, 2003.

Cooke, Graham. *A Divine Confrontation.* Shippensburg, Pennsylvania: Destiny Image Publishers, 1999.

__________. *The Language Of Love: Hearing And Speaking The Language Of God.* Grand Rapids, Michigan: Chosen Books, 2004.

Cramer, Dennis. *You Can All Prophesy.* Cedar Rapids, Iowa: Arrow Publications, 2003.

Cullis, Charles. *Faith Cures.* Boston: Willard Tract Repository, 1879.

Damazio, Frank. *Developing the Prophetic Ministry.* Portland, Oregon: City Bible Publishing, 1990.

Dayton, Donald W. *Theological Roots of Pentecostalism.* Grand Rapids, Michigan: Zondervan Publishing House, 1987.

Dedmon, Kevin. *The Ultimate Treasure Hunt: A Guide to Supernatural Evangelism Through Supernatural Encounters*. Shippensburg, Pennsylvania: Destiny Image, 2007.

Deere, Jack. *The Beginner's Guide to the Gift of Prophecy.* Ann Arbor, Michigan: Vine Books, 2001.

_________. Deere, Jack. *Surprised by the Power of the Spirit: Discovering How God Speaks and Heals Today.* Grand Rapids, Michigan: Zondervan Publishing House, 1996.

_________. *Surprised by the Voice of God: How God Speaks Today through Prophecies, Dreams, and Visions*. Grand Rapids, Michigan: Zondervan Publishing House, 1996.

Dennis, E. B. *The Duration of the Charismata: An Exegetical and Theological Study of 1 Corinthians 13:10*. Virginia Beach, Virginia: CBN University, 1989.

Eberle, Harold R. *The Complete Wineskin: Restructuring the Church for the Outpouring of the Holy Spirit.* Yakima, Washington: Winepress Publishing, 1993.

Egli, Jim. *Encounter God*. Houston, Texas: Touch Outreach Ministries, 2000.

Elliott, W. Winston. *Church Growth Leadership: Pastoral, Prophetic or Apostolic?* Singapore: Abundant Press, 1993.

Empereur, James L. *Prophetic Anointing: God's Call to the Sick, the Elderly, and the Dying.* Wilmington, Delaware: Michael Glazier, 1982.

Engle, Lou. and Catherine Paine. *Digging the Wells of Revival: Reclaiming Your Historic Inheritance through Prophetic Intercession.* Shippensburg, Pennsylvania: Revival Press, 1998.

Fee, Gordon D. *The Disease of the Health and Wealth Gospels.* Costa Mesa, California: The Word for Today, 1979.

Fish, Melinda. *The River is Here: Receiving and Sustaining the Blessing of Revival.* Grand Rapids, Michigan: Chosen Books, 1996.

Florida Department of Law Enforcement."Total Index Crime for Florida," Tallahassee, Florida: Florida Department of Law Enforcement. Database on-line. Available from http:// www.fdle.state.fl.us/ FSAC/ Crime_Trends/total_Index/index.asp.

Ford, M. *Charisma Reports: The Brownsville Revival*. Orlando, Florida: Creation House, 1997.

Foster, P. *Suggestibility, Hysteria and Hypnosis*. Cambridge: St. Matthew, 1997.

Foster, Richard J. *Celebration of Discipline: The Path to Spiritual Growth.* New York: HarperCollins Publishers Inc., 1998.

Frangipane, Francis. *Discerning of Spirits.* Cedar Rapids, Iowa: Arrow Publications, 2001.

Fuller Theological Seminary. *Papers Presented at the Symposium on Power Evangelism.* Pasadena, California: Fuller Theological Seminary, 1988.

Gardner, E. Clinton. *The Church as a Prophetic Community*. Philadelphia, Westminster Press, 1967.

General Council of the Assemblies of God. "Apostles and Prophets." A position paper. Springfield, Missouri, 2001.

General Council of the Church of God. "Resolution on the Ministry of Apostles and Prophets." *Agenda, International General Council, Church of God 70th International General Assembly, August 2-7, 2004.* San Antonio, Texas, 2004.

Geneva Study Bible. Available from http://bible.crosswalk.com.

Gentile, Ernest B. *Your Sons & Daughters Shall Prophesy: Prophetic Gifts in Ministry Today*. Grand Rapids, Michigan: Chosen Books, 1999.

Gerkin, Charles V. *Prophetic Pastoral Practice: A Christian Vision of Life Together.* Nashville: Abingdon Press, 1991.

Geyer, G. R. *Empowerment of the Laity with the Charismata for Renewal in a Traditional Congregation.* Rochester, New York: Crozer Theological Seminary, 1983.

Goll, Jim W. *The Beginner's Guide to Hearing God.* Ventura, California: Regal Books, 2004.

__________. *Kneeling on the Promises: Birthing God's Purposes Through Prophetic Intercession.* Grand Rapids, Michigan: Chosen Books, 1999.

__________. *The Seer: The Prophetic Power of Visions, Dreams, and Open Heavens.* Shippensburg, Pennsylvania: Destiny Image Publishers, 2004.

Goll, Jim W. and Michael L. Brown. *The Coming Prophetic Revolution: A Call for Passionate, Consecrated Warriors.* Grand Rapids, Michigan: Chosen Books, 2001.

Gordon, A. J. *The Ministry of Healing: Miracles of Cure in All Ages.* Boston: H. Gannett, 1882.

Gott, Ken and Lois Gott. *The Sunderland Refreshing*. London: Hodder & Stoughton, 1995.

Gott, Lois Gott. *The Glory of His Presence: Reaping the Harvest of the Sunderland Refreshing*. London: Hodder & Stoughton, 1996.

Grudem, Wayne. *The Gift of Prophecy in the New Testament and Today.* Westchester, Illinois: Crossway Books, 1988.

Hagin, Kenneth E. *The Gift of Prophecy*. Tulsa, Oklahoma: Kenneth Hagin Evangelistic Association, 1975.

__________. *How You Can be Led by the Spirit of God.* Tulsa, Oklahoma: Kenneth Hagin Evangelistic Association, 1978.

__________. *I Believe in Visions.* Tulsa, Oklahoma: Kenneth Hagin Evangelistic Association, 1972.

Hammond, Frank and Ida Mae Hammond. *Pigs in the Parlor: A Practical Guide to Deliverance*. Kirkwood: Impact Books, 1973.

Hamon, Bill. *Apostles Prophets and the Coming Moves of God: God's End-time Plans for His church and Planet Earth.* Santa Rosa Beach, Florida: Christian International, 1997.

__________. *Prophets and Personal Prophecy*. Santa Rosa Beach, Florida: Christian International, 1987.

__________. *Prophets and the Prophetic Movement: God's Prophetic Move Today.* Shippensburg, Pennsylvania: Destiny Image, 1990.

__________. *Prophets Pitfalls and Principles : God's Prophetic People Today.* Santa Rosa Beach, Florida: Christian International, 1991.

Hamon, Jane. *Dreams and Visions: Understanding Your Dreams and How God Can Use Them to Speak to You Today.* Ventura, California: Regal Books, 2000.

Hanegraaff, Hank H. Counterfeit Revival. *Nashville, Tennessee: Thomas Nelson, 1997.*

Harper, Michael. *Spiritual Warfare.* Plainfield, New Jersey: Logos International, 1970.

Harris, C. W. *Resist the Devil: A Pastoral Guide to Deliverance Prayer.* South Bend, Indiana: Greenlawn Press, 1989.

"Heraclitus." *The Internet Encyclopedia of Philosophy.* Available from http://www.utm.edu/research/iep/h/heraclit.htm; accessed 5 February 2005.

Hickey, Marilyn. *Devils, Demons and Deliverance.* Denver, Colorado: Marilyn Hickey Ministries, 1994.

Hilborn, D. *"Toronto" in Perspective: Papers on the New Charismatic Wave of the Mid 1990's*. Carlisle: Paternoster, 2001.

Hill, Clifford S. *Prophecy, Past and Present: An Exploration of the Prophetic Ministry in the Bible and the Church Today*. Ann Arbor, Michigan: Vine Books, 1991.

Horton, H. L. C. *The Gifts of the Spirit.* Springfield, Gospel Publishing House, 1975.

Jackson, R. E. *An Evaluation of the Evangelistic Emphasis of the North American Power Evangelism Movement, 1977-1997.* Southern Baptist Theological Seminary, 1999.

Jackson, Wayne. "Reflections on the Goodness of God." Available from https://www.ChristianCourier.com.

Jacobs, Cindy. *The Voice of God: How God Speaks Personally and Corporately to His Children Today.* Ventura, California: Regal Books, 1995.

Jamieson, R., A. R. Fausset, & D. Brown. "John 14:8-13." *A Commentary, Critical and Explanatory on the Old and New Testaments* [CD-ROM]. Oak Harbor, Washington: Logos Research Systems, Inc., 1997.

Joyner, Rick Joyner. *The Final Quest.* New Kensington, Pennsylvania: Whitaker House, 1997.

Joyner, Rick. *The Prophetic Ministry.* Wilkesboro, North Carolina: Morning Star Publications, 1997.

Kelsey, Morton T. *Healing and Christianity in Ancient Thought and Modern Times.* New York: Harper & Row, 1973.

Kettenring, T. O. *The Impact on Confidence for Personal Witnessing through Exposure to Power Evangelism.* Denver, Colorado: Denver Seminary, 2000.

Kittel, G. W. Bromiley, and G. Friedrich, eds. *Theological Dictionary of the New Testament*. 10 vols. Grand Rapids, Michigan: Eerdmans, 1964-1976.

Kuhlman, Kathryn. *I Believe in Miracles.* Englewood Cliffs, New Jersey: Prentice-Hall, 1962.

Land, Steven J. *A Passion for the Kingdom: An Analysis and Revision of Pentecostal Spirituality*. Atlanta, Georgia: Emory University, 1991.

__________. *Pentecostal Spirituality: A Passion for the Kingdom.* Sheffield, England: Sheffield Academic Press, 1993.

Last Days Ministries. "The History of Keith Green." Available from http://www.lastdaysministries.org/keith/history.html.

Lee, J. *Power Evangelism in the Third Wave Movement and Its Implications for Contemporary Church Growth*. Southwestern Baptist Theological Seminary, 2000.

Liardon, Roberts, ed., *John G. Lake: The Complete Collection of His Life Teachings.* Tulsa, Oklahoma: Albury Publishing, 1999.

Lindsay, Gordan. *All About the Gifts of the Spirit.* Dallas, Texas: Christ for the Nations, 1971.

__________. *The Gift of Discerning of Spirits*. Dallas, Texas: Christ for the Nations, 1972.

__________. *The Gift of Prophecy: The True and the False.* Dallas, Texas: Christ for the Nations, 1971.

__________. *Gifts of the Spirit*. Dallas, Texas: Christ for the Nations, 1963.

__________. *The Ministry of Casting Out Demons.* Dallas, Texas: Christ for the Nations, 1977.

__________. *Miracles in the Bible,* 7 vols. Dallas, Texas: Christ for the Nations, n.d.

Lowery, T. L. *Apostles and Prophets: Reclaiming the Biblical Gifts.* TL Lowery Global Foundation.

Lyne, Peter. *First Apostles, Last Apostles.* Tonbridge, Kent, England: Sovereign World, 1999.

MacNutt, Francis. *Deliverance from Evil Spirits: a Practical Manual.* Grand Rapids, Michigan: Chosen Books, 1995.

__________. *Healing.* Notre Dame, Indiana: Ave Maria Press, 1974.

__________. *The Power to Heal.* Notre Dame, Indiana: Ave Maria Press, 1977.

__________. *The Prayer that Heals.* Notre Dame, Indiana: Ave Maria Press, 1981.

Maher, J. F. *As the Spirit Wills: Leadership and Administration in the Local Church for the Manifestation of All the Gifts of the Spirit.* Pasadena, California: Fuller Theological Seminary, 1992.

Marcus, W. M. and Holy Smoke Productions. *Go Inside the Toronto Blessing.* Shippenburg, Pennsylvania: Destiny Image, 1997. Videocassette.

Martin, Trevor. *Kingdom Healing.* London: Marshalls, 1981.

McClung, Floyd, Jr. *The Father Heart of God.* Harvest House Publishers, 1985.

__________, Rickie Moore, Kelvin Page, et al. "The Prophetic Journey." A prophetic ministry conference, Westmore Church of God, Cleveland, Tennessee, 2005.

McQueen, Larry R. *Joel and the Spirit: the Cry of a Prophetic Hermeneutic.* Sheffield, England: Sheffield Academic Press, 1995.

Milligan, Ira. *Every Dreamer's Handbook: Simple Guide to Understanding Your Dreams.* Shippensburg, Pennsylvania: Destiny Image Publishers, 2000.

__________. *Understanding the Dreams You Dream.* Shippensburg, Pennsylvania: Destiny Image Publishers, 1997.

Mills, Dick. *He Spoke and I Was Strengthened.* San Jacinto, California: Dick Mills Ministries, 1991.

Mitton, Michael. *The Heart of Toronto: Exploring the Spirituality of the "Toronto Blessing"*. Cambridge: Grove Books Ltd., 1995.

Mongoven, Anne Marie. *The Prophetic Spirit of Catechesis: How We Share the Fire in Our Hearts.* New York: Paulist Press, 2000.

Morris, Danny E. and Charles M. Olsen. *Discerning God's Will Together: A Spiritual Practice for the Church.* Bethesda, Maryland: Alban Publications, 1997.

Niebuhr, H. Richard. *Christ and Culture.* New York: Harper and Row, 1951.

Norton, Robert. *The Restoration of Apostles and Prophets: in the Catholic Apostolic Church.* London: Bosworth & Harrison, 1861.

Odon, Don. *School of the Prophets.* Orlando, Florida: Daniels Publishing Company, 1976.

Origen. *Contra Celsus.*

Osborn, T. L. *Divine Healing Through Revelation, Faith, Power.* Tulsa, Oklahoma: T. L. Osborn, 1949.

__________. *Healing the Sick and Casting out Devils: the Message and Ministry of a Bible Disciple Now Living; Christ's Power of Attourney Exercised Today.* Tulsa, Oklahoma: International Headquarters of Evangelist and Mrs. T. L. Osborn, 1953.

Packer, J. I., G. S. Greig, et al., *The Kingdom and the Power: Are Healing and the Spiritual Gifts Used by Jesus and the Early Church Meant for the Church Today?: A Biblical Look at How to Bring the Gospel to the World with Power.* Ventura, California: Regal Books, 1993.

Parker, Stephen E. *Led by the Spirit: Toward a Practical Theology of Pentecostal Discernment and Decision Making*. Sheffield, England: Sheffield Academic Press, 1996.

Parsons, George and Speed B. Leas. *Understanding Your Congregation as a System.* Bethesda, Maryland: Alban Institute, Inc., 1993.

Penny, Steve. *Look Out, the Prophets Are Coming!* Sutherland, NSW Australia: Prophetic People International, 1993.

Perez, Pablo. *The Prophetic Worshiper: Heaven's Sounds in the Hearts of a Lovesick Generation.* Truth Press, 2004.

Pfeiffer, C. F. *The Wycliffe Bible Commentary.* Chicago: Moody Press, 1962.

Pierce, Chuck D. and Rebecca Wagner Sytsema. *Receiving the Word of the Lord.* Colorado Springs, Colorado: Wagner Publications, 1999.

__________. *When God Speaks: Receiving and Walking in Supernatural Revelation.* Colorado Springs, Colorado: Wagner Publications, 2003.

Pietersen, L. *The Mark of the Spirit?: A Charismatic Critique of the "Blessing" Phenomenon.* Carlisle: Paternoster Press, 1998.

Plüss, Jean-Daniel. *Therapeutic and Prophetic Narratives in Worship: A Hermeneutic Study of Testimonies and Visions: Their Potential Significance for Christian Worship and Secular Society.* New York: Verlag P. Lang, 1988.

Prince, Derek. *How to Judge Prophecy.* Fort Lauderdale, Florida: Derek Prince Publications, 1971.

Pytches, David. *Some Said It Thundered: a Personal Encounter with the Kansas City Prophets.* Nashville, Tennessee: Oliver-Nelson, 1991.

Randolph, Larry. *User Friendly Prophecy: Guidelines for the Effective Use of Prophecy.* Shippensburg, Pennsylvania: Destiny Image Publishers, 1998.

Riffel, Herman. *Dream Interpretation.* Shippensburg, Pennsylvania: Destiny Image Press, 1993.

Riss, Richard M. *A History of the Revival of 1993-1995.* Toronto: Toronto Airport Vineyard, 1995.

Robbins, S. C. *Charismata, Revelation, and the Authority of Scripture: A Theological, Philosophical, and Exegetical Study of the Implications of 1 Corinthians 12:8, 10.* Pasadena, California: Fuller Theological Seminary, 1999.

Rumble, Donald. *Apostolic and Prophetic Foundations: Giving the Lord Back His Church.* Clinton Corners, New York: The Attic Studio Press, 1996.

Runyon, T., ed. *What the Spirit is Saying to the Churches.* New York: Hawthorne Books, 1975.

Ruthven, Jon M. *On the Cessation of Charismata: The Protestant Polemic on Postbiblical Miracles.* Sheffield: Sheffield Academic Press, 1993.

Sandford, John Loren. *Elijah Among Us: Understanding and Responding to God's Prophets Today.* Grand Rapids, Michigan: Chosen Books, 2002.

Sarles, K. L. *An Appraisal of the Signs & Wonders Movement.* Dallas, Texas: Bibliotheca Sacra, 1988.

Schatzmann, S. S. *The Pauline Concept of Charismata in the Light of Recent Critical Literature.* Fort Worth, Texas: Southwestern Baptist Theological Seminary, 1981.

__________. *A Pauline Theology of Charismata.* Peabody, Massachusetts: Hendrickson Publishers, 1987.

Sheets, Dutch Sheets. *Intercessory Prayer.* Ventura, California: Regal Books, 1998.

Shepherd, D. H. *A Critical Analysis of Power Evangelism as an Evangelistic Methodology of the Signs and Wonders Movement.* Mid-America Baptist Theological Seminary, 1991.

Simpson, A. B. *The Gospel of Healing,* rev. ed. New York: Christian Alliance Publishing, 1915.

__________. *The Lord for the Body*. New York: Christian Alliance Publishing, 1925.

Society for Pentecostal Studies. *Gifts of the Spirit: Papers Presented at the 12th Annual Meeting of the Society for Pentecostal Studies, November 18-20, 1982*. Pasadena, California: Fuller Theological Seminary, 1982.

Smith, Gordon T. *Listening to God in Times of Choice: The Art of Discerning God'sWill.* Downers Grove, Illinois: InterVarsity Press, 1997.

Smith, Randall D. "The Life and Ministry of Jesus." A lecture series delivered on a pastors' study tour sponsored by Christian Travel Study Programs, Jerusalem, Israel, December 1996.

Sparks, Austin T. *Prophetic Ministry: A Classic Study on the Nature of a Prophet.* Shippensburg, Pennsylvania: Mercy Place, 2000.

Stephanoum, E. A. *The Charismata in the Early Church Fathers*. Brookline, Massachusetts: Holy Cross Orthodox Press, 1976.

Stone, Dwayne. *Gifts from the Ascended Christ: Restoring the Place of the 5-Fold Ministry.* Shippensburg, Pennsylvania: Destiny Image Publishers, 1999.

Stronstad, Roger. *The Prophethood of All Believers: a Study in Luke's Charismatic Theology.* Sheffield: Sheffield Academic Press, 1999.

Sullivant, Michael. *Prophetic Etiquette: Your Complete Handbook on Giving and Receiving Prophecy.* Lake Mary, Florida: Charisma House, 2000.

Tharp, D. T. *Signs and Wonders in the Twentieth Century Evangelical Church: Corinth Revisited.* Ashland, Ohio: Ashland Theological Seminary, 1992.

Thomas, Benny. *Exploring the World of Dreams.* New Kensington, Pennsylvania: Whitaker House, 1995.

Thomas, John Christopher. *The Devil, Disease and Deliverance: Origins of Illness in New Testament Thought*. Sheffield: Sheffield Academic Press, 1998.

Torres, Hector. *The Restoration of Apostles and Prophets: How it Will Revolutionize Ministry in the 21st Century.* Nashville Tennessee: Thomas Nelson Publishers, 2001.

Turpin, Jr. Randolph, Jr. *A Man Called King: The Life and Legacy of King Turpin, Jr.* Scarborough, Maine, 2010.

__________. "A Synthesis and Critique of 'The Prophetic Journey': The 2005 Prophetic Ministry Conference Conducted at Westmore Church of God." An unpublished paper, Church of God Theological Seminary, 2005.

__________. "A Training Model for Transitioning Classical Pentecostal Churches Toward the Intentional Integration of the *Charismata* in the Exercise of Prayer Ministry." D.Min. diss., Church of God Theological Seminary, 2004.

__________. *Gateway to the Christian College Experience.* Canal Winchester, Ohio: Declaration Press, 2015.

Underwood, B. E. *The Gifts of the Spirit: Supernatural Equipment for Christian Service.* Franklin Springs, Georgia: Advocate Press, 1967.

Unger, Merrill F. *Demons in the World Today.* Wheaton, Illinois: Tyndale House, 1971.

Wagner, C. Peter. *Apostles and Prophets: The Foundations of the Church.* Ventura, California: Regal Books, 2000.

__________, ed. *Pastors and Prophets: Protocol for Healthy Churches.* Colorado Springs, Colorado: Wagner Publications, 2000.

__________. *Signs and Wonders Today.* Wheaton, Illinois: Christian Life Magazine, 1983.

__________.*Your Spiritual Gifts Can Help Your Church Grow.* Ventura, California: Regal Books, 1997.

__________. *The Third Wave of the Holy Spirit: Encountering the Power of Signs and Wonders Today.* Ann Arbor: Servant Publications Vine Books, 1988.

Weaver, C. Douglas. *The Healer-Prophet, William Marrion Branham: A Study of the Prophetic in American Pentecostalism.* Macon, GA: Mercer University Press, 1987.

"The Welsh Revival: A History of 1904 and News of Today." Available from http://www.welshrevival.com.

Wentroble, Barbara. *Prophetic Intercession: Letting God Lead Your Prayers.* Renew, 1999.

Willard, Dallas. *Hearing God: Developing a Conversational Relationship With God.* Downers Grove, Illinois: InterVarsity Press, 1999.

__________. *In Search of Guidance.* Rev. ed. San Francisco, California: Harper, 1993.

Williams, Charles D. *The Prophetic Ministry for Today*. New York: The Macmillian Company, 1921.

Williams, D. *Signs, Wonders, and the Kingdom of God: A Biblical Guide for the Reluctant Skeptic.* Ann Arbor, Michigan: Vine Books, 1989.

Wimber, John. *A Brief Sketch of Signs and Wonders through the Church Age*. Placentia, California: Vineyard Christian Fellowship, 1984.

__________. *Signs and Wonders and Church Growth.* Placentia, California: Vineyard Ministries International, 1984.

Wimber, John and Kevin Springer. *Power Encounters.* San Francisco, California: Harper & Row, 1988.

__________. *Power Evangelism*. San Francisco, California: Harper & Row, 1986.

__________. *Power Healing.* San Francisco, California: Harper & Row, 1987.

__________. *Power Points.* San Francisco, California: Harper & Row, 1991.

Winiger, Daniel. "The Missions Command: A Commission to Discipleship, Fulfilled through the Five-fold Ministry." M.Div. thesis., Church of God School of Theology, 1992.

Woodhouse, J., P. Barnett, et al. *Signs & Wonders and Evangelicals: A Response to the Teaching of John Wimber.* Homebush West, NSW, Australia: Lancer Books, 1987.

Yocum, Bruce. *Prophecy: Exercising the Prophetic Gifts of the Spirit in the Church Today.* Ann Arbor, Michigan: Word of Life, 1976.

Paperback: 90 pages
Language: English
Dimensions: 8 x 5 inches

Available in both Paperback and Kindle formats.

For ordering information, visit DeclarationPress.com.

101 Prayer Models

J. Randolph Turpin, Jr.

This book is both personal and missional. It is a practical resource to help Christians jump-start their personal prayer lives. It is a concise collection of ideas to help small groups and churches mobilize for the ministry of prayer. It is for anyone seeking to link the power of prayer with the fulfillment of the Great Commission.

101 Prayer Models is a catalog of models designed to involve everyone. Presented as a set of annotated lists, the models are arranged in four categories: personal and family models, small group models, congregational models and evangelistic models.

The author, Dr. J. Randolph (Randy) Turpin, has been training congregants, pastors and students for the ministry of prayer for over twenty years. For years, he distributed handouts listing ways to cultivate a culture of prayer. In February of 2011 he decided to compile those lists and make them available as a published booklet—*101 Prayer Models*.

Dr. Turpin serves as president of Valor Christian College in Columbus, Ohio. Previously he served as lead pastor of Royal Ridge Church of God in Scarborough, Maine. He also served as an adjunct faculty member with the Pentecostal Theological Seminary teaching subjects related to leadership, ministerial practice and prayer. He is an ordained bishop in the Church of God (Cleveland, Tennessee) and has earned a B.A. degree in Biblical Studies from Lee University and M.Div. and D.Min. degrees from the Pentecostal Theological Seminary.

Randy's calling to minister to leaders has taken him to South America, Africa, Asia and various training venues in North America. He and his wife, Kerry, have devoted their lives to promoting prayer, spiritual renewal and the Spirit-empowered life.

Paperback: 150 pages
Language: English
Dimensions: 8 x 10 inches

For ordering information, visit DeclarationPress.com.

Prayer Strategy

A Planning Workbook

J. Randolph Turpin, Jr.

This workbook is designed to help ministry teams develop the ministry of prayer in local churches and ministry organizations. It is formatted as a retreat guide, but it can also be used in other settings. The process is presented in three parts: pre-retreat, retreat and post-retreat.

Part One, Pre-retreat, provides a guide for an initial orientation meeting, a personal prayer inventory and a congregational assessment instrument.

Part Two, Retreat, directs the team through four steps of a five-step planning process: (1) assess, (2) set goals, (3) plan a course of action and (4) agree and celebrate—a covenant-making step. Integrated with these steps is a process for the shared discernment of God's will.

Part Three, Post-retreat, fulfills the final step in the five-step process: work the plan. Through a series of follow-through meetings combined with work conducted between meetings, the team pursues the goals set during the planning retreat.

Dr. Turpin serves as president of Valor Christian College in Columbus, Ohio. Previously he served as lead pastor of Royal Ridge Church of God in Scarborough, Maine. He also served as an adjunct faculty member with the Pentecostal Theological Seminary teaching subjects related to leadership, ministerial practice and prayer. He is an ordained bishop in the Church of God (Cleveland, Tennessee) and has earned a B.A. degree in Biblical Studies from Lee University and M.Div. and D.Min. degrees from the Pentecostal Theological Seminary.

Randy's calling to minister to leaders has taken him to South America, Africa, Asia and various training venues in North America. He and his wife, Kerry, have devoted their lives to promoting prayer, spiritual renewal and the Spirit-empowered life.

Paperback: 314 pages
Language: English
Dimensions: 8 x 10 inches

For ordering information,
visit DeclarationPress.com.

Behold the Son

A Study of the Gospel of John

J. Randolph Turpin, Jr.

BEHOLD THE SON has been prepared as a resource for personal study and as a tool for teachers walking their students through a study of the Gospel of John. These pages contain the complete text of the Gospel According to John. The commentary in the footnotes features technical notes, cross references, sermon notes and the author's personal reflections. To further assist in the study, tables have been inserted providing a harmony of the Gospels in those places where such information might prove relevant and helpful.

Dr. Turpin declares this blessing over all who work through this study: "May you behold the Son of God with every turn of the page, with every word that you ponder, and with every prayer that you pray in response to the message of this amazing Gospel."

Dr. Turpin serves as president of Valor Christian College in Columbus, Ohio. Previously he served as lead pastor of Royal Ridge Church of God in Scarborough, Maine. He also served as an adjunct faculty member with the Pentecostal Theological Seminary teaching subjects related to leadership, ministerial practice and prayer. He is an ordained bishop in the Church of God (Cleveland, Tennessee) and has earned a B.A. degree in Biblical Studies from Lee University and M.Div. and D.Min. degrees from the Pentecostal Theological Seminary.

Randy's calling to minister to leaders has taken him to South America, Africa, Asia and various training venues in North America. He and his wife, Kerry, have devoted their lives to promoting prayer, spiritual renewal and the Spirit-empowered life.

Paperback: 192 pages
Language: English
Dimensions: 8 x 10 inches

For ordering information,
visit DeclarationPress.com.

Shared Discernment

A Workbook for Ministry Planning Teams

J. Randolph Turpin, Jr.

"Shared discernment" guides ministry teams through a planning process that involves (1) listening for the Spirit's voice, (2) sharing what has been heard and (3) discerning what it means. Teams then set goals and draft plans for the work to which God is calling them.

This manual facilitates strategic planning in retreat or planning settings. Parts Two, Three and Four are a workbook—a practical tool for the team's journey.

The text has been divided into four parts: (1) Introducing Shared Discernment, (2) Pre-summit, (3) The Ministry Planning Summit and (4) Post-summit.

Part One, Introducing Shared Discernment, explains the four phases of the shared discernment process.

Part Two, Pre-summit, involves an initial orientation meeting with the planning team.

Part Three, The Ministry Planning Summit, covers four of five steps: (1) assess, (2) set goals, (3) plan a course of action and (4) agree and celebrate.

Part Four, Post-summit, is the final step in the five-step process—Work the Plan. Through follow-through meetings and work conducted between meetings, the team pursues the goals set during the planning.

Dr. Turpin serves as president of Valor Christian College in Columbus, Ohio. Previously he served in pastoral ministry. He also served Pentecostal Theological Seminary teaching on leadership, ministerial practice and prayer. He is an ordained bishop in the Church of God (Cleveland, Tennessee) and has earned a B.A. degree in Biblical Studies from Lee University and M.Div. and D.Min. degrees from Pentecostal Theological Seminary. Randy's calling to minister to leaders has taken him to South America, Africa, Asia and various training venues in North America. He and his wife, Kerry, have devoted their lives to promoting the Spirit-empowered life.

Made in the USA
Monee, IL
25 January 2023